Evolving from Digital Transformation to Digital Acceleration Using The Galapagos Framework

Brian Harkin

CRC Press
Taylor & Francis Group
Boca Raton London New York

CRC Press is an imprint of the
Taylor & Francis Group, an **informa** business

AN AUERBACH BOOK

Designed cover image: Michael Soremi of UXD Financial Ltd.

First edition published 2024
2385 NW Executive Center Drive, Suite 320, Boca Raton FL 33431

and by CRC Press
4 Park Square, Milton Park, Abingdon, Oxon, OX14 4RN

CRC Press is an imprint of Taylor & Francis Group, LLC

© 2024 Taylor & Francis Group, LLC

ISBN: 978-1-032-51111-5 (hbk)
ISBN: 978-1-032-51848-0 (pbk)
ISBN: 978-1-003-40421-7 (ebk)

DOI: 10.1201/9781003404217

Typeset in Garamond
by SPi Technologies India Pvt Ltd (Straive)

Evolving from Digital Transformation to Digital Acceleration Using The Galapagos Framework

Evolving from Digital Transformation to Digital Acceleration Using The Galapagos Framework challenges established thinking and offers a new way to deliver digital change. It introduces The Galapagos Framework, which is a new, innovative, and human-centric approach to transformational change. The framework allows organizations to move from digital transformation to digital acceleration, resulting in the creation of exciting and groundbreaking products as well as having a positive impact on the motivation and well-being of their teams.

Digital Acceleration is an iterative process that allows organizations to deliver transformations and demonstrate continual progress at pace. Rather than tackling the transformation as one large single event, Digital Acceleration enables organizations to improve one or, at most, two discrete areas of the business quickly and then move onto the next area needing improvement.

Presenting a detailed guide to The Galapagos Framework, the book also highlights solutions to common issues, expert case studies, and The Galapagos Roadmap. It discusses how the framework provides the key to increasing productivity, delivery velocity, and performance while reducing cost and complexity, ultimately resulting in digital and business success. The book demonstrates how The Galapagos Framework operates in practice to provide clear solutions to common issues that are classified into Human Elements, Organizational Factors, and the Delivery Aspects. The book also explains why the current approaches to digital transformation are failing and shows how digital leaders and organizations can:

- Increase productivity
- Reduce costs
- Improve delivery performance
- Reduce operational, financial, and delivery risks
- Increase profits
- Deliver digital transformation success

Brian Harkin is a highly collaborative and trusted digital leader who leverages over 30 years' experience across the financial services sector, principally global markets, asset management, and investment banking. Prior to creating The Galapagos Framework, Brian served in a variety of leadership roles and delivered numerous Digital Transformation programs across a range of business domains (e.g., digital channels, ecommerce, data and risk analytics). In addition to his freelance work, Brian is a passionate coach/mentor/educator and is a visiting lecturer at City University of London's Bayes Business School. He also writes and presents extensively on Digital Transformation and Leadership.

For
Alex, Roisin, Aaron, and Indy ♡

Contents

SECTION I OVERVIEW

SECTION II   HOW THE GALAPAGOS FRAMEWORK RESOLVES THE COMMON ISSUES

A. THE HUMAN ELEMENT

C. THE DELIVERY ASPECTS

SECTION III UNDERSTANDING THE FUNCTION OF THE GALAPAGOS FRAMEWORK

SECTION V   CONCLUSIONS

SECTION VI   CASE STUDIES

Acknowledgments

The large number of individuals who have in some way or another been on this journey with me, from the creation of The Framework itself through to the writing of the book, are a many, varied, and very helpful bunch.

Some of these I've known since my first days at IBM, well over 30 years ago, and others I've known for a much shorter period of time, but all have made valuable contributions to my thinking and writing.

Firstly, I'd like to extend my gratitude to John Wyzalek, my editor, who took a bet on a first-time author and provided sage guidance throughout the writing process.

Phil Jarratt and Tony Williams, despite living almost 6,000 miles apart and never having met each other, set me off on this odyssey and deserve special thanks. Tony for planting the seed of the idea by commenting, *Have you thought about writing a book on this?* and Phil for his inspirational *Galapagos* naming suggestion and assistance with the original book proposal (along with Rowan).

I am profoundly grateful to Dr. Anne-Marie Bremner for her help in shaping the text and her patience and good humor throughout the many, many iterations of write and re-write. This book is undoubtedly better for her expert input.

The unenviable task of reviewing my early writings fell to Jo Power, and I'd like to thank her for her honest feedback and suggestions on how the text might be improved (I'm still not sure I've managed to *put more Brian into the text*).

My heartfelt appreciation also goes to Gee Paw Hill, Steve Duesbury, Justin Marcucci, and Dr. Charlotte Webb for taking the time to speak with me and/or providing their insightful views and experience which I have included in the book.

The credit for suggesting the idea of the *Just Do This*, quick reference sections, goes to Tony Bland, a longtime friend and tea drinker extraordinaire.

Sarah Patel and Richard Jeffreys have also provided their time, effort, and suggestions (with Sarah providing some of the text on aligning incentives, and Richard providing the idea of culture, kindness, and abundance). I am delighted to know them and the rest of the People Centric Transformation LinkedIn group.

My gratitude must also be extended to Michael Soremi for his incredible work on the cover design and to Ket Patel for his outstanding work on the branding of The Galapagos Framework and of DigitalXform Ltd.

The support that my family has provided throughout the writing process has been enormous, and the patience that my wife, Alex, has (mostly) demonstrated has been exceptional. Roisin's incredible culinary skills have ensured that we've all remained fed on the occasions when I've *forgotten* to cook, and I'm exceptionally proud that my daughter has demonstrated such thoughtfulness. This pride extends to Aaron, my son, who has shown maturity and resilience beyond his years with the transition to a new school, and navigating all that entails, at a time when I have been sitting at the kitchen table writing and not affording him all of the attention that he so richly deserves. I will rectify this situation going forward. It has been great having Indy 🐾 curled up at my feet as I write, and to her, I promise not to cut short any more walks.

Charles and Paul have proved a welcome distraction from time to time with their unique brand of humor; however, I still struggle to understand how Sam and Brenda put up with them.

Finally, to the friends (*It's just like writing a big report, isn't it?*; *We never thought you'd actually finish it*) and family that surround me and everyone who has contributed to the thinking behind The Framework and this book I will be forever grateful.

Thank you,
Brian.

Preface

70% of digital transformations fail, and by 2026 there will be an annual enterprise spend of **$2.3 trillion** globally that does not deliver success.

There can be no clearer warning that organizations are failing to transform, or failing to transform effectively enough, to cater for the challenges and disruptions of the digital age.

This inability to execute effective digital change is an existential threat, as some organizations will be too slow to respond and will be replaced by smaller, more agile companies. Other organizations will understand the need for change and will be embarking on digital transformation strategies, but these initiatives are unlikely to succeed due to structural problems in the approach taken.

The Galapagos Framework has evolved out of a working lifetime of practical experience in digital transformations and addresses the key issues that plague these ventures.

With the advent of the digital era, organizations are finding themselves in the peculiar position where technology adoption (be that AI, big data analytics, cloud, IoT, mobile, etc.) is exposing issues with the way in which these businesses are fundamentally set up.

The approaches that are currently being taken to transformational change, combined with outdated operating models, are stifling innovation, hampering growth, and negatively impacting organizational health.

The Galapagos Framework has been designed to address the issues that lie at the heart of transformational failure and to present a positive way forward for organizations embarking on these programs.

Delivering a fundamental rethink of the way in which organizations approach digital transformations (across the Human, Organizational, and Delivery dimensions), this book will demonstrate how The Galapagos Framework allows digital leaders and organizations to increase productivity, reduce costs, improve delivery performance, reduce operational, financial and delivery risks, increase profits, and deliver digital transformation success.

Brian Harkin
Surrey, England

OVERVIEW

1

Chapter 1

Introduction, Overview, and Definitions

Introduction

70% of Digital Transformations Fail – You Can Do Something About It!

This book challenges the established thinking and offers a new way to deliver digital change – The Galapagos Framework is a new, innovative, and human-centric approach to transformational change.

This Framework allows organizations to move from digital transformation to Digital Acceleration, resulting in the creation of exciting and groundbreaking products, and a positive impact on the motivation and well-being of their teams.

Covering solutions to the common issues, expert case studies, The Galapagos Roadmap, and a detailed guide to The Galapagos Framework itself, this book provides the key to increasing productivity, delivery velocity, and performance while reducing cost and complexity, ultimately resulting in digital and business success.

EVERYTHING YOU KNOW ABOUT DIGITAL TRANSFORMATIONS IS WRONG

- *Multiple, parallel streams of work get you to your end goal faster –* **WRONG**.
- *Running a digital transformation from inside your (predominantly) non-digital organization will work –* **WRONG**.
- *More communication is better –* **WRONG**.
- *Leading a digital transformation program requires a complex matrix management structure –* **WRONG**.
- *Young, enthusiastic, and ambitious teams deliver success –* **WRONG**.
- *You must avoid failure –* **WRONG**.

DOI: 10.1201/9781003404217-2

This book demonstrates how The Galapagos Framework operates in practice to provide clear solutions to the common issues (classified into the *Human Elements, Organizational Factors,* and *Delivery Aspects*), and details why the current approaches to digital transformation are failing.

Further, the book will show how The Galapagos Framework allows digital leaders and organizations to:

■ Increase productivity	■ Reduce costs
■ Improve delivery performance	■ Reduce operational, financial, and delivery risks
■ Increase profits	■ Deliver digital transformation success

Overview

The Case for Change

Huge Spend Does Not Equal Huge Success

There is a vast amount of strategic spend on digital transformations against a backdrop of limited success. There is, however, significant potential for future market growth.

In 2020, the total enterprise spending on digital transformations was $1.3 trillion.[1]

Respondents to a McKinsey survey[2] reported that circa 70% of transformations fail to deliver successful outcomes, which is corroborated by independent research from the Boston Consulting Group (BCG).[3]

---

[1] Statista, 'Worldwide Digital Transformation Market Size', Statista.com (2022). Available at: https://www.statista.com/statistics/870924/worldwide-digital-transformation-market-size/ [accessed August 29, 2023].

[2] McKinsey & Company. 'Common pitfalls in transformations: A conversation with Jon Garcia'. mckinsey.com, 2022. Available at: https://www.mckinsey.com/capabilities/transformation/our-insights/common-pitfalls-in-transformations-a-conversation-with-jon-garcia [accessed: June 19, 2023].

[3] BCG delivers the same 70% failure rate for digital transformations:
Boston Consulting Group, 'Increasing the Odds of Success in Digital Transformation', bcg.com, (2020), https://www.bcg.com/publications/2020/increasing-odds-of-success-in-digital-transformation [accessed June 19, 2023].

The global digital transformation market is projected to grow at a compound annual growth rate (CAGR) of more than 16% between 2020 and 2025/26,[4] with the International Data Corporation (IDC) forecasting that global spending on digital transformations will reach $3.4 trillion in 2026.[5]

Given the 70% failure rate highlighted above, by 2026 there could be a total annual enterprise spend of over **$2.3 trillion** that did not deliver anticipated results.

Every Mass Extinction Results in a New Beginning

It is surprising that some organizations have no sense of urgency to evolve; they either do not see the need to change or are simply unaware of the size and speed of the digital juggernaut that is heading toward them. Large and currently stable organizations may not be nimble enough to change trajectory and as such will struggle to survive and may be replaced by smaller, more agile companies.

In terms of how far organizations have progressed through their digital transformation journey, there is a significant disparity between geographic regions, industry sectors within those regions, and organizational size.

The McKinsey Global Institute (MGI) Industry Digitization Index (as highlighted in *McKinsey Global Institute Digital America: A Tale of the Haves and Have-Mores*[6]) shows that sectors such as Media, Finance, and Insurance are advanced in their overall digitization efforts. The laggards in digital transformation span a diverse range of sectors including Construction, Agriculture, Education, and Government. Similarly, at a regional level, MGI has shown[7] that, in terms of digital transformation progress, the European Union (EU) is lagging behind the United States (although there is significant variance between EU member nations).

Somewhat surprisingly, the MGI Industry Digitization Index also shows that smaller companies lag larger firms in terms of their digital adoption, though this may be changing/has changed with the arrival of FinTech organizations and other start-ups where technology is fundamental to their business model.

---

[4] FinancesOnline, '72 Vital Digital Transformation Statistics: 2023 Spending, Adoption, Analysis & Data', FinancesOnline.com, (2023), https://financesonline.com/digital-transformation-statistics/ [accessed June 19, 2023].

[5] IDC, 'Global Digital Transformation Spending Guide', idc.com, (2022), https://www.idc.com/getdoc.jsp?containerId=prUS49797222 [accessed June 19, 2023].

[6] McKinsey Global Institute, 'Digital America: A tale of the haves and have-mores', mckinsey.com, (2015), https://www.mckinsey.com/~/media/mckinsey/industries/technology%20media%20and%20telecommunications/high%20tech/our%20insights/digital%20america%20a%20tale%20of%20the%20haves%20and%20have%20mores/mgi%20digital%20america_executive%20summary_december%202015.pdf [accessed June 19, 2023].

[7] McKinsey Global Institute (@McKinsey_MGI). 'Industries & countries digitize at different rate. Here's how #Europe can increase the pace'. Twitter, October 12, 2017. Available at: https://twitter.com/mckinsey_mgi/status/918446314681192448?lang=de [accessed: June 19, 2023].

The Galapagos Framework is crucial in this era of rapid change, as it allows organizations to become more agile without a wholesale overhaul of their core processes and capabilities.

A Human-Centric Approach to Transformational Change

The COVID-19 pandemic has caused profound changes in the relationship between the employee and employer. There are huge sections of the workforce that think life is too short to be working in a company/culture/role that they do not enjoy and are giving much more consideration to the question: *Is this really where I want to be?*

Companies may well think that a level of staff attrition is a healthy thing from an organizational perspective, especially if the individuals involved are not happy in their roles. Unhappy staff are likely to be demotivated, not very productive and will often be bringing the rest of the team down.

But let's turn that on its head for a moment: what happens if it's the organizational culture or the structure in which the individuals are operating that is causing employee dissatisfaction?

In this instance, there could be a situation where brilliant employees are leaving the company because it's just not a great place to work, does not meet their needs, and because they can.

This leaves behind those staff that, for whatever reason, can't move, resulting in a workforce that may not be skilled or motivated enough to deliver an effective transformation.

Digital transformation programs present opportunities for companies to reinvent themselves as somewhere that great staff want to work.

Definitions

Digital Transformation: A Definition

The term *digital transformation* is used widely and, depending on who you speak to, can mean anything from the development of a website to wholesale organizational and technological change. What is clear is that, wherever you are on this spectrum, digital transformation is a journey rather than a finite point of delivery of a product or service.

The increasing pace of customer demand and expectation means that organizations need to be more light-footed and more adaptable to an ever-changing landscape of consumer behavior. Digital transformation has a key role to play in ensuring that organizations remain relevant in the face of these increasing external challenges.

Given the above, it is worthwhile looking at some definitions of what this book means by digital, transformation, and most importantly, digital transformation.

Digital

Paraphrasing the words of Chris Micklethwaite at 3pointsDIGITAL,[8] *Digital* is the convergence of people and technology. Technology is all pervasive and how this is integrated into our daily lives is increasingly the driver for what is now called *Digital*.

Transformation

Transformation is not the same as re-organization, and to paraphrase Lou Gerstner (ex-IBM CEO), *re-organization is shuffling boxes around. Transformation is fundamentally changing the way the organization thinks, responds, and leads.*[9]

Digital Transformation

Given the above definitions, and to ensure that we progress on a sound footing, this book defines digital transformation as:

The means by which organizations use technology, people, and processes to find new business models and revenue streams, given the accelerating and increasing customer expectations around the products and services they receive.

Linear Transformation

Currently, most digital transformations are linear[10] in nature. They are finite (rather than evolving) and follow a direct path toward a predetermined end goal. Often multiple linear, but interrelated, transformations are set in progress concurrently.

Digital Acceleration

The Galapagos Framework is a new approach to digital transformations that challenges the established dogma of doing everything right first time using multiple, parallel, interconnected, and linear streams of program delivery.

---

[8] 3pointsDIGITAL, 'Home', 3pointsdigital.com, (no date), https://www.3pointsdigital.com/ [accessed June 19, 2023].

[9] Gerstner, L. (2004) 'In Focus: Lou Gerstner'. Interview with R. Quest. Available at: https://edition.cnn.com/2004/BUSINESS/07/02/gerstner.interview/ (Accessed: 27th November 2023).

[10] Linear in this instance means non-iterative. Organizations may be running multiple, parallel, and interrelated streams of work, with these streams being predominantly linear and long running in approach, and not iterative and incremental.

In order to move from digital transformation to Digital Acceleration, organizations need to reconsider their approach to these change initiatives. Digital Acceleration strategies are not linear (i.e., there is no digital end state; they are iterative and incremental in approach) and do not involve heavily parallel, programs of work; instead, they are more cyclical and evolutionary in nature.

Digital Acceleration is an iterative process that allows organizations to deliver transformations and demonstrate continual progress, at pace. Rather than tackling the transformation as one large single event, organizations will improve one (or at most two) discrete area(s) of the business quickly and then move on to the next.

Given the above, this book defines Digital Acceleration as:

An iterative, incremental, and mostly sequential approach to the delivery of digital transformations, that changes one (or at most two) distinct area(s) of the business before moving on to the next transformation objective.

The Fourth Industrial Revolution (4IR)

Digital transformation is a significant part of what has become known as the *Fourth Industrial Revolution (4IR)*, that is, the fusion of advances in physical, digital, and biological technology that is transforming society and the economy.

Advances in automation, artificial intelligence (AI), the Internet of Things (IoT), 3D printing, cloud computing, big data, blockchain, Web 3.0,[11] robotics, and other digital technologies are enabling new levels of productivity and connectivity that are marking this new age.

The convergence of these emerging technologies will lead to the development of more autonomous systems, more intelligent machines, and more sophisticated data analytics and will drive disruption in existing markets and exponentially change the way organizations operate, and the way in which we live.

Volatility, Uncertainty, Complexity, and Ambiguity

Given the advances highlighted previously, we now live in a world where *Volatility, Uncertainty, Complexity, and Ambiguity (VUCA[12])* are not only prevalent in the business world but are also part of everyday life.

---

[11] See Appendix D for definitions of AI, IoT, 3D Printing, etc.

[12] Warren Bennis and Burt Nanus, Leaders: The Strategies for Taking Charge (New York: Harper & Row, 1985), p. 20.

This requires a fresh approach to the leadership of digital transformations. The Galapagos Framework will give organizations and individuals a new orientation to deliver positive results under changing circumstances.

The Framework provides the structure to improve the delivery of business demands by eliminating complexity and allowing individuals to utilize their skills, in a collaborative environment, to produce more qualitative and quantitative results.

Chapter 2

Digital Transformations: The Common Issues

This chapter covers some of the common issues with digital transformation initiatives. The solutions to these issues are presented in *Chapters 7 to 12*.

There appear to be some consistent themes across those digital transformations that do not deliver success over anything beyond the very short term. The common issues that are presented here have been categorized into the following themes: *Human Elements*, *Organizational Factors*, and *Delivery Aspects*, and are explored below.

A Brief Word on Leadership

One school of thought is that every failed digital transformation is a failure in leadership. This is too broad a view to be useful, and there are some key elements of leadership that require special attention.

To address the leadership-specific issues, each of the *Human, Organizational, and Delivery* categories contains a *Failures in Leadership* section.

The Human Elements

The most significant factors that lead to a lack of success in transformation programs revolve around people. Some organizations appear to have forgotten that it's the people within the company, their relationships, and how they are led and managed that drive transformational change.

   DOI: 10.1201/9781003404217-3

The success, or otherwise, of any digital transformation change initiative is predominantly dependent on the organizational will to put *the human* at the center of the change story.

The Human Elements discussed in this section are broadly divided into Culture, Failures in Leadership, Communication, and Skills Issues.

Culture

Some organizations simply do not have the culture that is required for successful digital transformations. The lack of an open, healthy/positive working culture that is conducive to successfully delivering change is a significant factor in increasing the risk profile of the transformation.

Issue – Toxic culture[1]

What is surprising about poor corporate cultures is that a lot of leaders are blissfully unaware of the problem or don't see it as enough of an issue to warrant intervention. Business leaders seldom recognize that their organization's negative culture is reducing productivity, impacting morale, causing sickness, increasing staff attrition, and putting program deliveries at risk.

If the organizational culture is already having a negative impact on business performance, then the delivery of any transformation strategy is highly unlikely to realize positive outcomes.

How can this be? How can senior leaders not know (or in some instances not care) that sections of their organization have a toxic culture? Culture is driven from the top down, isn't it?

The extract below is from an article that was written for Fintech Futures, where the topic of *the dinosaur café – the impact of a toxic culture on digital transformation* is discussed.[2]

The master manipulators that are middle management

Most sizeable organizations will have several very competent managers that have, over time, been promoted into leadership positions.

They have reached these stations due, in no small part, to the fact that they are political experts and extremely skillful in "managing the

---

[1] The solution to this issue is presented in *Chapter 7 – How the Galapagos Framework Resolves the Common Issues: – The Human Element – Culture.*

[2] Fintech Futures. 'The Dinosaur Café: The impact of a toxic culture on digital transformation'. fintechfutures.com, 2023. Available at: https://www.fintechfutures.com/2023/04/the-dinosaur-cafe-the-impact-of-a-toxic-culture-on-digital-transformation/ [Accessed: June 19, 2023].

message". That is, they carefully control and manipulate the communications that flow upwards and outwards from their fiefdom.

The messages emanating from these groups go through so many layers of filtration that by the time the communication hits the senior leadership team any trace of contamination is removed, and a shiny and spotless message has been crafted and is ready for consumption.

The elephant in the room is actually a dinosaur

Individuals in these positions of power remain too focused on the operational and delivery detail to provide effective leadership.

Over the years, they create an authoritarian regime where there is no desire to foster broad collaboration. They evolve a siloed structure which leads to fractionalization, division, and a situation where the political game playing, at which they excel, is rife.

In "Team Flow The psychology of optimal collaboration", Jef J. J. van den Hout & Orin C. Davis express their views on this type of management: "*You can get the right talent in the room, give them a clear, meaningful goal, and then stick a dinosaur brain at the head of the table. You know the type: it roars loudly, ignores what people say, does what it wants, stomps around looking to see what it can snag, and generally makes a nuisance of itself. …Whatever the case: bad leader, bad team.*"

Delivery? Absolutely! But at what cost?

The very fact that these managers are so focused on the detail of delivery means that, more often than not, they do actually deliver.

What they deliver might not be exactly what was asked for or might be a bit late, but they do deliver.

Closing thoughts

A toxic culture will have a direct financial effect which can be difficult to quantify especially if it is obscured. There are human costs, delivery inefficiencies and waste which all have a negative impact on the efficiency and effectiveness of the transformation function.

A human centric approach to transformational change combined with incentives, that cover "how" delivery is achieved as well as "what" is delivered, are required to allow organizations to effectively identify and challenge the toxic culture.

Tackling the dinosaurs will result in positive improvements in delivery and the overall organizational health of the company.

The main take-home message from this extract is that you might have a dinosaur at the head of the table, and that person/group of people could be jeopardizing your program delivery and, over the longer term, will be holding your organization back.

Cultural Red Flags

Some warning signs of a toxic organizational culture are outlined below.

Lack of a Collaborative Environment

Some organizations are heavily siloed, inhibiting cross-functional collaboration. This type of environment often creates an atmosphere where internal politics and fear thrive, which severely inhibits the easy collaboration required to make any transformation successful. There may also be a lack of systems/tools in place to encourage and enable either individuals or whole teams to work together and share information freely.

Fear of Failure

Fear of failure not only stifles innovation but slows the pace of change execution.

An environment where there is no appetite for failing fast (or any degree of failure) results in significant inefficiencies and stifles innovation. Staff spend an inordinate amount of time and effort checking minor details of, relatively insignificant, work to avoid being reprimanded should something be found to be wrong. Inevitably, this results in delivery impacts and missed opportunities.

The Transformation Is Seen as an Unwanted Distraction From The Core Business

Individuals/teams and functions can perceive the transformation as *just another* new initiative, sometimes overplaying the impact on the core business of delivering the transformation.

Ensuring everyone is bought into the transformation and taken along on the journey is critical to success. The strategy and direction might be clear but if those that are tasked with implementing it are not fully on board, then the chances of success are low.

Obstructive Individuals/Teams/Functions

There will always be resistance to change with any transformation initiative.

In some instances, this resistance can slow down the implementation of the strategy, negatively impact staff morale, and increase costs. In extreme cases, this resistance can cause the transformation itself to fail.

Junior executives and middle managers (who have been promoted into these positions due, in no small part, to their political expertise) can control the narrative that is disseminated within their department. This, in turn, can have a negative impact on the delivery of the transformation. However, any adverse impact on delivery will be explained away and blamed on external factors using the outstanding manipulation skills that these individuals have built up over the years.

It only takes a very small number of junior executives/middle managers, adopting a similar approach to the one outlined above, to cause serious issues with the implementation of the transformation strategy.

Failures in Leadership

> **Issue: Strategy and direction are not clear and are not anchored in the business's core values and competencies[3]**

It is important for staff to understand where they are heading and why. Leaders need to make it clear to all employees that the transformation is aligned with the core values of the company and that this transformation will enhance the overall business. A significant proportion of staff will, no doubt, be working for the organization because the corporate values align with their own personal values. It is, therefore, imperative that the members of the leadership team that are driving the strategy ensure that it is grounded in, and aligned to, the values of the business.

> **Issue: Professional/corporate ambiguity[3]**

There are some instances where a degree of ambiguity is expected, but if the leaders of the function that is tasked with delivering on the strategy (particularly with regard to the scope of the transformation) don't provide clarity of focus, then this will lead to delay, mistrust, and in some instances, failure. After all, if the team is not clear on the direction of travel, it makes it very difficult to get to the destination.

A level of uncertainty suits a lot of executives as it allows them to change their mind on any number of factors (e.g., requirements/delivery scope/approach, etc.) without losing face but this does not help the organization deliver effective digital change at pace.

> **Issue: Leadership vacuum[3]**

In some instances, the *dinosaurs* mentioned in the article above are highly competent managers who have been in the organization for a long time and have been promoted into leadership positions.[4] In certain cases, these individuals are so focused on the operational and day-to-day delivery detail that they fail to provide effective leadership.

---

[3] The solution to this issue is presented in *Chapter 7 – How the Galapagos Framework Resolves the Common Issues: – The Human Element – Failures in leadership.*

[4] N.B: The vast majority of leaders that have been promoted through the managerial ranks are excellent at what they do and are not the dinosaurs referred to here.

The resulting leadership vacuum can be extremely difficult to identify as delivery output is maintained, and messaging produced out of these areas is carefully managed.

Communication

Targeted communication is, of course, critical to the success of any transformation initiative. However, there is all too often a scattergun approach to communication which can cause more problems than it solves.

Issue: The approach to communication[5]

The style of communication across the organization needs to be fit for purpose and support free collaboration and information sharing but must not result in everyone receiving a deluge of information that is not directly related to the relevant aspects of the transformation.

Issue: The frequency, method, and volume of communication[5]

The perceived wisdom that *more communication is better* generally results in many employees suffering from information overload. Constant communication can leave some staff members feeling overwhelmed, especially if their workload is already high.

When team members are bombarded by instant messages, emails, phone calls, and meetings, there will be a direct and negative impact on productivity which will reduce the overall efficiency of those tasked with delivering the transformation.

It is not uncommon for individuals to receive many hundreds of, sometimes lengthy, emails per day as well as instant messages and telephone/conference/video calls. Unsurprisingly, this impacts directly on delivery and performance as staff are diverted from getting on with their actual job.

Clear, unambiguous, and targeted communication is critical during any digital transformation, and care must be taken to ensure that employees involved in the delivery of each initiative are not receiving a flood of irrelevant information.

Skills Issues

If the organization does not have the required skills profile in the right locations or does not direct these skills correctly, then the organization will struggle to deliver effective digital change and the strategy is unlikely to succeed.

---

[5] The solution to these issues is presented in *Chapter 8 – How the Galapagos Framework Resolves the Common Issues: – The Human Element – Communication.*

Issue: Lack of the right type/number/level/mix of skills in the right location[6]

Skills gaps can be difficult and time-consuming to fill. So identifying the skills that are missing, the size (the number of skilled individuals required), the level (expert, mid-level, junior), and geographic location of these skills gaps is important. Having skills gap data will inform the decision as to whether the organization either partners with a trusted third party (in a resource augmentation capacity) or goes to market directly to fill the gaps.

Issue: Digital leaders are not on the top team[6]

The successful execution of any digital transformation requires digital leaders (CDO/CIO/CTO/CXO) to drive the strategy forward. The cross-functional/cross-departmental nature of these transformations requires these leaders to be highly collaborative in their approach.

There is a strong case for the appointment of a Chief Transformation Officer (abbreviated to CTO/CTrO depending on the company) for large and complex transformations. This is a C-suite, executive role that will lead and manage transformation initiatives and any associated organizational changes required. The specific responsibilities of the role will vary from organization to organization but will include activities such as developing the transformation strategy, capability building, ensuring cross-functional collaboration, fostering innovation, and so on.

Issue: Incentives not aligned to the transformation strategy[6,7]

Incentives can be a powerful tool, and when used correctly, they will support a strong collective purpose and a highly engaged team.

Historically, the various functions and roles involved in digital transformations have been incentivized differently. This is due to many factors (e.g., the sales team will be incentivized on revenue generation, the delivery teams will be incentivized on product build, and other supporting functions may not be 100% allocated to the transformation itself, etc.).

Goals and incentives show where the organization is focusing effort and priorities. Conflicting, or misaligned, incentives pull people to different north stars, dilute clarity on what success looks like, and increase risk. This has a negative impact on the efficiency and effectiveness of the transformation by creating silos, inhibiting collaboration, and sowing the seeds of disunity across the entire transformation function.

---

[6] The solution to these issues is presented in *Chapter 9 – How the Galapagos Framework Resolves the Common Issues: – The Human Element – Skills issues.*

[7] Extracts taken from *Digital transformations: aligning incentives to the transformation strategy.* Brian Harkin & Sarah Patel: April 2023.

Organizations also rely on commonly tracked program metrics and success indicators (such as schedule, scope, milestones, budget, etc.) and mandated organizational drivers (e.g., mission statement, company values, standards adherence, and so on) to contribute to employee incentive packages.

However, used in a disjointed way, these simply don't work. Incentives must be aligned to the transformation strategy which, in turn, must be anchored in the core business values and competencies.

The Organizational Factors

Every digital transformation is unique, as each evolves out of the dynamic nature and *ecology* of the parent organization and, though less significant than the *Human Elements*, the organizational considerations require serious attention.

Organizational Structure

> **Issue: The structure of the organization is not conducive to effective digital change[8]**

Many large organizations maintain a complex organizational structure that has evolved over time and is seen as either too difficult, too risky, or too costly to redesign.

In some instances, the structures themselves lead to political chicaneries, conflict, and defensive behavior, stemming from heavily siloed operating structures that inhibit open communication and prevent the high degree of collaboration that is required to deliver successful digital transformations.

Failures in Leadership

> **Issue: Lack of senior executive sponsorship[8]**

There is clearly a significant issue surrounding senior executive sponsorship of digital transformation initiatives. As discussed in *The Human Elements* section, a digital leader needs to be included in the top team. In addition, however, it is crucial that the CEO has a key role in driving the digital transformation forward.

Research reported by financesonline.com[9] indicates that only 23% of CEOs own or sponsor digital transformation initiatives. Furthermore, 37% of people think that the CEO or board of directors are actually *holding back* digital transformation

---

[8] The solution to these issues is presented in *Chapter 11 – How the Galapagos Framework Resolves the Common Issues: – The Organizational Factors – Organizational structure.*

[9] FinancesOnline, '72 Vital Digital Transformation Statistics: 2023 Spending, Adoption, Analysis & Data', FinancesOnline.com, (2023), https://financesonline.com/digital-transformation-statistics/ [accessed June 19, 2023].

initiatives. Given that the total enterprise spend on digital transformations is likely to hit **$3.4 trillion**[10] by 2026, it is staggering to think that CEOs are not at the forefront of these changes.

The underlying reasons behind CEOs' reticence to drive digital transformation initiatives are unclear. It has been suggested that these programs are inherently risky, and as such CEOs would rather play it safe and not take the chance of any personal/professional reputational damage that may be incurred if things don't go well. This may in turn be why many organizations employ third parties to deliver on digital transformation strategies.

Digital transformations must not only be driven from the top but also *be seen* to be driven from the top – by the CEO or as close to the CEO as possible. The sponsoring executive must communicate to the entire organization the reasons why the transformation initiative is of strategic importance and communicate this message consistently and, in the early stages of the change, frequently. This will reduce the chances of issues arising as the transformation progresses.

Issue: Complex and sometimes conflicting reporting lines[11]

Organizational orthodoxy (i.e., the established practices that inform and guide the way companies function) has resulted in a situation where many organizations operate in a matrix management structure (where staff may report to several different managers). This is not necessarily a bad thing and can, in many instances, lead to more efficient use of resources and improved flexibility.

However, as businesses grow, matrix structures can result in situations where the lines of responsibility become blurred and conflicting priorities arise. This ambiguity can lead to situations where accountability and delivery are compromised by confusion over who is answerable for which deliveries leading to inter-managerial conflict.

We touched on *The frequency, method, and volume of communication* earlier, and a complex matrix management structure can exacerbate the information overload on staff. The organizational structure itself often requires an extensive communication matrix to support it which can consume significant amounts of people's time that would be better spent on delivery.

---

[10] IDC, 'Global Digital Transformation Spending Guide', idc.com, (2022), https://www.idc.com/getdoc.jsp?containerId=prUS49797222 [accessed June 19, 2023].

Issue: The right mix of "C" level leaders are not involved early enough[11]

Digital transformation requires cross-function/cross-department collaboration driven by the CEO, CTrO, CIO/CTO/CDO, CPO, CHRO[12] *et al.* Frequently, the technology functions have early input into the transformation process, but HR is either late to the table or in some instances not included at all.

Given that the most significant factors that lead to failure in transformation programs revolve around people, any transformation initiative must have HR involvement at an early stage. The HR function will not only assist with cultural transformation but will also help in defining the Workforce Strategy and identifying and filling skills gaps that the organization needs to drive the transformation forward.

The Delivery Aspects

Digital transformation programs are often run within the context of complex, dynamic, multi-faceted businesses, but are delivered in a way that does not cater to the inherent uncertainty and volatility of these environments.

Failures in Leadership

Issue: Strategy review cycles are too long[13]

The perfect strategy doesn't exist, and even if it did, by the time any strategy is executed on the ground the world has moved on. Having a mid- to long-term strategy is clearly still required. However, the frequency with which the strategy is reviewed must increase.

Issue: Strategy reviews are not data-driven[13]

Often, feedback cycles from transformation initiatives either do not exist or do not deliver clear enough metrics to allow strategic programs to change course. There is, therefore, a need for better quality, and improved timelines of, information to facilitate more accurate, data-driven decision-making.

---

[11] The solution to this issue is presented in *Chapter 11 – How the Galapagos Framework Resolves the Common Issues: – The Organizational Factors – Organizational structure.*

[12] CEO – Chief Executive Officer, CTrO – Chief Transformation Officer, CIO – Chief Information Officer, CTO – Chief Technical Officer, CDO – Chief Digital Officer, CPO – Chief Product Officer, CHRO – Chief Human Resources Officer.

[13] The solution to these issues is presented in *Chapter 12 – How the Galapagos Framework Resolves the Common Issues: – The Delivery Aspects – Failures in leadership.*

Businesses can no longer rely on subjective, gutfeel, and often knee-jerk, pronouncements from leaders. Even if these are based on extensive experience, they have in the past, often resulted in many poor and sometimes catastrophic decisions being taken. Leadership decisions should not be based solely on experience; they must be informed and supported by the data.

Orchestrating the Transformation

Many change programs are still run on the basis that the executives and delivery leadership teams know, and have accounted for, every possible situation that will occur over the course of the transformation (even if the delivery of this is expected to run for a very long time).

The assumption that everything can be known, or accounted for is, of course, not true. There are many factors both internal and external to the transformation (and in many instances external to the organization itself) that will affect the delivery of the strategy, and the best that program directors/managers can do is plug in some arbitrary contingency time to cater for things that may/may not happen.

When the stakes are so high and the spending is so large, this does not seem like a very satisfactory way to deliver a fundamental change to the way the business thinks, responds, and leads.

Issue: Managing change and transformation activities[14]

All companies have sections of their business that are running at different speeds, with some delivering moon shots (the higher end of what the digital transformation aims to achieve) and others covering roof shots (regular change activities) and the core Business As Usual (BAU) changes required to support the ongoing functioning of the business. The delivery of these endeavors often falls to the same (relatively small) group of individuals.

The skills required to manage the full range of transformation activities can often be very different from those required to deliver regular or BAU changes. Concentrating the responsibility for the delivery of all these transformation and change processes on a small number of individuals can lead to drops in efficiency and effectiveness, as well as the human cost of employee fatigue and burnout.

Scope

A clearly defined, and limited, scope of the transformation is critical for success. There is always a push to deliver more over shorter timeframes and a certain amount of challenge in this area is healthy.

---

[14] The solution to this issue is presented in *Chapter 12 – How the Galapagos Framework Resolves the Common Issues: – The Delivery Aspects – Orchestrating the transformation.*

However, leaders will often ignore what they are being told about what is achievable, by when, and either dig their heels in or push harder. This, in turn, leads to a huge increase in pressure on the delivery teams, over a sustained period, which significantly increases the risk of failure. More bloated scope leads to more complexity, more cost, and more delay.

By asking for less, leaders will, over the medium and long term, get more. Shorter and more iterative delivery cycles will result in more consistency of what can be expected at the end of a delivery iteration. When delivery pressure remains at an *indefinitely* **sustainable** *level*, the organization reduces the risk of staff attrition and burnout and increases the likelihood of success.

Issue: Scope is too broad[15]

The scope may involve multiple functions/business units or the whole enterprise. 80% of respondents to a McKinsey survey said their recent change efforts either involved multiple functions/business units or the whole enterprise.[16]

As will be covered later, parallelism is never free. Attempting to transform multiple, interrelated areas of the business concurrently will result in any perceived benefit being quickly outweighed by the increasing complexity of the transformation program.

Issue: Scope is too deep[15]

Attempting to solve significant issues with the entire organization's operating model, as part of a digital transformation initiative, will dramatically increase the complexity of the change.

Minimizing the impact of the transformation on the wider organization is key to ensuring the stability of core business functions. Targeted changes to the operating model may be necessary to drive success (e.g., removing silos), but care needs to be taken to confirm that wholesale operating model change is not included within the scope of the transformation.

---

[15] The solution to this issue is presented in *Chapter 12 – How the Galapagos Framework Resolves the Common Issues: – The Delivery Aspects – Scope.*

[16] McKinsey & Company, 'Unlocking success in digital transformations', mckinsey.com, (2018), https://www.mckinsey.com/business-functions/organization/our-insights/unlocking-success-in-digital-transformations [accessed June 19, 2023].

Linear/Non-iterative Approach

Digital transformations are still predominantly run in a linear fashion, where there is a large amount of analysis and decision-making performed before the transformation itself moves forward.

Issue: A linear approach to the transformation[17]

In linear transformations, there is a single end goal and a straight path to get there, with little to no room for adjustment along the way. Also, in an attempt to shorten delivery timelines, these initiatives are also run in a mostly parallel way (i.e., lots of interdependent workstreams in flight at the same time) and highly complex delivery plans are produced to demonstrate that the end goal can be achieved within the timeframe and budget available.

These linear delivery plans look great on a slide but often fail to take into account the messy reality of transformational change in a complex business environment.

A linear approach to transformational change will significantly increase the risk of failure. Organizations are essentially rolling the dice and hoping that all the work and assumptions that were taken at the start of the program are still valid at the time of delivery and that everything still works together as it should. All of this without the ability to validate the technical feasibility, or test any of the preliminary assumptions that were made, until very late in the delivery process. Of course, leaving it until near the end (or worse at the end) of the process to validate the up-front assumptions is a very high-risk approach.

Heavy-Weight Governance[18]

When digital transformation programs hit setbacks, or look like they might be getting into trouble, the dinosaur brains invariably throw more governance at the problem.

This is never the right way forward.

---

[17] The solution to this issue is presented in *Chapter 12 – How the Galapagos Framework Resolves the Common Issues: – The Delivery Aspects – Linear/Non-iterative approach.*

[18] Extracts taken from Fintech Futures. 'Digital transformations: the negative impact of heavy-weight governance'. fintechfutures.com, 2023. Available at: https://www.fintechfutures.com/2023/08/digital-transformations-the-negative-impact-of-heavyweight-governance/ [accessed: August 1, 2023].

> **Issue: Heavy-weight governance is increasing costs and reducing delivery efficiency[19]**

In every digital transformation, it is inevitable that there will be obstacles and challenges to overcome, and some of these will be significant.

However, when bumps in the road are encountered, and sensing potential trouble ahead, the dinosaurs get involved, and in an attempt to wrestle back some control, they throw more governance at the program.

Hierarchies of steering committees and delivery boards lurch into existence, and these beasts need feeding.

Individuals who should be delivering the transformation are diverted from their day job to serve up a banquet of slides and delivery updates for the committees and boards to consume (or in some instances ignore).

Bureaucracy and red tape are liberally applied to the entire program resulting in the slowing down of many processes.

Yet the transformation typically remains in the same position and most of the same issues exist, but the misguided approach taken to *fix the problem* has now exacerbated the situation.

The positive impact of any changes that have been applied pale into insignificance against a backdrop of rising costs, and the decreasing pace of delivery, resulting from the multiple layers of inefficiency that have been added.

It is understandable, expected, and right that senior leaders will take an active interest in programs that are hitting turbulent times; after all, they are accountable for the program spend.

Nevertheless, the overzealous approach that can be adopted by some often makes the situation worse, and in some instances, almost impossible to recover from.

---

[19] The solution to this issue is presented in *Chapter 12 – How the Galapagos Framework Resolves the Common Issues: – The Delivery Aspects – Heavy-weight governance.*

Chapter 3

Introduction to The Galapagos Framework

What Is The Galapagos Framework?

The Galapagos Framework takes a holistic approach to digital transformations by solving the human, organizational, and delivery problems that plague many of these programs.

The Framework provides the scalability and flexibility to allow organizations of any size to deliver successful transformational changes against a backdrop of an increasingly uncertain and ever-changing operating environment.

A Human-centric and Inclusive Approach to Deliver Successful Transformations

Every digital transformation will be unique, as each evolves out of the dynamic nature and *ecology* of the parent organization.

There is, however, one constant across all transformation initiatives – *the human*. The Galapagos Framework puts people at the center of the change strategy (be that the staff within the organization, the end customers, the suppliers, or other third parties), encouraging collaboration, creativity, and positive cultural transformation.

Putting *the human* at the heart of the transformation will drive positive behavioral and organizational changes, resulting in more successful outcomes for transformation programs.

DOI: 10.1201/9781003404217-4

The Island[1]

One of the principal structures of The Galapagos Framework is The Island. This is a discreet, dedicated innovation environment, free from existing business influence and risk, which promotes the fast evolution of ideas and deliveries resulting in a stronger end state. Thus, imitating nature through an iterative cycle of many, small incremental changes, micro A-B competitions between ideas, instant feedback loops, and constant course corrections delivered at speed.

The Island structure is protected from the broader business, resulting in an environment where experimentation and testing are continuous, there's no fear of failure, and ideas fit for purpose win through and survive to the next stage.

Consisting of a cross-functional group of individuals tasked to deliver, initially, on a single well-defined business objective, the staff on The Island will be the agents of transformational change; they will not be afraid to challenge the status quo, will be passionate about their mission, and have the skills, resources, and motivation to effect positive change.

We will look at The Island again in *Chapter 4, The Function of The Galapagos Framework*, and explore it in more detail in *Chapter 14, The Island*.

Why *Galapagos*?

The use of *Galapagos* is, of course, in reference to the Galapagos archipelago where Charles Darwin conducted some of the research that led to the writing of the *Origin of Species*. Being approximately 600 miles off the coast of Ecuador, the unique biodiversity found on the Galapagos Islands is due, in no small part, to their geographic isolation from other land masses.

Darwin's ideas on evolution were not a flash of inspiration but rather developed over time and not along a linear trajectory: *When Darwin arrived at cognitive impasses, he sought alternative routes.*[2] Furthermore, Darwin did not work in isolation but rather collaborated with other naturalists to refine his work.

The relevance of geographic isolation, transformations following a nonlinear trajectory, and collaboration are some of the key themes of The Galapagos Framework.

---

[1] The island is the organizational structure that delivers fast product evolution toward a stronger end state, imitating nature through an iterative cycle of many small incremental changes.

[2] "...small islands were particularly conducive to the engendering and transmutation of species." De Paolo, C. (2010). 'Darwin and the Galápagos Islands: An Annotated Guide to the Primary Texts', Victorian Web. Available at: https://www.victorianweb.org/science/darwin/depaolo2.html (accessed: 5th September 2023).

Why a Different Approach Is Required

Increasing Costs and Complexity

In many organizations, digital transformations cut across a large number of different streams of activities, functions, and departments (e.g., organizational change, leadership and strategy, culture and communication, skills, technology, etc.).

With an already complex transformational landscape, most companies approach this type of change initiative by attempting to *transform the organization, … rather than transforming departments in isolation, or sequentially.*[3] This approach significantly increases the risk profile of the program of work.

It is, therefore, no surprise that organizations find themselves in a position where the complexity of the transformation is significant, the risk profile is increasing, and where the scope, and therefore costs, are snowballing.

Cost and Complexity Are Nonlinear

Given that businesses are looking to transform the entire organization, and that *time is money*, they naturally try to run many streams of transformation activity in parallel in an attempt to shorten delivery timelines.

This, however, is a false economy.

Multiple concurrent, interrelated streams of activity have a nonlinear cost curve, when run in the context of an existing business structure that is delivering products and services in a predominantly non-digital way. In other words, the costs of interdependent parallel work streams don't just steadily increase; they skyrocket exponentially as the number of work streams or dependencies increase.

The complexity of running multiple interrelated streams of work is also nonlinear. This complexity also comes with other hidden costs.

Human Cost

There is an inherent and significant human cost to increasing the complexity of any transformation program, and this must be considered. Communication overload and complex interdependencies between departments, functions, and teams increases the risk of unintended consequences when changes are delivered and can lead to employees suffering from transformation fatigue. Significant amounts of time will be spent on impact analysis to ensure that changes made in one area don't inadvertently impact other areas, which will leave staff feeling frustrated and overwhelmed.

---

[3] Prophet. 'The 2021 State of Digital Transformation'. prophet.com, 2021. Available at: https://prophet.com/2021/10/the-2021-state-of-digital-transformation/ [accessed: June 19, 2023].

There are broad and far-reaching human costs of delays to program delivery stemming from increasing complexity (e.g., loss of confidence in the team(s) delivering the changes, internal/external reputational damage, etc.). The knock-on effect of this damage will lead to a downward spiral of overthinking, excessive planning and, generally, more bloat[4] and more delay.

The Most Efficient Path Is Not a Straight Line

The counterintuitive idea that *The most efficient path is not a straight line (nor is it multiple parallel streams of work)* is a key principle of The Galapagos Framework (see "Sequential Transformation" below).

The Framework proposes that the most efficient execution path for digital transformations is nonlinear. Further, The Framework suggests that starting a large transformation program with multiple concurrent, interrelated streams of work, covering multiple business areas is *not* the most effective or efficient means of a successful or timely delivery.

The Galapagos Framework approaches digital transformations from a very different perspective, and how this works is covered in the later chapters of the book.

The Galapagos Principles

The Galapagos Framework has at its core, a set of principles that guide how The Framework operates.

Principle 1: Culture Is King

The right culture is driven from the top down and therefore requires strong and consistent leadership. Key aspects of a positive culture include:

Collaboration	– A high degree of collaboration must be encouraged.
Communication	– Open, honest, and friendly two-way communication must become the norm.
No Fear of Failure	– Failing fast is fine as long as the cause is understood, and lessons are learned. Failing quickly minimizes the cost of failure; it also minimizes the impact of failure, ensuring that drastic consequences do not result.

---

[4] In this context, referring to throwing more governance or heavy-weight processes at the problem.

Principle 2: Customer Proximity

We must shorten feedback loops and reduce the distance between the end customer and the engine room of delivery. That is, we must minimize the links in the chain between the end customer and the product development and delivery functions.

The Customer Proximity principle of The Galapagos Framework sates the following:

Minimizing the number of links between the end customer and the product development and delivery functions will reduce costs and increase profit. Increasing the number of links will have the opposite effect.

In essence, this principle works on the basis that every additional link between the customer and the organization carries a point of inefficiency.

At small scale, bringing the customer closer to the company could involve more direct contact with the end customer, but at larger scales (where this is not possible) a similar effect could be achieved by collecting and analyzing more data about how the customer interacts with both the organization and its products.

The Customer Experience Function (covered in *Chapter 14, The Island*) is the driver of the *Customer Proximity* principle and it is the role of this function to define the mechanics of how this principle is implemented within the organization.

This principle is covered in more detail in *Chapter 26, The Customer Proximity Principle*.

Principle 3: Geographic Isolation

The Island does not have to be physically separated from the parent organization but must (where possible) be unencumbered by the processes, procedures, tooling, and ways of working of the parent company.

These operational mechanisms have often been developed over many years/decades and in several cases do not lend themselves to a digital way of working. The Island must also have all the resources, tools, and technologies to allow it to succeed.

In short, The Island must be set up for success.[5]

---

[5] This is a strange phrase that is used frequently in many different organizations (e.g., "we've got to set this individual/team up for success") the implication being that other teams/individuals have either been set up to fail or set up to retain the status quo.

Principle 4: Sequential Transformation

The most efficient path is not a straight line (nor is it multiple parallel streams of work).

In the natural world, as well as the business world, *actual change is never linear. Change exists in a complicated, ever changing, multidimensional environment.*[6]

The only way to successfully execute transformations in today's complex business environment is to use fast, iterative cycles of delivery (*Digital Acceleration*) focusing on one (or at most two) area(s) of the business at a time, in a mostly sequential fashion (viz. *Sequential Transformation*).

Parallelism is never free, and having many parallel and interdependent streams of work negates any benefit from running streams concurrently.

Principle 5: Transformation Context

The Island exists within a *Transformation Context*,[7] and there should only ever be one Island within a Transformation Context. The Island should deliver one (and under very specific circumstances,[8] at most two) digital transformation(s) at a time.

Increasing the number of parallel streams of work, or the dependencies between these streams, even by a small amount increases the complexity, cost, and risk profile of the delivery significantly.

Managing interdependencies relating to resources, schedules, technical requirements, or any of the other myriad factors that affect delivery becomes extremely complex. The lines of communication also increase significantly, resulting in more delay, more scope for confusion, and ultimately results in a vicious cycle of increasing complexity.

The concept of the Transformation Context is covered in more detail in *Chapter 4, The Function of The Galapagos Framework.*

Principle 6: Senior Executive Sponsorship Is a Must

Many digital transformations fail because there is a lack of *visible sponsorship* from the CEO (or a senior executive who is as close to the CEO as possible).

---

[6] Hill, G. 'Many More Much Smaller Steps: First Sketch'. geepawhill.org, 2021. Available at: https://www.geepawhill.org/2021/09/29/many-more-much-smaller-steps-first-sketch/ [accessed: June 19, 2023].

[7] There are many global organizations where subsidiaries or business units exist that have different operating models, tools, processes, and technologies to deliver on their specific business objectives. The Galapagos Framework regards each of these as a different transformation context.

[8] Two concurrent transformation initiatives can be undertaken by a single instance of The Island in situations where there are zero, or close to zero, interdependencies between these initiatives.

Resistance to change is prevalent in all too many transformation programs, but the impact of this can be minimized if there is clear support for the initiative from the CEO. The support of senior executives for the change strategy will also make it easier to align staff incentives to the goals of the transformation and ensure that everyone is pulling in the same direction.

Principle 7: Clarity Is Key

Professional/corporate ambiguity suits a lot of executives and managers as it allows them to change their minds regarding approach or delivery scope, or any number of other factors, without losing face.

There are some instances where a degree of ambiguity is expected, and indeed necessary (e.g., vision/mission statements). However, if ambiguity exists in the communication of the transformation strategy or The Delivery or Go-To Market Functions (see *Chapter 4, The Function of The Galapagos Framework – The Island Structure*), particularly with regard to scope, then this will lead to delay, mistrust, and in some instances failure.

Principle 8: The Right Balance of Skills and Experience

Each organization needs to find its *Goldilocks Zone* of experience and skills to deliver the transformation.

Considering the large number of start-ups that have not survived beyond a year or two gives some indication that having a young, ambitious, and enthusiastic team is not enough to deliver success. On the flip side of this particular coin, there are several large organizations headed by very experienced leaders that have struggled to adjust to an ever-changing commercial environment.

Delivering the right balance (which will be different for each organization) of youth, ambition, and experience will be a key factor in driving success.

Principle 9: Establish and Automate Metrics and Reporting Early

It is important that agreement is reached at the earliest opportunity as to what metrics (Key Performance Indicators, Objectives and Key Results etc.) and reporting will be used within The Island and for onward communication of progress/updates to the parent organization.

Once an agreement has been reached, effort needs to be placed into ensuring that this reporting is automated as far as possible. Program management functions need to focus on delivery and not on report production. Spending countless hours changing report formats and content for slightly different audiences is not a productive use of anyone's time, let alone those who are tasked with keeping the transformation on track and within budget.

Principle 10: Three Rules of Three

The Island operates on the *Three rules of three* principle.

There are only ever three roles in The Leadership Function: The Accountable Executive (AE), The Business Head, and The Delivery Head.

There are only ever three Go-To Market and Delivery Functions: The Customer Experience Function, The Product Function, and The Technology Function.

There are only ever three areas on The Island: The Nucleus, The Ancillary Go-To Market Functions and the Integration Specialist(s); these areas are covered in *Chapter 4, The Function of The Galapagos Framework.*

Chapter 4

The Function of The Galapagos Framework

The Galapagos Framework provides the structures, scalability, and flexibility to drive successful digital transformations and resolves the common problems that these programs suffer from.

The Framework operates at any scale, from small companies up to globally distributed multinational organizations, and allows these businesses to change direction/focus in the face of a rapidly changing environment.

Successful Delivery

The purpose of the Galapagos Framework is to deliver successful digital transformations faster, whist at the same time reducing the operational, financial, and delivery risks associated with these programs.

There is no need to bet the house on a single, organization-wide, transformation event; The Framework delivers success by approaching the challenge differently.

A Means of Tackling the *Common Issues*

As touched on in *Chapter 2, Digital Transformations: The Common Issues*, there are a number of organizational, human, and delivery factors that impact the success of digital transformations.

The Galapagos Framework addresses these issues by setting up The Island, a structure that is largely unencumbered by the heavyweight processes of the main

DOI: 10.1201/9781003404217-5

organization but still has solid links to the parent company. By doing this, The Island has the freedom to explore new approaches, techniques, and technologies to solve the common issues in a more efficient and effective way.

The Island

As touched upon in *Chapter 3*, The Island is the organizational structure that is tasked with creating and realizing the transformation strategy and is wholly responsible for the execution and delivery of the entire digital transformation. The Island is the entity that satisfies *Galapagos Principle 3: Geographic Isolation*:

The Island ... must be (where possible) unencumbered by the processes, procedures, tooling, and ways of working of the parent company.

The Island Location

At this point, is it worth exploring where The Island could be located.

The Island may exist in the same office as the parent organization. In contrast, The Island could be in a totally different building from the parent organization, or it may be 100% virtual (i.e., made up of teams and individuals that work in a fully remote way).

Similarly, the staff on The Island may spend 100% of their time physically located in the same office, work in a hybrid model (with staff in the office some days and working remotely on other days), or work in a fully remote style.

The location of The Island, and the approach to where the staff on The Island work, is not as important as adhering to the principle of *Geographic Isolation*.

A New Method of Delivery

Rather than take a *systems thinking* approach (where the whole system/current operating model is analyzed and improved) which may increase cost, complexity, and risk of failure, the Galapagos Framework tackles the problem in a new way.

The Island transforms one (or at most two) discreet area(s) of the business in a mostly sequential fashion, adhering to *Galapagos Principle 4: Sequential Transformation*[1] which states that:

---

[1] See *Chapter 3 – Introduction to The Galapagos Framework: The Galapagos Principles.*

Parallelism is never free and having many parallel, and interdependent streams of work, negates any benefit from running streams concurrently.

Greenfield[2]

The Island is essentially a greenfield structure that predominantly operates outside of the constraints of the parent organization. This makes it ideal for creating or using new processes/procedures/technologies and establishing a more collaborative and communicative culture and way of working, without being hindered by the burden of existing processes or other limitations (in this sense, The Island could be considered as something of an oasis).

The Island is free from the routine constraints of the parent organizational structure; however, if the processes/procedures/technologies of the parent company are fit for purpose, then these can, and should, be used on The Island. There is no point in implementing new approaches, ways of working, or technologies just for the sake of it. In addition, each new element created within The Island will, at some point, need to be easily reintegrated back into the parent organization.

The Island Structure

Figure 4.1 shows The Go-To Market and Delivery Functions of The Island and illustrates how The Island interacts with the end customer and the parent organization via The Customer Experience Function and Integration Specialists, respectively. These are some of the key elements that differentiate The Galapagos Framework from other frameworks in this field.

The Island simplifies the structure that will deliver the digital transformation as much as possible while ensuring a highly collaborative and communicative engagement model that will enhance delivery capabilities.

---

[2] In this context, *Greenfield* means a blank canvas or a clean sheet. The Island is creating something new outside of the structures of the parent organization.

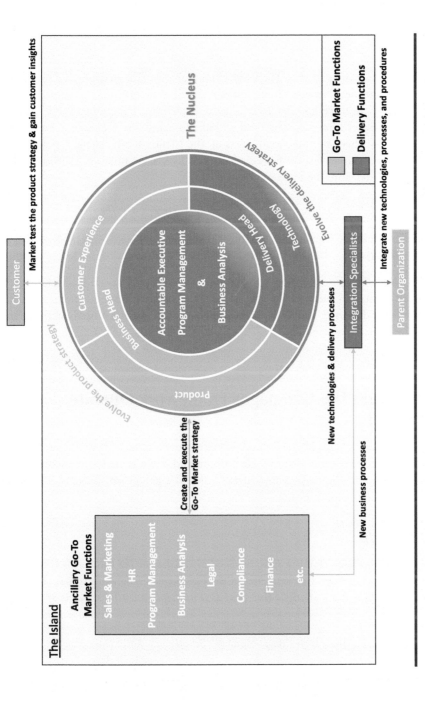

Figure 4.1 The Island structure.

Three Is the Magic Number

The Island operates on the principle of *The three rules of three*; after all, three is the magic number.[3]

1. There are three roles in The Leadership Function: The Accountable Executive, The Business Head, and The Delivery Head.
2. There are three key Go-To Market and Delivery Functions: The Customer Experience Function, The Product Function, and The Technology Function.
3. Finally, there are three main areas of The Island: The Nucleus, The Ancillary Go-To Market Functions (i.e., those Go-To Market functions outside of The Nucleus), and The Integration Specialists.

Each of these will be covered in more detail in *Chapter 14 – The Island.*

The Model

The Island will define and deliver a clear, user-friendly, and easy-to-understand digital transformation model (*The Model*) that will describe how the transformation was/is being delivered. It is essentially the operating model that is used on The Island to deliver the transformation.

The model is described in detail in *Chapter 19 – The Model.*

How Does The Galapagos Framework Operate at Scale?

One of the key benefits of The Galapagos Framework is its scalability. The Framework has been designed to allow it to scale both up and down to make it suitable for use in Small and Medium-sized Enterprises (SMEs) right up to globally distributed multinational organizations.

Scaling Up

As touched on above (and in *Chapter 3 – Introduction to The Galapagos Framework: The Galapagos Principles*), a key tenet of the Galapagos Framework is that: *The most efficient path is not a straight line (nor is it multiple parallel streams of work).*

---

[3] Bob Dorough, "Three is the Magic Number," Schoolhouse Rock! (American Broadcasting Company, 1973).

But more famously to people of a certain generation, De La Soul, "The Magic Number," track 7 on 3 Feet High and Rising, Tommy Boy/Warner Bros., 1989, CD.

Scalability, in this sense, does not mean massive parallelism, in terms of large numbers of interdependent streams of work that are in-flight simultaneously.

Scaling up, in this instance, uses the concept of the *Transformation Context*.

The Transformation Context

There are many global organizations where subsidiaries or business units exist that have different operating models, tools, processes, and technologies to deliver on their specific business objectives. The Galapagos Framework regards each of these as a different *Transformation Context*.

The Island exists within a *Transformation Context*, and there should only ever be one Island within a *Transformation Context*.

However, there will inevitably be some situations where there will be a need for more than one transformation to occur at the same time within a single *Transformation Context* (e.g., two distinct business areas with zero, or close to zero, interrelationships that need to be transformed at the same time) and under these specific conditions The Island can increase in size to accommodate a second transformation.

Please note that there should not be more than two concurrent transformations taking place within a single *Transformation Context*, as these transformations will be delivered by a single instance of The Island. As mentioned in *Chapter 3 – Introduction to The Galapagos Framework*, increasing the number of parallel streams of work, or the dependencies between these streams, even by a small amount increases the complexity, cost, and risk profile of the delivery significantly.

There will be many situations where the digital transformation strategy will cover multiple business areas. In these situations, and once the first transformational objective is nearing delivery, the organization would begin to increase the size of The Island to allow it to tackle two delivery streams concurrently.

It should be noted that additional resources will reduce the delivery velocity of The Island in the short term, but that is okay; delivery can slow down initially, to go faster later.

Note that handling two concurrent transformations doesn't mean that the size of The Island needs to double. The rationale for this is that the processes and procedures that The Island has implemented in the first transformation will be functioning well and will already be starting to be bedded into the organization. At this stage of the delivery, The Island will be becoming more efficient and the delivery velocity increasing.

So, the addition of another transformation stream to The Island will allow it to deliver two concurrent transformations (with zero or close to zero interdependencies) but will not double the number of staff on The Island.

The aim of limiting the number of concurrent streams to two is, first, to minimize the complexity introduced by increasing the management of dependencies/

interdependencies and, second, to minimize impacts on multiple other streams of activity (e.g., Business As Usual, BAU, day-to-day work).

This could be thought of as analogous to a house and garden *transformation*, in which there can only ever be a maximum of two concurrent (and unrelated) work-streams going on at any one time. So, for example, the inside of the house could be being painted while the garden is landscaped.

The house and garden transformation strategy is created and led by one Leadership Function and the entire delivery of the transformation is handled by one instance of The Island, and in the example above, The Island is executing two unrelated streams of work concurrently (i.e., the internal painting of the house and the landscaping of the garden).

Multiple Transformation Contexts

For large-scale transformations, there may be multiple Transformation Contexts (each with its own Island) and, in these situations, it is the responsibility of The Leadership Functions of the various Islands to liaise with each other to ensure that there is some commonality of approach (especially regarding culture, collaboration, and communication) to the transformations being undertaken.

Scaling Down

It is important to be mindful that the roles that exist on The Island are just that, roles, they are not individuals. On this basis, multiple roles could be performed by one individual, and for small businesses, this is likely to be the case.

For example, it could be that The Delivery Head, Program Management, and Business Analysis roles are all performed by one individual and The Accountable Executive and Business Head roles are performed by another individual.

Equally, The Integration Specialists and The ancillary Go-To Market Functions may/may not exist for smaller businesses.

Flexibility

The Galapagos Framework is extremely flexible, particularly in its ability to scale up/down from micro/small businesses to multinationals. The Framework can be applied to the smallest of businesses (with just a few employees) to the largest of organizations. In fact, for large organizations, The Island could be an entirely separate business unit or a separate Legal Entity.

Chapter 5

Moving from Digital Transformation to Digital Acceleration[1]

With three-quarters of digital transformations being undertaken to improve efficiencies or to meet the ever-increasing pace of changing customer expectations[2] (40% and 35%, respectively), it is crucial to success that organizations not only improve the pace of these changes but also effectively manage the risks associated with this type of initiative.

What Is Digital Acceleration?

Digital Acceleration is the process that underpins *Galapagos Principle 4: Sequential Transformation*, which states, *The most efficient path is not a straight line (nor is it multiple parallel streams of work).*

The use of fast iterative cycles of delivery drives behavioral change and benefits beyond improving the quality and timeliness of the deliveries themselves. It has a positive effect on morale as staff, and stakeholders, see continuous progress with teams and individuals working at a rate that is sustainable over the long term.

---

[1] This chapter is based on the output of an interview with Marcucci J., CDO: endava (July 8, 2022).

[2] FinancesOnline, '72 Vital Digital Transformation Statistics: 2023 Spending, Adoption, Analysis & Data', FinancesOnline.com, (2023), https://financesonline.com/digital-transformation-statistics/[accessed June 19, 2023].

The overall wellbeing of the organization will also be improved and the company's ability to perform effectively over a prolonged period will be enhanced. Similarly, the organizations' ability to adapt to change will be improved as will employee satisfaction and engagement.

The Benefits of Digital Acceleration vs. Linear Transformations[3]

Those who have experience in Agile delivery will no doubt understand the benefits of an iterative and incremental approach to product development. Taking the iterative and incremental approach into the domain of digital transformation also results in several clear advantages compared to large-scale linear transformations.

Risk Management

Linear transformations require a significant amount of up-front analysis and decision-making. Essentially, organizations are placing a bet for 6/9/12 months ahead (or sometimes longer) that the up-front assumptions and prework are still accurate at the time of delivery, and that all the processes and technology still work together within the newly transformed environment.

There are only two outcomes in these situations, either the bets are not correct – which leads to failure – or the bets and assumptions made are so low-risk that what is eventually delivered is underwhelming.

Many large transformation programs that have been unsuccessful have often tried innovation and failed due to their adoption of a pre-defined, linear approach.

The iterative nature of Digital Acceleration allows for improved management of the risks associated with the execution of conceptual ideas. Hypotheses are tested and developed quickly in a real-world environment and either succeed or fail fast. Failing fast allows for the early identification of issues and quick responsive corrections to take place.

In the worst-case scenario (i.e., a major flaw is found), the organization will not have wasted significant time, effort, and money on developing a concept all the way through to delivery and then finding the failure. In the best-case scenario (i.e., everything works), an innovative idea will have been successfully validated in a real-world environment allowing further investment to develop the concept further.

This improved, iterative risk management process gives teams the confidence to drive more innovation. The delivery teams can fully understand and trust what has been implemented so far and use this as a firm basis for exploring new ideas.

---

[3] Linear, in this instance, means noniterative. Organizations may be running multiple, parallel, and interrelated streams of work, but these streams are linear and long running in approach, and not iterative and incremental.

Validation and Innovation

Adopting a Digital Acceleration approach allows organizations to test assumptions, check technical feasibility, and validate transformation concepts much faster than using a wholesale, linear method.

The outcomes in the Digital Acceleration scenario are much more favorable than in a fixed, linear environment; either the bets and assumptions are correct, which allows another set of risks to be taken to drive innovation a little bit more, or they are incorrect, and the issues found are resolved in the next delivery iteration.

In the words of Justin Marcucci (CDO of endava), this is like *save points* in a video game: if there is no option to save your progress, your approach will be much more risk averse; if you can save your progress, you are much more willing to try more creative approaches to solve a problem.

There Is No Digital End State

Large transformation programs can encourage a race-to-the-finish mentality. Once the initiative is delivered, everything is going to be better. Organizations don't see past the finish line, so when the product is delivered, there is a valley of morale when results don't match (or exceed) expectations.

Digital Acceleration means that companies stop this mentality of placing big bets and trying to win the lottery. The organization understands that the next iteration of the transformation will not solve the world. However, it will improve a small part of your business; it's one step of many on the transformation journey.

This iterative approach sets an expectation of continual progress so that the organization is not betting the house on a single, major event. Therefore, everyone is pleased when something works but if it does not work, then it can be adjusted in the next delivery iteration.

This stepped approach delivers an organizational health benefit as people feel more engaged by ongoing delivery success and less anxious compared to the high-stakes strategy.

Vaporware/Slideware and Theoretical Debate

Many transformation programs set off on the wrong foot, early in the process, by expending large amounts of time and effort producing slide deck presentations, which look great but fail to deal with the often-messy reality of complex change initiatives. These slide decks are delivered to teams in an effort to *sell* the transformation outcomes but are often regarded as slideware or vaporware by the people that they are supposed to be engaging (i.e., a sales pitch presentation for a concept with no substance or proven effectiveness).

This slideware then feeds into a process where time and effort are spent debating theoretical concepts that act as a distraction from the job at hand (i.e., the practicalities of delivering a successful transformation).

The vaporware and theoretical debate approach is often a by-product of overly deep hierarchies. The increasing distance between the vision creators and those making the vision happen is too large and this disparity creates many of the issues that are seen in transformation programs today.

Empathy for the Customer

Focusing any digital transformation from the perspective of the customer is always going to yield a better outcome. It is surprising how often organizations forget that the customer is a key stakeholder in their digital transformation strategy. The customer does not care how an organization's internal processes or systems work; they care about the product they have bought and/or the service they receive.

There are a lot of products in the market that are structured based on the internal organizational model of the company that produces them or how their internal technology estate is organized. The experience received may not meet the needs of the customer, which can drive them to competitors that have systems designed to be more user-friendly and tailored to deliver the elements that are of most value to the customer. If there is a bad experience between making a purchase and calling customer service, this is possibly because the internal teams are using different systems which leads to a disjointed customer experience.

Some organizations focus on customer-first *user episodes*, asking the questions, *What problem the user is trying to solve at a broad level?* and *How do we define this user episode, empathetic to the state of mind that the user is in, plus, what are they trying to solve first?*

They then move on to outline a system that answers these questions in as few steps as possible. This may result in a solution that is more difficult to implement but will solve the right problem for the user.

If we are not solving the correct problem as experienced by the customer, then what are we doing in the first place?

Diversity[4]

The modern workplace should be a place where diversity (in all its forms) is embraced. This is not just because it's the *right thing to do* but also because of the richness that it brings to the working environment.

---

[4] Views on diversity are based on the output of an interview with Dr. Webb C. – Senior Lecturer, Creative Computing Institute: August 25, 2022.

Organizations should be designing products that work for all of the different groups within their potential market(s), and if these groups are not represented within the company itself, then there is little chance of achieving this goal.

Diversity will encourage innovation and creativity, support talent attraction and retention, and improve decision-making but the primary reason that Digital Acceleration embraces diversity is because it is *the right thing to do*.

What Does It Mean To Be Diverse?

Diversity can mean a lot of different things to lots of different people.

Some would argue that diversity has been emptied out of meaning due to over-use in organizational contexts, some might say that it represents a struggle toward equality, in particular, gender equality and racial equality, while others may suggest that it is important not to be lazy by using the term to tick some boxes or to *diversity wash* what's going on within organizations.

However, from an organizational perspective, diversity refers to the presence of a wide range of variation in the workforce. This can include but is not limited to differences in race, gender, ethnic group, age, personality, cognitive style, education, background, and more.

Why Is Diversity Important in the Modern Workplace?

If diversity is viewed as meaning more equal opportunities for people to hold sway in institutional contexts, it's important that those people who are underrepresented start to be more equally represented.

Diversity and representation both within the business and the design processes that fuel business are crucial. If organizations don't have the interest of different groups represented, they can't design things that work for those groups. That is, organizations will make products and services that don't serve people's needs equally.

It is imperative to say, however, that diversity should not only be promoted in the sense of it being useful for building more effective products. Organizations should also be tackling the challenges of structural and systemic inequalities.

Diversity is becoming a fundamental key to staff retention. Organizations may find that they are losing talented people because the environment doesn't support individuals' needs equally. Lack of diversity can result in missing out on the full range of talent available both from within underrepresented groups but also from people who actively want to work in a forward-thinking, diverse environment.

Thus, a lack of diversity can result in a situation where companies are producing bad products and services coupled with running the risk of losing the very people who can help the business be more profitable.

What is vital is that organizations are able to recognize and celebrate differences and promote a vision for a more equal future.

Diversity of Thought

There is huge interdisciplinary value that comes from bringing people together that have different perspectives. For example, the tolerance that is built when people are open to working with others who have different religious or political beliefs is crucial.

Some organizations fail to build diverse, cross-functional, multidisciplinary teams and they fail to realize that there needs to be a lot of people, from a lot of different backgrounds, in the room to triangulate the best solution.

In the words of Justin Marcucci (CDO of Endava), *if you put ten plumbers into a house to fix a problem, you're going to get ten plumbing-based solutions.* (Interview with Marcucci J., CDO: endava (July 8, 2022))

Within The Galapagos Framework, the diversity of the team must stretch from The Leadership Function across all other Go-To Market and Delivery Functions.

Chapter 6

Emerging Better Practices

Overview

This book has already touched on some of the reasons behind the lack of success in digital transformation programs.

However, before moving on to discuss how The Galapagos Framework resolves these issues, it is worth examining some emerging better practices and discussing how these can contribute to the successful delivery of transformation initiatives.

The better practices covered in this chapter will provide some useful techniques to improve the effectiveness of transformation initiatives.

Many More Much Smaller Steps (MMMSS)[1]

The Many More Much Smaller Steps (MMMSS) approach states that *If you want more value faster, take Many More Much Smaller Steps*.

The MMMSS approach suggests that there should be a short period at the beginning of a program of work to establish a *walking skeleton* (i.e., the bare bones of a functional delivery) followed by a somewhat meandering path,[2] from left to right over time, which counterintuitively, is the most efficient path and is shown in Figure 6.1.

---

[1] GeePaw Hill, 'Many More Much Smaller Steps: First Sketch', geepawhill.org, (2021), https://www.geepawhill.org/2021/09/29/many-more-much-smaller-steps-first-sketch/ [accessed June 19, 2023].

[2] This meandering path is a set of incremental deliveries that put flesh on the bones of the *walking skeleton*.

DOI: 10.1201/9781003404217-7

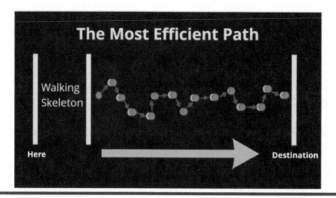

Figure 6.1 The Most Efficient Path.[3]

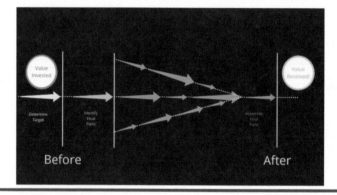

Figure 6.2 Today's Popular Idea.[4]

The Most Common Approach to Delivery

The approach to the delivery of change that is most common today is centered around making everything more efficient which makes for a path that looks more like the one in Figure 6.2.

The approach in Figure 6.2 looks a lot straighter, cleaner, more orderly, organized, coordinated, and is frankly better-looking on a slide.

---

[3] Hill, GeePaw. (2021) "Figure showing the most efficient path." Online figure. Available at https://www.geepawhill.org/2021/09/29/many-more-much-smaller-steps-first-sketch/ [accessed June 19, 2023].

[4] Hill, GeePaw. (2021) "Figure showing the today's popular idea.", online figure. Available at https://www.geepawhill.org/2021/09/29/many-more-much-smaller-steps-first-sketch/ [accessed June 19, 2023].

The Uncomfortable Reality

However, actual change is never linear. Change exists in a complicated, ever-changing, multidimensional environment.

Wherever a central function plans, monitors, and coordinates multiple streams of activity, this has a sharply rising nonlinear cost curve, at even very small numbers of streams.

Parallelism is never free, and the cost isn't linear as the size of the problem goes up.

It doesn't just get harder when we add more streams, it gets significantly more difficult, quickly swamping any benefit it might deliver.[5]

The 60-Minute Strategic Action Session

In the 60-Minute Strategic Action Session,[6] Steve Duesbury states that companies that hit trouble with digital transformations *end up creating bloated roadmaps and wish lists that lead to a lack of clear direction and decisions, chaotic activity, wasted effort and frustration*, resulting in little hope of achieving the promised outcomes or finding a clear path to success.

He goes on to suggest that

> *Most companies will then respond to being stuck with even more thinking and planning, trying to come up with a better strategy, and the result is more cowbell[7]... more bloat, delay, and frustration. More Transformation Fatigue.*

The 60 Minute Strategic Action Session may be a way to avoid the issues above. The principal elements of the strategic action session are:

■ No more than five decision-makers.
■ We decide rather than deliberate.
■ The outcomes are actions NOT ideas.
■ We prioritize the most important ideas that we will act on NOW, this is not a roadmap session.

---

[5] GeePaw Hill, "Many More Much Smaller Steps: First Sketch," geepawhill.org, (2021), https://www.geepawhill.org/2021/09/29/many-more-much-smaller-steps-first-sketch/ [accessed June 19, 2023].

[6] Duesbury, S. "How the Top Companies Turn Ideas into Action Fast." LinkedIn, 2019. Available at: https://www.linkedin.com/pulse/how-top-companies-turn-ideas-action-fast-steve-duesbury/ [accessed: June 19, 2023].

[7] Superfluous or unnecessary elements that, while originally intended to enhance a process, instead contribute to inefficiency.

The diagram shown in Figure 6.3 shows the basic Value vs. the Effort Required framework.

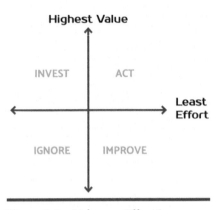

Figure 6.3   Value vs. Effort.[8]

ACT: Do these things right now because they are the most valuable, easiest to execute, and provide valuable early results and momentum.

INVEST: These are high value, but you lack the resources to execute them. Do not spend time on these unless you have fully ensured needed funding, resources, time, etc.

IMPROVE: These are easy to do but are of low value and not worth the effort. Do not do these unless you find a way to make them more valuable.

IGNORE: Don't spend any more time on these. They have the least chance of ever succeeding.

The structure of the strategic action sessions is designed to create focus and to force decisions to be taken and actions to be produced, and though this approach is not new, the difference is that the process is dramatically accelerated.

How Do These Approaches Align with The Galapagos Framework?

Many More Much Smaller Steps

The MMMSS approach is very closely aligned with The Galapagos Principle of *Sequential Transformation* which states that *The most efficient path is not a straight line (nor is it multiple parallel streams of work).*

The Galapagos Framework suggests that, in the domain of digital transformations, as the number of interdependent, parallel streams of transformation work increase, the complexity and cost will also sharply (exponentially) increase, quickly outweighing any benefits of running the streams concurrently in the first place.

[8] Duesbury, S. (2019), "Figure showing The Quadrants," online figure. Available at: https://www.linkedin.com/pulse/how-top-companies-turn-ideas-action-fast-steve-duesbury/?trackingId=%2FH0MAIeZQduDkB5Jp3URbA%3D%3D [accessed: June 19, 2023].

The premise that no advantage is delivered from transformation programs running highly parallel and interdependent workstreams is supported by the significant failure rate with digital transformation initiatives,[9] and the fact that the majority of transformational change efforts involved multiple functions/business units or the whole enterprise.[10] Undoubtedly, these unsuccessful initiatives will have used multiple parallel streams of work to deliver the change.

The 60-Minute Strategic Action Session

Improving the efficiency of processes and moving from digital transformation to Digital Acceleration are fundamental precepts of The Galapagos Framework.

The highly focused nature of the 60 Minute Strategic Action Sessions makes them ideal for use within a transformation initiative, and as such, The Galapagos Framework uses them in two key areas:

- As part of The Galapagos Strategy Review Cycle.[11] Where the Strategic Action Sessions feed into the creation of the Transformation Strategy and provide for revisions to the strategy itself, the Transformation Roadmap derived from the strategy, and the Transformation Actions carried out as part of the execution of the roadmap.
- Within the scope of the **iterative** delivery process contained in The Galapagos Roadmap. Discussed and covered in detail in Chapter 13 – *How Does The Galapagos Framework Work in Practice?*

It should be clear at this point that the ideas of reducing parallelism, improving efficiency, and accelerating processes are central tenets of The Galapagos Framework.

---

[9] McKinsey & Company. "Common pitfalls in transformations: A conversation with Jon Garcia." mckinsey.com, 2022. Available at: https://www.mckinsey.com/capabilities/transformation/our-insights/common-pitfalls-in-transformations-a-conversation-with-jon-garcia [accessed: June 19, 2023].

BCG delivers the same 70% failure rate for digital transformations:

Boston Consulting Group, "Increasing the Odds of Success in Digital Transformation," bcg.com (2020), https://www.bcg.com/publications/2020/increasing-odds-of-success-in-digital-transformation [accessed June 19, 2023].

[10] McKinsey & Company, "Unlocking success in digital transformations," mckinsey.com (2018), https://www.mckinsey.com/business-functions/organization/our-insights/unlocking-success-in-digital-transformations [accessed June 19, 2023].

[11] This is covered in more detail in *Chapter 12 – How The Galapagos Framework resolves the common issues: The Delivery Aspects – The Galapagos Strategy Review Cycle*

HOW THE GALAPAGOS FRAMEWORK RESOLVES THE COMMON ISSUES

THE HUMAN ELEMENT

The most significant factors that lead to a lack of success in transformation programs revolve around people.

Chapter 7

The Human Element – Culture

Culture

The first principle of The Galapagos Framework states that *Culture is king.*

It is people who deliver transformational change, but they can only do so effectively if the company culture supports them in this endeavor.

To deliver successful transformations, companies need to create a culture that encourages and rewards collaboration, open, honest, and friendly communication, supports creativity and innovation, and where fear of failure does not exist.

Inspiring individuals, teams, and organizations to nurture these behaviors will not only give companies the best chance of success but will also provide them with a larger portfolio of opportunities to create products and services that customers love.

Presiding over a toxic organizational culture is a significant failure of leadership and as such is given special consideration here ahead of some other, human-related *Failures in Leadership* discussed at the end of this chapter.

Issue: Toxic culture

One of the most perplexing things about this type of failure is that a lot of leaders are either unaware that they are leading an organization (or parts of an organization) where the culture is reducing productivity, or worse, are aware of it but do not see the issue as significant enough to merit intervention even though it will be placing deliveries at risk.

DOI: 10.1201/9781003404217-10

Resolution: The Leadership Function must tackle the cultural red flags

Culture can, and often does, take a long time to change, especially in larger organizations or organizations where key members of staff have been around for a long time.

Having said this, one of the reasons that The Island is largely separated from the parent organization is to allow for a fresh approach to cultural change to be adopted.

Culture is predominantly driven from the top down, and so the responsibility for setting the appropriate culture on The Island lies with The Leadership Function.

There are many cultural *red flags* that The Leadership Function needs to be aware of, and tackle, to provide an environment where teams and individuals can thrive, and that is conducive to delivering rapid transformational change.

Some cultural *red flags* and potential solutions to these are covered below.

Lack of a Collaborative Environment

Ego and fear drive internal politics[1] which in turn inhibit a culture of collaboration.

Resolution – The Leadership Function Must Promote Trust and Respect, and Lead by Example

To create a collaborative environment, individuals and teams on The Island must operate on the basis of mutual trust and respect. The Leadership Function will lead by example to promote these behaviors. Leaders must not just *talk the talk* they must also demonstrate that they embrace the culture they are implementing by *walking the walk* and personifying the culture that they want others to adopt.

Further, by highlighting the shared goal(s) that The Island has been created to deliver on, and by encouraging close cooperation between teams and individuals The Leadership Function will foster an environment of collective success/failure and will remove organizational silos.

Fear of Failure

Innovation cannot thrive under the Sword of Damocles.

Resolution – The Island Operates as a Unified TEAM!

One result of operating in an environment where fear of failure is prevalent is that the pace of change execution is slowed. As such, The Island must operate as a unified *TEAM!*[2] where the principles of collective success/failure are central to the way the

---

[1] Examples of internal politics include forming cliques, undermining colleagues, manipulation of others to influence decisions, and information hoarding to maintain control/power over a situation etc.

[2] In upper case and italics deliberately to emphasize the importance of the *TEAM!*

team operates and thus build stronger team cohesion. This topic is covered in more detail in the *TEAM!* section of *Chapter 10 – From Culture to Competitive Advantage.*

Providing a psychologically safe environment is central to encouraging more creativity, more innovation, more measured risk taking, and a faster pace of transformational change execution. As already stated, creating an environment that operates using the approaches of mutual trust and respect, combined with an open, honest, and friendly approach to communication will assist in creating an atmosphere that will contribute significantly to removing any fear of failure.

Other factors such as showing empathy, encouraging curiosity, providing constructive feedback, and taking an active interest in the well-being of the team will also contribute to creating a psychologically safe environment.

The Transformation is Seen as an Unwanted Distraction from the Core Business

The dinosaurs sow seeds of doubt and fear by overplaying the impact on the core business of the transformation.

The dinosaurs (as mentioned in the extract from a Fintech Futures article in *Chapter 2 – Common Issues – The Human Element*) can wreak havoc and severely impede the execution of any transformation strategy. One technique that is often employed by the dinosaurs is to overplay the impact on the core business of delivering the transformation.

They will often say that other strategically important initiatives will have to be delayed, or not delivered, if the transformation proceeds or that the core business will suffer as a direct result of the transformation.

Resolution 1 – The Island Structure Minimizes the Impacts On the Core Business

One of the rationales behind The Island structure is to counter just this sort of middle management objection. By creating a structure that is largely detached from the core business, and core business processes, the impact of the transformation on these elements of the operation will be minimized whilst other areas of the business are transformed.

Resolution 2 – CEO Sponsorship

Senior executive sponsorship (the CEO or as close to the CEO as possible) will also make a significant impact in removing any blocks or objections raised by middle managers, to the transformation itself. It is, therefore, critical that all senior executives (including those **not** assigned to The Island) make clear the rationale behind the transformation strategy and how it relates to the core business of the organization.

This will help to bring everyone along on the same journey and mitigate the risk of non-cooperation from others within the wider organization.

Obstructive Individuals/Teams/Functions

Resistance to change.[3]

There have been many situations where strategies have been defined by senior executives, but these have not been successfully implemented due to the sluggish adoption of the strategy by junior execs and middle managers, who either disagree with the direction or just do not see the value in the implementation of the strategy.

It is rare that outright opposition to transformational change is voiced openly, and much more common for quiet reticence to gain traction via water cooler conversations.

Resolution – Create Feedback Loops between The Leadership Function and Those Implementing the Strategy On the Ground

The Leadership Function needs to understand what sections of the organization will be receptive to the proposed changes and those that may be averse. Strategies will then need to be developed to counter any resistance to the transformation and encourage all members of staff to move in the right direction.

To address the main issue of resistance to change, and the potentially slow implementation of the strategy, feedback loops need to be in place between those setting the strategy (The Leadership Function) and those staff members on the ground who are implementing the strategy.

These feedback loops could be as simple and informal as Management By Walking Around (MBWA[4]) or occasionally taking part in daily stand-up meetings. They could also be something slightly more structured such as 1:1 meetings with staff or formal team meetings.

---

[3] "According to Darwin's Origin of Species, it is not the most intellectual of the species that survives; it is not the strongest that survives; but the species that survives is the one that is able best to adapt and adjust to the changing environment in which it finds itself."
Megginson, L. C. (1963) 'Lessons from Europe for American Business', *Southwestern Social Science Quarterly* (now known as The Social Science Quarterly), 44(1), p. 3–13.

[4] Peters, T.J., Waterman, R.H. (1982) *In Search of Excellence.* New York: Harper & Row.
When used carefully, this technique improves communication, relationship building and demonstrates an approachable and inclusive leadership style.

The Leadership Function needs to hear, and manage, the concerns of the wider team on The Island by keeping staff engaged and preventing misplaced niggles from developing into larger issues.

Just Do This: Toxic Culture

Situation

The organizational culture is not conducive to digital transformation change initiatives.

Create a Collaborative Environment

Promote mutual trust and respect amongst all team members.

Everyone is in this together, everyone is driving towards the same goal, and everyone has a part to play in successful delivery.

Encourage close collaboration.

Inspiring teams and individuals to share ideas, or work together to solve particularly gnarly problems, will form the basis of a collaborative working style.

The same north star

Set a clear and consistent strategy that everyone understands and can get behind to ensure that everyone is pulling in the same direction.

Fear of Failure & Psychological Safety

Lead by example

The Leadership Function must be the model for the type of behavior that is expected on The Island.

Communication

Encourage open, honest, and friendly communication at all times (this is covered in more detail in the *Communication* section of *Chapter 8 – How Does The Galapagos Framework Resolve the Common Issues?*).

Promote respect of the individual

Ensure that everyone's view is respected, regardless of grade/level/seniority. This will help to build a trusting environment.

Think About This: Toxic Culture

Overstating Impacts to the Core Business

Visible and well-communicated CEO sponsorship of the transformation strategy, coupled with senior executives being well versed in why The Island structure exists and how this minimizes the impact on the core business areas of the transformation, will help to mitigate the risk of the *dinosaurs overplaying the impacts on the core business.*

Obstructive Individuals/Teams/Functions

To ensure that the strategy is being executed, set up feedback loops between The Leadership Function and those teams and individuals on the ground that are implementing the strategy. This will mitigate the risk of middle management blocking or slowing the pace of the transformation.

These feedback loops could be as simple and informal as Management By Walking Around (MBWA)[5] or occasionally taking part in the daily stand-ups. They could also be something slightly more structured such as 1:1 meetings with staff or formal team meetings.

Where obstructive individuals/teams/functions are found, then the following questions need to be answered.

> *Why are they being obstructive?*
> > *Fear of change? Fear for their role? Concerns about navigating the new digital world?*
> *How can we bring them along on the transformation journey?*
> *What levers can we pull to bring these individuals/functions around to get behind the transformation?*
> *Can we circumvent these individuals/functions?*

Failures in Leadership

To some extent or another, all failed transformations are failures in leadership.

Having said that, leadership is a complex, multidimensional activity that requires different skills at different times covering the different needs of the individual (coaching, mentoring, developing, etc.) and of the group (team building based on a common purpose). It is, therefore, too broad a view to say that a failed transformation is down to failures in leadership.

---

[5] Peters, T.J., Waterman, R.H. (1982) *In Search of Excellence*. New York: Harper & Row.

A finer-grained approach is required to understand what elements of leadership are most likely to cause the most significant issues.

Issue: Strategy and direction are not clear and are not anchored in the business's core values and competencies

As mentioned previously, the rationale behind the strategy and how this relates to the core business of the organization must be made clear.

All staff both inside and outside of The Island need to understand the direction of travel and why this transformation is important for the business. Creating this understanding will help to mitigate any resistance to change from areas outside of The Island but on whom The Island must rely for the successful completion of its mission (e.g., integration with the parent organization's systems, etc.).

Resolution: Zero ambiguity in the strategy and communicate it often

Galapagos Principle 7 states that *Clarity is key* (see *Chapter 3 – Introduction to The Galapagos Framework, Galapagos Principles*) and so clear, consistent, and frequent (in the early stages of the transformation) communication of the strategy must be delivered by a, or a number of, very senior executive(s) to the broader organization to ensure that all functions outside of The Island are cooperative.

The frequency of this communication can be reduced over time, but the message must be communicated clearly and often, in the early stages of the transformation, to ensure that the message is embedded in the corporate psyche.

Issue: Professional/corporate ambiguity

Ambiguity may exist outside of the strategy definition, and there are sometimes instances where it suits leaders/managers to consciously deliver vague messages, as it allows them to change their position on delivery scope/approach without losing face.

On other occasions, it may be because the leaders/managers themselves are not clear as to exactly what they require and use uncertainty as a tactic to allow them time to think things through.

The underlying reasons for this corporate ambiguity are less important than the impact, which can be severe, leading to delay and wasted effort as delivery teams start work based on a best guess as to what needs to be delivered. This ultimately results in rework when the leaders/managers deliver the *that's not what I asked for…* message.

Leaders being open about what they don't know at a specific point in time is not a sign of weakness (quite the contrary). This openness engenders a feeling of respect amongst team members and, as well as presenting a more human side, builds trust and improves engagement.

Resolution: The Leadership Function must eliminate professional/corporate ambiguity

Where ambiguity exists, it needs to be highlighted as a delivery risk/issue and removed as soon as possible. It is inevitable that there will be some areas of uncertainty in any program of work, and as long as these are identified, impact assessed, and prioritized for resolution, they should not cause a significant issue.

Within The Galapagos Framework, it is incumbent upon The Accountable Executive (AE), Business Head, and Delivery Head to ensure that clarity is sought in all matters and that this message is conveyed to all teams and individuals on The Island, and beyond.

Issue: Leadership vacuum

Those individuals in leadership positions can be so focused on the operational and day-to-day delivery details that they fail to provide effective leadership.

The resulting leadership vacuum can be extremely difficult to identify as delivery output is maintained, and messaging produced out of these areas is carefully managed.

This is not a new problem, and most organizations have put in place checks and balances to mitigate this (e.g., leadership training and development, anonymous employee surveys, exit interviews, and so on), but it still occurs all too frequently.

Results and rewards for results are often about the what not the how. Managers who drive results often don't concern themselves about how they get them and of course for all the HR work (training, surveys, exit interviews, and so on), in too many organizations, this lacks teeth and performance remains one dimensional.[6]

Resolution 1: Align incentives to how delivery is achieved

In the short-term ensuring that incentives are targeted on *how* delivery is achieved as well as *what* is delivered will allow organizations to effectively identify and respond to the leadership vacuum.

Challenging the dinosaurs that are creating the vacuum will result in positive improvements in delivery, and the overall organizational health of the company.

---

[6] Tony Williams – business transformation advisor.

Resolution 2: Develop/hire new leaders

Over the longer term, there may be a need to develop new leaders, with younger or newer members of staff presenting the best candidates as they are less likely to be steeped in the old traditions.

However, if a leadership vacuum is having a significant and immediate impact on the effectiveness of delivery, then there may be a need to hire new leadership talent into the organization.

Chapter 8

The Human Element – Communication

Communication

Communication and collaboration go hand in hand when creating an environment that fosters productivity and values employee satisfaction.

Issue: The approach to communication

The organization does not support a style of communication that improves the level of collaboration required to deliver the transformation.

Resolution 1: Foster open, honest, and friendly communication based on trust

---

It is vitally important that The Leadership Function promotes and nurtures an open, honest, and overall, friendly approach to communication, based on mutual trust and respect.

Building on the foundations of *respect for the individual* will allow staff to constructively disagree or have difficult conversations and move on.

Progress requires diversity of thought and for different opinions to be aired freely. By inhibiting these behaviors, companies stifle creativity and create a bland working environment where innovative solutions to problems could well be missed.

DOI: 10.1201/9781003404217-11

Resolution 2: Employ the use of digital communication channels

Post the COVID-19 pandemic, working from home or working in a hybrid environment has become the norm. It is, therefore, important that The Island employs the use of digital communication channels to improve the effectiveness of communication. By providing a more accessible approach to knowledge sharing across the organization, these tools will enable individuals and teams to work together to distribute information freely and encourage more effective communication and collaboration (see *Appendix B – Example Technology Matrix* for examples of some of these).

Issue: The frequency, method, and volume of communication

A constant flood of instant messages, emails, telephone calls, video calls, and meetings will divert staff away from the core business of delivering the transformation and leave some staff feeling overwhelmed.

Resolution: Implement a targeted communication strategy

Stem the flood of communication that is not directly related to the transformation.

The Island must engage with the rest of the organization, and external third parties, to successfully deliver the transformation. However, The Island must also reduce (or stop totally) the deluge of information, that is not related specifically to the transformation itself. There is a need to maintain targeted communication to keep all parties meaningfully engaged and the HR function will assist in developing a strategy that covers communication lines both into and out of The Island.

The *Communication Strategy* is a key artifact of The Model (see *Chapter 19 – The Model*) that, if implemented effectively, will allow The Island to streamline the flows of communication, ensure that the messaging is clear and consistent, remain focused on the job in hand, and protect the core delivery teams from overzealous communications.

Two-way Communication within The Island

As part of the *Communication Strategy*, two-way communication needs to become the new norm on The Island. Top-down/one-way communication will still be required on occasion; however, an open-door, interactive approach to communication across all levels of staff needs to be actively encouraged.

Celebrate Success

It is imperative that, as part of the broader approach to engagement, successes are celebrated and communicated. This will not only remind key stakeholders of the value that is being delivered but will ensure that staff feel appreciated for the work that they are doing.

Communicate the Reasons for the Change to Those Outside of The Island

It's not just communication between the teams and individuals on The Island that is important to the successful delivery of the transformation. The change story needs to be made clear in order to help everyone (employees, customers, and third parties) understand what it is changing, and why these changes are important.

Just Do This: Communication Problems

Situation

Staff are swamped and suffering from information overload. All levels of staff are receiving huge numbers of emails, instant messages, telephone, and video calls every day as well as regular team meetings, daily standups, etc.

Method of Communication

Stop emails being sent between team members.

Unless there is a very good reason as to why an email must be sent (e.g., a file needs to be attached), then other forms of communication should be used.[1]

If an email must be sent, then ensure it does not have a CC list. Emails need to be person to person, if there is a CC list then the wrong communication method is being used.

Encourage face-to-face verbal communication so that this becomes the norm.

The hierarchy of communication should be face-to-face, video conference, telephone, instant messaging and, only after all of these options have been considered, email.

---

[1] It is estimated that people spend approximately 28% of their working week managing email. McKinsey & Company, 'The Social Economy: Unlocking Value and Productivity Through Social Technologies,' McKinsey & Company, [2012], accessed [23 August 2023], https://www.mckinsey.com/industries/technology-media-and-telecommunications/our-insights/the-social-economy.

Think About This: Communication Problems

Frequency and Volume of Communication

*More communication is **not** better communication.*

Encourage people to think before they send a written communication. Is this message likely to result in a reply and then another response from me? If so, speak to the person rather than send a message.

Can we reduce the number of emails coming from central sources?

Chapter 9

The Human Element – Skills

Any organization planning to embark on a digital transformation must conduct a sober analysis of the existing skills, capabilities, and resources available to deliver the strategy.

Where gaps are identified, the organization should recruit/develop/re-train staff to build the capabilities that will be required for transformation to succeed, and then extend these capabilities to develop talent throughout the organization, and thus build the workforce of the future.

> **Issue: Lack of the right type, right number, right level, or the right mix of skills in the right location**

In order to solve the issue of not having the right number, right type, or right mix of skills in the right locations, you first need to assess what skills are required, what skills the organization currently has available, and where these skills are located.

> **Resolution: Produce and act upon a Workforce Strategy**

One of the first artifacts to be produced from The Island will be the *Workforce Strategy* (which will be contained in The Model, see *Chapter 19 – The Model*). This would naturally be produced as part of a *Digital Transformation Readiness Review* or a *Digital Maturity Assessment* (these are covered in more detail in *Chapter 25 – Digital Transformation Strategy, Readiness, and Maturity*) ahead of any decision to progress with the transformation is taken.

   DOI: 10.1201/9781003404217-12

The *Workforce Strategy* will be used to determine the skills and capabilities required to meet the short, medium, and long-term transformation goals, and assess these against the existing skills and capabilities that the organization currently has.

In order to progress with the transformation strategy, the organization needs to ensure that there is a clear *and achievable* plan to close any identified skills gaps, in a timeframe that will not jeopardize the delivery timelines of the transformation. This may require a well-funded and robust approach to talent acquisition.

If the skills gaps are too large or the cost of closing these gaps is prohibitive, then the Transformation Strategy itself will need to be reviewed to understand if any sections of the Strategy can still be achieved with the existing skills or a smaller investment in talent acquisition.

Given the above, it should come as no surprise that the *Workforce Strategy* will be a key artifact in any *Go/No-Go* decisions regarding the transformation.

Issue: Digital leaders are not on the top team

To drive strategic change in a digital environment, The Island must contain leaders that are digitally savvy and who have a broad understanding of the importance of data-driven decision-making, agile techniques, DevOps, customer/user experience, cloud, cyber security, process automation, and so on.

Resolution: Add digitally knowledgeable leaders to The Leadership Function

These digital leaders must be highly collaborative individuals who can garner cross-functional/departmental support for the transformation and cross these boundaries easily. These individuals may come from one of the following roles – CDO/CIO/CTO/CTrO/CXO.

Issue: Incentives not aligned to the transformation strategy

Aligning team and employee incentives to the strategic goals of the transformation is crucial to the successful delivery of the strategy.

When incentives are misaligned, this creates discord within the teams delivering the transformation, drives undesirable behavior, and increases the risk of failure, with individuals and teams pulling in different directions.

Aligning incentives and compensation strategies to the strategic goals and direction of the transformation is critical to delivering a successful outcome.

Resolution: CEO sponsorship will make it easier to align incentives to the goals of the transformation[1]

As mentioned in the *Culture* section of *Chapter 7 – How Does Galapagos Framework Resolve the Common Issues?*, senior executive sponsorship (CEO, or as close to the CEO as possible) will ensure that the transformation is not seen as a pet project, and this will help remove barriers to aligning incentives to the strategic goals of the transformation.

The full range of incentive tools should be used to push alignment of recognition and reward to the Critical Success Factors (CSFs) of the transformation program. Organizations must also include transformation-focused objectives as part of individual's annual performance targets.

Incentives don't always have to be financial. Securing opportunities for individuals to take on development opportunities is highly motivating as are milestone celebrations, gamification[2], and heartfelt appreciation.

Organizations need to step back and review the transformation program to assess how teams and individuals are currently incentivized. For those teams and individuals on The Island and those that will interact with it, incentives could be weighted to align to the strategic goals of the transformation and the impact of this approach assessed and revised as necessary.

Incentives are a potent tool, and when used thoughtfully, they can work to support a strong collective purpose with a highly engaged team.

However, misaligned incentives (or when used as a blunt tool) can act as a distraction or create conflicts within the transformation program leading to poor behavior and increasing the risk of non-delivery on program objectives.

Aligning incentives and compensation strategies to the vision underpinning the transformation and tying compensation to collaboration are essential to ensuring that all functions/teams and individuals are pulling in the same direction.

Beyond incentives, The Leadership Function of The Island must also ensure that there is regular recognition for both those fully immersed in transformation and those contributing to key parts of it. A regular routine of recognition may not be a bad thing.

---

[1] Extracts taken from Digital transformations: aligning incentives to the transformation strategy. Brian Harkin & Sarah Patel: April 2023.

[2] The application of game-design principles to encourage engagement and make processes more fun, thus increasing motivation and continued participation.

Integration Specialists

At this point, it is worth touching on The Integration Specialist role. This role exists to ensure a smooth integration of tools, technologies, and processes back into the parent organization. This role acts as a bridge between the more traditional parts of the parent business and the digital functions that exist on The Island.

The Integration Specialists role is, by definition, multiskilled. The individual(s) performing this role must be cognizant of the tools, technologies, and processes being used on The Island and must also be fully aware of the existing landscape of tools, technology, and processes in use in the parent organization. This will allow them to form an opinion and plan as to how the elements used on The Island can be integrated into the parent organization.

Individuals in this role will also help foster stronger internal capabilities among colleagues in the parent company and, by acting as a guide to what the future holds, they can, in conjunction with HR, steer the education and training of employees in the parent organization to bolster skills and create the workforce of the future.

There is a risk that The Island could be perceived as an ivory tower by those staff in the parent organization. Thus, another part of The Integration Specialist role will be to reduce this risk by acting as a window into what is happening on The Island and keeping individuals in the parent organization informed of the developments that are taking place with respect to new tools, technologies, and processes.

Just Do This: Skills Issues

Situation

The organization does not have the right number, level, or mix of skills, in the right locations, to successfully deliver the digital transformation.

Perform a Skills Gap Analysis

The magnitude of the issue needs to be understood. Therefore, a serious assessment of the skills that the organization currently has and the gaps that exist across locations needs to be conducted.

The question of *What is the organization missing?* in terms of the type of skills, at what level of seniority, in what numbers, and in which locations, needs to be answered.

Plan to Close the Skills Gaps

Once the size of the problem is understood, then a clear and credible plan needs to be put in place to fill any skills gaps identified. Further, an impact assessment must be conducted to assess the effect on the transformation given the timelines included in the plan.

Think About This: Skills Issues

Filling the Skills Gap

The following questions must be answered.

Does the organization have time to go to market and hire these skills?
Are there other areas of the organization that have the required skills?
If so, can we temporarily transfer/second these skills to where they are required?
Can trusted third parties be used to supply these skills?
Is there enough budget to cover filling the skills gaps?

Chapter 10

The Human Element – From Culture to Competitive Advantage

Survival of the Friendliest[1] (Or the Most Collaborative)

In keeping with the evolutionary theme of this book, and The Galapagos Framework itself, it is worth considering the following questions:

Why did Homo sapiens survive against competition from the many other types of human[2] and What has this got to do with digital transformation?

Survival of the Friendliest...

First, let's look at one possible reason for *Homo sapiens* surviving against the other types of human.

A new idea is emerging that it was Homo sapiens' *ability to network with strangers: the survival of the friendliest...* and their *...unparalleled ability to form alliances beyond their immediate group* that led to them flourishing.

---

[1] Kate Ravilious, 'The last human.', New Scientist, 252/3362, (2021), pp. 38–41.
[2] At the time when our lineage first evolved in Africa some 300,000 years ago, there were at least five other species in the human genus.

DOI: 10.1201/9781003404217-13

...Or Most Collaborative

Now let's examine why is this relevant to digital transformation.

Networking and building *alliances* are important elements that come under the general umbrella term of collaboration.

Extending the *survival of the friendliest* idea to the realm of digital transformations, it is not too much of an intellectual leap to see that, when operating in a group context, teams and individuals have an instinctive need to cooperate as, at a very basic level, they know that it leads to success.

Individuals may not naturally be all that collaborative, but groups function better when they are in an environment that encourages and facilitates broad cooperation, which leads the teams to want to collaborate more frequently and a virtuous cycle ensues.

This virtuous cycle comes back to the points raised previously on culture: an open, honest, friendly (well mostly), and collaborative culture is critical for the delivery of digital transformation programs. After all, this is a transformation **not** a re-organization, and again using the words of Lou Gerstner (ex-IBM CEO) ... *Transformation is fundamentally changing the way the organization thinks, responds, and leads.* Thus, culture is central to success.

Collaboration and interaction with others outside of their own immediate group not only strengthens the cohesion of those on The Island but also encourages behavior and thinking consistent with moving the transformation program forward.

A highly collaborative, cohesive, and communicative Island ensures that when things get tough (and they will get tough), The Island will be resilient and flexible enough to weather the storms.

Culture + Kindness = Abundance[3]

Culture + Kindness

In the biggest ever public science project on kindness, carried out by the BBC and the University of Sussex[4], it was found that the most common act of kindness is to help people when they ask.

If individuals on The Island do not feel able to ask for assistance when they need it, then this will slow down progress and, in some cases, can lead to blocks in delivery that could have been removed if only the right culture had been in place.

---

[3] Thanks to Richard Jeffreys, founder of CX ALL for his input on this.
[4] BBC Radio 4. "The Anatomy of Kindness." (09 Mar 2022).

The ability to ask for and receive help fosters a culture of kindness that is critical to creating a psychologically safe space. This, in turn, removes any barriers to communication and encourages increased levels of cooperation and collaboration and allows teams and individuals to become enablers of change.

Creating the right culture not only improves the efficiency of the entire function but also increases employee wellbeing. It is easy to see how this might, in turn, lead to improved staff retention rates and less illness.

Kindness really does add value, and those individuals that are kind or generous with their time should be highly valued members of staff.

Does Excessive Pressure Reduce Kindness?

It is no surprise that people operating under excessive pressure may not be as generous with their time as one would hope for, and this may result in a reduction in acts of kindness and lower levels of collaboration.

It is the responsibility of the Delivery and Business Head roles to ensure that the other functions of The Island are operating under a level of pressure that can be sustained over the long term. These roles also need to insulate the other functions from the external pressures that they themselves endure.

= Abundance

Of Goodwill

An abundance of goodwill drives support, collaboration, innovation, and creates a culture of trust that encourages employees to share ideas, take risks, and gives staff a sense of purpose for the work they are undertaking.

Of Opportunity

We can never create certainty but by using the techniques and structures outlined above, we can create an abundance of opportunity. More opportunities for successful delivery, more opportunities to solve problems in an efficient and effective way, and more opportunities for innovation and creativity.

Working hard does not necessarily create an abundance in the portfolio of opportunities available, but working creatively, collaboratively, and supportively does. Nothing can be created or predicted with absolute certainty; however, *organizations can increase the likelihood of something happening by creating more opportunities for it to happen.*

Creating a supportive and friendly environment on The Island enables teams to devise creative solutions to problems and develop new products and ideas. A congenial atmosphere helps foster a sense of ownership, which can lead to increased productivity and motivation.

Of Talent

The environment, as outlined above, will help to attract, and retain talented employees, which will allow the teams and individuals on The Island to become the agents of change, and for the transformation to be led through them.

Retaining talent will also support the dissemination of skills across the team, as highly skilled individuals being generous with their time will bring more junior members of staff up the learning curve faster.

The Serious Business of Not Being Too Serious

Any large transformation program is a serious business, and with significant global spend not always yielding the anticipated (or promised) benefits, the pressure to deliver can be, and often is, high.

The Leadership Function will be fully aware of what must be achieved within the ever-present budget and ever-tightening time constraints, the risks associated with transformational change, and the pressure to deliver.

However, one of the many roles of The Leadership Function is to shield all elements of The Island from the weight of this pressure as much as possible. A certain amount of pressure is always required to ensure that things get done, but care must be taken not to let the full weight of this fall on the other functions of The Island.

An occasional dash of levity, coupled with some generosity of time, will lead to a sense of spirit on The Island which in turn will improve delivery. A lightness of leadership touch infused with a modicum of humor will bond people together when they are facing difficult situations and will help to release the pressure valve when things get tough.

TEAM!

It is outside the scope of this book to cover team formation and teamwork in any detail.

However, it would be remiss not to touch on the subject as The Island is fundamentally a unified team, put in place to deliver the transformation initiative.

The TEAM![5] is central to any delivery where the work cannot be delivered, in a specified time, by one individual. In the context of The Island, the notion of a unified TEAM! is crucial to ensuring successful delivery.

---

[5] Deliberately in upper case and with an exclamation mark to emphasize its criticality.

Collective Success, Collective Failure

In order to forge team cohesion, The Leadership Function must ensure that the TEAM! operates in an environment of collective responsibility. No individual succeeds and no individual fails, only the TEAM! succeeds/fails.

The approach requires strong leadership as, when things go wrong, there will be pressure to point fingers and identify individuals. The leadership *must not* allow this to happen and no individual should be singled out.

To successfully eliminate a blame culture, it is important that when things go wrong, the focus is on correcting the problem and moving on, rather than dwelling on who was at fault.

The approach described above provides the TEAM! with a safe space where team members are encouraged to cooperate and fail fast (see the *Chapter 3 – The Galapagos Principles - Culture is king – No Fear of Failure*).

Trust

The TEAM! exists in a trusting environment where individuals are free to voice concerns or ideas, there is no discomfort in disagreement, and constructive conflict occurs without the burden of fear. This approach is central to building team cohesion which, in turn, allows the TEAM! to build consensus and move forward when issues are encountered.

You cannot build cohesion in a team that is constantly changing. It is therefore important that as far as possible stability is sought in team membership for as long as possible (see section *Culture + Kindness = Abundance* ➜ *Of talent*).

Direction

Without clarity of purpose and a well-defined objective, a team does not exist. We just have a collection of individuals with no sense of the direction of travel or what needs to be achieved. It is the leadership of the team that provides this clarity, and as such it is imperative that the right leadership is in place to support and direct the team appropriately, ensuring that each team member understands that their role is important and has value.

THE ORGANIZATIONAL FACTORS

B

Chapter 11

The Organizational Factors

The Organizational Factors

For many companies, the organizational structure itself can impede the delivery of successful transformational change. The Island structure of The Galapagos Framework simplifies the organizational model and improves the effectiveness of the entire transformation.

Organizational Structure

> **Issue: The structure of the organization is not conducive to effective digital change**

It is often the situation that organizations work in a complex operational structure which has evolved over time and ends up actually promoting conflict. Teams are working inside their own silos, which is creating an atmosphere of mistrust leading to defensive behavior and political shenanigans.

> **Resolution: The Island structure simplifies the organizational model and removes silos**

The Island structure of The Galapagos Framework (which is explored in detail in *Chapter 14 – The Island*) has been designed to resolve the issues surrounding poor organizational structures. The Island removes silos and promotes a highly

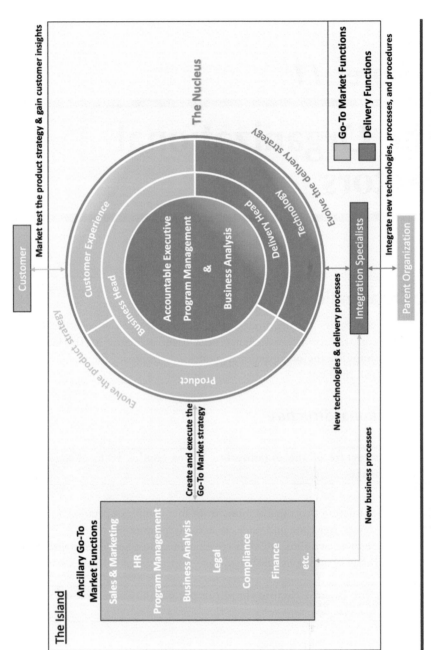

Figure 11.1   The Island Structure.

collaborative and communicative engagement model that will enhance delivery capabilities (Figure 11.1).

Failures in Leadership

The complex nature of leadership has been covered previously and the need for a finer-grained approach has been highlighted. The following section will examine the specific leadership failings that apply to the needs of the organization.

Issue: Lack of senior executive sponsorship

Outside of *the Human Elements*, the single biggest leadership failing in digital transformation programs is a lack of sponsorship from the CEO.[1]

Resolution: Senior executive sponsorship is in place before the transformation starts

Senior executive sponsorship is a must (see *Chapter 3 – Introduction to The Galapagos Framework, Galapagos Principles* ➔ *Principle 6: Senior executive sponsorship is a must*) is one of the principles of The Galapagos Framework, and as such The Framework mandates that senior executive sponsorship is in place and communicated *before* the transformation process fully kicks off.

The Accountable Executive and The Leadership Function of The Island need to have the full *and visible* backing of the CEO. This sponsorship must be clearly and unambiguously communicated to all functions that are likely to encounter The Island transformation team.

Issue: Complex and sometimes conflicting reporting lines

Accountability, transparency, and delivery can be compromised by overly complex/conflicting reporting lines, resulting in managerial tension and communication issues.

Resolution: The Island structure removes complex/conflicting reporting lines

The Island has a relatively flat reporting structure with The Business Head and Delivery Head reporting to The AE and an entirely flat structure below The Business Head and The Delivery Head (Figure 11.2).

---

[1] Or a senior executive who is as close to the CEO as possible.

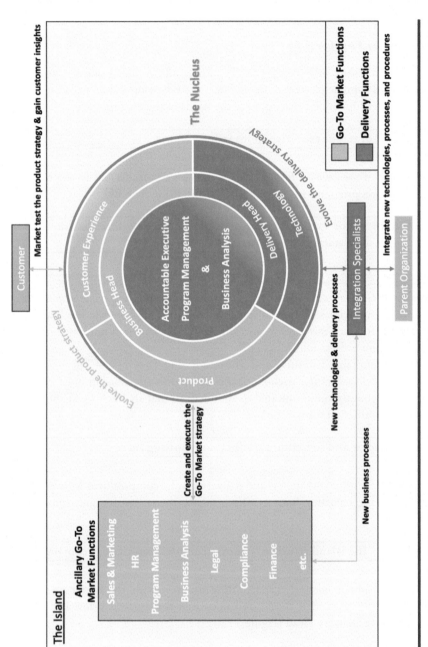

Figure 11.2 The Island Structure.

The Business Head is responsible for all activities required to get the product to market (i.e., all The Go-To Market Functions). The Go-To Market Functions may comprise of Product, Sales & Marketing, Legal & Compliance, Finance, etc., and the coordination of all these activities lies with the Program Management team of The Go-To Market Functions.

The Delivery Head is responsible for all activities required to build, test, and deploy the product. *Delivery* may comprise Program Management, Business Analysis, Testing and Technology, etc., and the coordination of all these activities lies with *Delivery*.

The Go-To Market and Delivery Functions may have their own Program/Project Management teams. If this is the case, these will be coordinated by a Program Director role that resides within The *Delivery* Function.

The Galapagos Framework does not prescribe if the Program Director role and The Delivery Head role are performed by the same person.

The rationale for the very small hierarchical structure between The AE and The Business and Delivery Heads is to allow quick decision-making to take place and for The AE to arbitrate in situations where there are differences of opinion between The Business Head and The Delivery Head that cannot easily be resolved.

The entirely flat structure below The Business and Delivery Heads facilitates open and honest communication and collaboration across all the other different functions and allows all parties to observe the challenges that the other teams are facing and the decisions that they are taking, thus furthering team cohesion.

The structure above lends itself easily to the use of 60 Minute Strategic Action Sessions (*Chapter 6 – Emerging Better Practices*) by limiting the number of people responsible for setting the direction of the transformation to The AE, The Business Head, The Delivery Head, and any two other roles (as required).

Issue: The right mix of "C" level leaders are not involved early enough

---

Digital transformations are complex initiatives that often span multiple functions/departments. These are not, as is often thought, technology-centric changes (though technology will certainly have a role to play); they are human-centric change initiatives. As such, the organization must ensure that the right mix of leaders are involved early in the process.

Resolution: Assign HR and digital leaders to The Island

Involve Human Resources (HR) from Day One
Given that people are at the heart of every transformational change initiative, it seems odd that the HR function is often a last-minute consideration. The most significant factors that lead to a lack of success in transformation programs

revolve around people, and involving HR late in the process appears to be a strange approach.

One of the first artifacts to be produced from The Island, the *Workforce Strategy*, will be the responsibility of the HR function, and this will be an essential item in any decision as to whether to progress, delay, reduce the scope, or not move forward with the transformation at all.

Therefore, The Galapagos Framework mandates that the HR function is involved from day one of The Islands creation.

The rationale behind HR being outside of The Nucleus of The Island is due to the fact that the HR function will be involved heavily in the early stages of the transformation, with their involvement tapering off as the transformation progresses towards its goal.

Even though, from the perspective of the Framework, the HR function is considered an ancillary function this does not reduce or negate its importance.

Digital Leaders – Drive Innovation and the Transformation Forward

There are many corporate roles that cover digital leadership (e.g., CIO/CTO/CPO) and good arguments can be made for the creation of the Chief Transformation Officer (CTrO) and Chief Digital Officer (CDO) to add to the list of digital leadership roles. Whether or not some or all of these corporate roles exist within the same transformation program is a moot point; there needs to be a digital executive to drive innovation and the transformation forward, and one or more of these roles are good candidates.

Whichever corporate role(s) is selected to be added to the top team must be placed into the appropriate Leadership Function role (e.g., Accountable Executive, Business Head, or Delivery Head).

Just Do This: Failures in Leadership

Situation

The organization is suffering from failures in leadership. These types of issues are the most difficult and politically sensitive to solve as there may not even be an awareness that the leaders are not operating effectively.

CEO Sponsorship

The CEO must clearly communicate to all parties that the digital transformation is strategically important and has their full backing.

This message may have to be communicated frequently in the early stages to ensure that the message is thoroughly understood by all.

Think About This: Failures in Leadership

Strategy and Direction

There must be no ambiguity in the strategy and the direction of travel.

Communicate the strategy and explain why this is important to the future of the business.

The transformation story must be rooted in the core values and competencies of the organization.

Complex and Sometimes Conflicting Reporting Lines

The use of The Island structure itself removes complex/conflicting reporting lines.

The Right Mix of "C" Suite Leaders

Ensure that the organization has the right mix of "C" suite leaders (digital, HR, etc.) involved at the earliest opportunity.

Professional/Corporate Ambiguity

The Leadership Function must seek to eliminate professional/corporate ambiguity.

THE DELIVERY ASPECTS

C

Chapter 12

The Delivery Aspects

The Delivery Aspects

Having covered solutions to the *Human Elements* and the *Organizational Factors* that impact on transformation programs, this chapter covers solutions to some of the issues that may be encountered with the *Delivery Aspects* of the transformation strategy.

Failures in Leadership

The section below explores two important leadership failings and a single solution to both of these issues from a delivery perspective.

Issue: Strategy review cycles are too long

Annual and quarterly strategy reviews are not fit for purpose in the dynamic digital age. Reviewing the direction of travel, to facilitate course corrections and tactical adjustments, needs to be much more frequent whilst at the same time maintaining a mid-term and long-term strategy view.

Issue: Strategy reviews are not data-driven

The subjective decision-making of the past is not suitable for the digital age, and this remains the case even when decisions are backed up by the extensive experience of leaders. Opinion-based decision-making often occurs in situations where feedback cycles from transformation initiatives do not provide enough accurate, or actionable, metrics to allow data-driven decisions to be taken.

DOI: 10.1201/9781003404217-17

It is critical that strategy reviews are data-driven, that is, they should be based upon timely and accurate metrics that will allow better quality decisions to be taken.

Resolution: The Galapagos Strategy Review Cycle

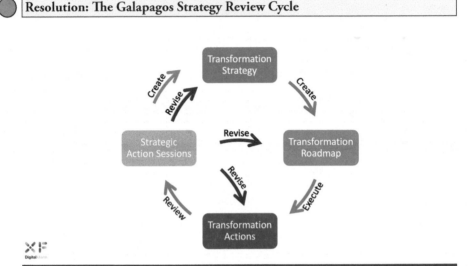

Figure 12.1 The Galapagos Strategy Review Cycle.

Shortening the Review Cycles

The Galapagos Framework supports the use of a revised strategy review process – *The Galapagos Strategy Review Cycle* – which is an iterative, and relatively frequent, review process that covers the creation of the *Transformation Strategy, Transformation Roadmap,* the execution of the *Transformation Actions* (tasks on the roadmap that will deliver on the strategy), and the reviewing of the status of these actions in the Strategic Action Sessions (*Chapter 6 – Emerging Better Practices*).

The outputs of the Strategic Action Sessions may include revisions of the approach to the *Transformation Actions* (or alter the actions themselves), revisions to the *Transformation Roadmap,* or indeed revisions to elements of the *Transformation Strategy* itself.

It should be noted that the *Transformation Strategy* and *Transformation Roadmap* are living artifacts that are contained within The Model, and as such are subject to change as a result of the outputs of the Strategic Action Sessions.

The Galapagos Framework does not specify the frequency of the Strategic Action Sessions, but it is suggested that these take place at least once every month.

Data-driven

The Strategic Action Sessions are key elements in *The Galapagos Strategy Review Cycle* and will allow adjustments to be made, at pace, to the strategy itself or the execution of the strategy. The Strategy Review Cycle will embrace and drive change on a continual basis and the Strategic Action Sessions will be informed by the metrics and reporting outputs of The Island on a near real-time basis.

Combining the above process with *Galapagos Principle 9: Establish and automate metrics and reporting early* will ensure that the decisions made in the Strategic Action Sessions will be data-driven, thus removing (or reducing) the predominantly subjective decision-making of the past.

Figure 12.1, shows the four key processes of *The Galapagos Strategy Review Cycle*, namely, **Create**, **Execute**, **Review**, and **Revise**.

From the *Transformation Strategy*, the *Transformation Roadmap* is created. *Transformation Actions*, that support the delivery of the strategy, are then executed and the impacts of these are assessed in the Strategic Action Sessions.

The data-driven, decision-oriented nature of these sessions allows revisions to the *Transformation Actions*, the *Transformation Roadmap*, or the *Transformation Strategy* itself to be applied to cater for what is happening on the ground rather than what should be happening on a plan.

Orchestrating the Transformation

Transformation and regular change activities invariably occur at the same time and ensuring that both of these undertakings happen without negative impacts to the business is critical to success.

Issue: Managing regular change and transformation activities

The organization is running at different speeds covering Moon Shots (the higher end of what the digital transformation aims to achieve), Roof Shots (regular change activities), and Business As Usual (BAU, change to support the ongoing functioning of the business). The delivery of these change activities often falls to the same (relatively small) group of individuals.

Resolution: Allocate experienced delivery leads to focus solely on the digital transformation

Having multiple different types of change activity happening concurrently in an organization is simply the nature of business. However, there are ways to lessen the impact of this on the transformation process.

Organizations may, for example, consider allocating one (or more) experienced delivery lead(s) to focus solely on the digital transformation (the Moon Shots) and leave existing change managers to cover the regular change and BAU activities. This will ensure that the delivery leads allocated to the transformation initiative are not distracted by other change activities and can focus solely on the job at hand (i.e., the successful delivery of the transformation).

Scope

While some companies claim to have *known for years that a comprehensive approach to organizational transformation is more conducive to lasting change* ... they seem surprised that ... *the average success rate has remained persistently low.*[1]

With digital transformations being even more difficult to successfully deliver than traditional change efforts, it seems astonishing that companies still believe that wholesale organizational change is the right way forward.

Whilst it is possible to argue that correlation does not necessarily equal causation (i.e., wholesale organizational change ≠ transformation failure), this seems to be unlikely in the case of digital transformations.

Issue: Scope is too broad

As mentioned in *Chapter 2 – Digital Transformations: The Common Issues*, most change efforts involve multiple functions/business units or the whole company. This significantly increases the risk of delivery failure.

Resolution: There should be a maximum of two concurrent transformations

The concept of the *Transformation Context*, and the fact that there should only ever be one Island within a *Transformation Context* was introduced in *Chapter 4 – The Function of The Galapagos Framework – How does The Galapagos Framework operate at scale.*

In most instances, The Island will only ever undertake one transformation at a time. However, there are instances where two concurrent transformation initiatives can be undertaken by a single instance of The Island. This allows The Island to operate with a remit of transforming one (or at most two) specific functions whilst being cognizant of other areas of the organization that are likely to be future candidates for transformation.

The Island should not try to solve for other transformations in the first instance but should put in place processes and procedures that are lightweight and flexible enough to be easily modified to cater to the needs of future transformations.

---

[1] McKinsey & Company, 'Successful transformations', mckinsey.com, (2021), https://www. mckinsey.com/capabilities/people-and-organizational-performance/our-insights/successful-transformations#/ [accessed June 19, 2023].

Issue: Scope is too deep

Attempting to solve significant issues with the entire organization's operating model[2] with a digital transformation program is like trying to boil the ocean. Increasing the scope of the transformation to cover the whole company's operating model is setting the transformation up to fail from the outset.

Resolution: Leadership Function controls the scope and the production of The Model

The underlying philosophy of The Galapagos Framework is to target the transformation strategy on a small area and minimize the impact of the transformation on the operating model(s) of the wider business. It is the responsibility of The Leadership Function to ensure that wholesale operating model change is not in scope as part of the transformation initiative.

There will almost certainly be changes required to the operating model of the *Transformation Context*, but care must be taken to ensure that these changes can be reintegrated back into the parent organization and the Integration Specialist role will be key to this process.

The evolutionary nature of The Galapagos Framework means that, over time, the entire organization's operating model may change, but this will be done in a controlled, iterative, and incremental fashion.

The production of a new, and hopefully simplified, operating model will be one of the outputs of The Island and will be contained in The Model – this artifact is covered in detail in *Chapter 19 – The Model* – but a summary of this is provided below for context.

The Model

The Model is a lightweight and comprehensive guide to the transformation that is taking place and will cover key elements of the new operating model that is being adopted by The Island. This artifact will be used by subsequent transformations as a starting point for their own journey and it is envisaged that each will make amendments to The Model to cater to their specific needs, as such, each Model will be unique to the business domain within which it was created (though there will be some common elements that will apply across business domains).

---

[2] McKinsey & Company, 'Unlocking Success in Digital Transformations', mckinsey.com, (2018), https://www.mckinsey.com/business-functions/organization/our-insights/unlocking-success-in-digital-transformations [accessed June 19, 2023].

One of the aims of The Model is to make subsequent transformations more efficient as they will not be starting from scratch.

The Model contains the following elements: the Leadership Guide, Workforce Strategy, Organizational Structure, Culture Guide, Transformation Strategy, Transformation Roadmap, Digital Transformation Readiness Review and/or Digital Maturity Assessment (DMA), Communication Strategy, Metrics, Technologies Matrix, Processes and Procedures, Integration Process, Plan and Costs, and Lessons Learned. *Each transformation will determine the elements of The Model that are most appropriate and may remove or add elements as required.*

Linear/Noniterative Approach

Adopting a linear approach to any digital transformation will increase the risk profile of the initiative. Organizations are essentially placing a bet that all of the upfront analysis and assumptions taken at the start of the program are still correct at the time of delivery.

Issue: A linear approach to the transformation

Significant numbers of interdependent transformation initiatives are in flight concurrently. These streams are linear, rather than iterative in nature, and each will have spent significant time and effort in up-front analysis and decision-making prior to the transformation beginning.

There is no easy way to confirm the technical feasibility or test the decisions that were taken at the start of the program are still valid until late in the delivery process. This lack of flexibility increases the risk of unexpected issues or delivery failures.

Resolution: Digital Acceleration

Galapagos Principle 4: Sequential Transformation states that *The most efficient path is not a straight line (nor is it multiple parallel streams of work)* and is underpinned by the process of Digital Acceleration, which is defined as:

An iterative, incremental, and mostly sequential approach to the delivery of digital transformations, that changes one (or at most two) distinct area(s) of the business before moving on to the next transformation objective.

As covered in *Chapter 5, Moving from Digital Transformation to Digital Acceleration*, the use of fast, iterative, and incremental cycles of delivery improves the management of risk within a *Transformation Context*, facilitates early validation of technical feasibility and assumptions, and drives increased levels of innovation.

In short, Digital Acceleration encourages organizations to improve one small part of their business quickly and then move on to the next.

The highly iterative nature of the activities in *The Galapagos Roadmap* and *The Galapagos Strategy Review Cycle* demonstrates that the entire Framework is founded on the basis of an iterative and incremental approach to the delivery of transformational change.

Heavy-Weight Governance[3]

Throwing more processes, more procedures, and more (often lengthy) meetings at the issues the digital transformation is encountering, is never the right solution.

> **Issue: Heavy-weight governance is increasing costs and reducing delivery efficiency**

To take control of a situation that may (or may not) develop into a real problem for the transformation, some leaders install many layers of process, bureaucracy, and red tape into the program.

In taking this approach, these leaders (often unwittingly) deliver a significant and detrimental effect on the entire transformation.

Costs increase, productivity decreases, and the overall efficiency of the transformation falls off a cliff. This negates any positive impact that the additional layers of governance may have produced.[4]

> **Resolution 1: Present the facts**

Gathering solid metrics on the time and cost impacts of the current heavy-weight governance processes is key.

The cost of satisfying the insatiable appetite of multiple committees/boards, not just in terms of the time spent on producing artifacts, but also in terms of the time diverted away from delivery tasks, needs to be quantified.

Similarly, a sober assessment of the efficiency of stand-ups and other meetings, often containing a *cast of thousands*, needs to be conducted, and associated costs attached.

---

[3] Extracts taken from Fintech Futures. 'Digital transformations: the negative impact of heavy-weight governance'. fintechfutures.com, 2023. Available at: https://www.fintechfutures.com/2023/08/digital-transformations-the-negative-impact-of-heavyweight-governance/ [accessed: August 1, 2023].

[4] See *Chapter 17,-Good Governance ≠ More Governance.*

In the interests of balance, metrics will also need to be gathered on the positive impact of any changes that have been applied using the current heavy-weight process.

Leaders will respond if they see the financial and delivery impact of adopting an overly onerous approach to governance.

> **Resolution 2: A balanced/lighter touch governance model**

Light-touch governance does not mean no-touch governance and striking the right balance is critical.

Adopt a Risk-based Approach

Clearly, the same level of scrutiny should not apply to the hire of a single additional resource that will assist in improving delivery velocity, and where budget is clearly available, as will be required for onboarding a new vendor.

Having said this, leaders trying to maintain a tight grip on the program often adopt a disproportionate response, requiring minutiae to be reviewed and approved as well as any big-ticket items.

Principles Should Guide Decisions Rather Than Rules

In the fast-paced world of digital transformations, applying strict governance rules is neither appropriate nor effective.

The flexibility provided by a principles-based approach, where the program is guided by broad principles that provide direction but also allow for adaptation to specific circumstances, is much more suited to the complex and rapidly changing digital environment.

> **Resolution 3: Lead, don't dictate**

Those closest to the problem are invariably those best placed to solve the issue.

Despite this, teams and individuals can become so focused on delivery that they lose sight of the big picture but, more often than not, providing a gentle nudge in the right direction will be enough to correct course.

When leaders dictate how to solve a particular problem, this shows a lack of trust in their teams to deliver and *when leaders don't trust in their teams to deliver, their teams don't deliver.*

Just Do This: Issues with delivery

Situation

There are many issues with the delivery of the transformation ranging from failures in leadership to issues with scope.

Failures in Leadership: Strategy Review Cycles are Too Long and Are Not Data Driven

Use The *Galapagos Strategy Review Cycle* focusing on the functions of **Create**, **Execute**, **Review**, and **Revise** across the Transformation Strategy, the Transformation Roadmap, and Transformation Actions.

Ensure that the Strategic Action Sessions are decision-oriented and data driven.

Orchestrating the Transformation: Issues with Managing Regular Change and Transformation Activities at the Same Time

Assign one (or more) experienced delivery lead(s) to focus solely on the digital transformation and leave existing change managers to cover the regular change and BAU activities.

Scope: Solve One Problem Well

The Galapagos Framework mandates that the scope of the transformation is limited to one (or at most two) concurrent transformations per Transformation Context.

This ensures that the scope of the transformation is limited to one or two well-defined business area(s)/function(s) and the transformation solves for these.

Scope: Wholesale Change to the Organization's Operating Model Must Not Be Considered

The Leadership Function must ensure that operating model changes are targeted and contained only within the *Transformation Context*.

The Model is a living artifact and should be modified throughout the lifecycle of the transformation.

Linear/Non-iterative Approach

Adopt a Digital Acceleration approach to the transformation. Focusing on the use of fast, iterative, and incremental cycles of delivery.

Heavy-weight Governance

Gather metrics to quantify the cost of adding additional layers of inefficiency.

Adopt a lighter touch governance model (i.e., risk-based and/or principles-based). Demonstrate leadership and trust; do not dictate solutions.

Think About This: Issues with delivery

Flexibility

Are the processes/procedures and operating model changes that are being used on The Island lightweight and flexible enough to be applied to other business areas/functions?

UNDERSTANDING THE FUNCTION OF THE GALAPAGOS FRAMEWORK

III

Chapter 13

How Does The Galapagos Framework Work in Practice?

The Galapagos Roadmap

Figure 13.1 shows the key elements of The Galapagos Roadmap. The Roadmap is highly iterative in nature and contains two phases (viz. *Bringing The Island to life* and *Delivery*), and four decision points (viz. *Integrate into the parent organization, Continue to transform, Start the next transformation*, and *Tear down & Stop*).

Each of the phases, the steps contained within these, and the four key decisions will be covered in the following sections.

Overview: Bringing The Island to Life

The activities involved in bringing The Island to life are principally concerned with defining the transformation strategy, direction, and culture, assigning people to the various roles of The Island (via internal transfer/secondment, external hires, etc.), identifying performance metrics, establishing automated monitoring, and reporting systems, and the setting up of digital communication channels to facilitate collaboration and communication.

Most of the tasks within this section are iterative and will run for some time, quite possibly overlapping (in terms of timeline) with the delivery activities.

DOI: 10.1201/9781003404217-19

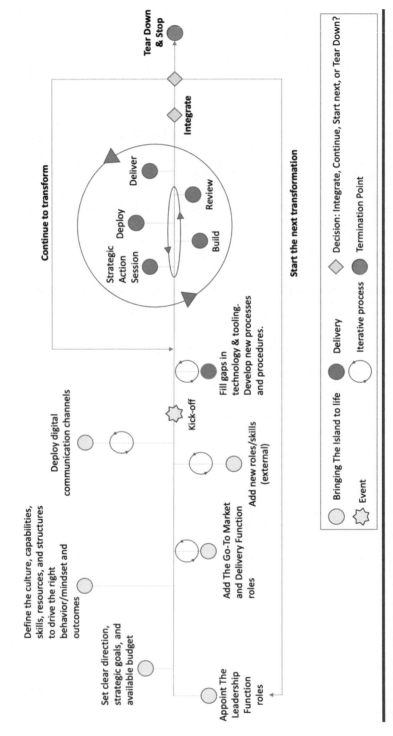

Figure 13.1 The Galapagos Roadmap.

◗ *Overview: Delivery*

The delivery activities predominantly relate to setting up The Island with the right tooling, processes, procedures, and building and delivering the product(s).
All the tasks within the *Delivery* phase are fully iterative and incremental.

◇ *Decision: Integrate into Parent Organization*

At the end of every delivery cycle a decision must be taken as to whether some/all of the new tools, technologies, processes, and procedures, etc. in use on The Island are in a stable enough state to allow them to be integrated back into the parent organization and, if they are, is now the right time to embark upon that integration activity? This area is touched on again in the *Integration* section at the end of this chapter.

◇ *Decision: Continue to Transform*

If there are additional elements of the current transformation initiative that need to be delivered, as is likely to be the case, then The Island simply moves on to the next iteration of the transformation journey.

◇ *Decision: Start the Next Transformation*

In the situation where there are other transformation initiatives in the pipeline, the organization may choose to start the next of these once the first is nearing completion. Please remember that The Island can run, at most, two transformation initiatives concurrently and only if these cover two distinct business areas with zero, or close to zero, interrelationships (see *Chapter 4 – The Function of The Galapagos Framework – Scaling up – The Transformation Context*).

Some elements of The Island will remain the same across different transformations. For example, it is anticipated that several staff will remain on The Island to provide consistency of approach, and it is likely that the digital communication channels that have been adopted by The Island for previous transformations will be fit for future initiatives.

Equally, the culture that has been set on The Island should be the same (or very similar) regardless of the transformation that is taking place.

Having said this, however, there may be a need to appoint additional roles, and there will certainly be a need to set direction, goals, and available budget for each new transformation.

Given the above, the *Start the next transformation* flow from the second *Decision* point of The Galapagos Roadmap goes back to the first action of *Appoint The Leadership Function roles*.

◇ *Decision: Tear Down and Stop*

In some situations, there may be no further transformation activities planned.

In these cases, there should also be an integration process (assuming this has not already been completed in previous iterations), but instead of moving on to the next transformation, or continuing with the current one, the company dissolves the structures of The Island itself returning the business to its original organizational state plus any new processes, procedures, tools, and technologies that have been integrated.

It is anticipated that this would be an unusual situation; however, the *Tear Down & Stop* termination point is included in The Galapagos Roadmap for completeness.

We will discuss the above processes in more detail in the following sections.

◯ Bringing The Island to Life

Once the decision has been made to progress with the digital transformation using The Galapagos Framework, we must breathe life into the structures that will support the delivery of the strategy.

Create The Island and Empower Individuals to Execute on the Strategic Goals[1]

Taking some quality time at the start of the digital transformation journey to define a clear strategic direction, the culture that is being targeted, and the profile of The Leadership Function will be time well spent and the Chief Human Resources Officer (CHRO) will be an invaluable asset in this activity.

Appoint The Leadership Function Roles

The Leadership Function comprises only three roles (discussed in more detail in *Chapter 16 – The Island Go To Market and Delivery Functions – The Leadership Function*); The Accountable Executive (AE) – who bears ultimate responsibility for the entire transformation, the Business Head – who is responsible for getting the product to market and generating revenue from this, and the Delivery Head – who is responsible for the product build and the implementation of any new technologies, tools, processes, and procedures to be used on The Island.

---

[1] Those closest to any problem will be in the best position to solve the issue. The Leadership Function must set a clear direction and empower The Island to execute on this.

Digital Executive(s)

Digital transformations fundamentally change the way companies operate and how they deliver value to their customers. The breadth and depth of this type of transformation means that it is imperative that there is at least one digitally savvy executive in a Leadership Function role.

This digital executive must be technically adept and understand the current technology landscape, to allow them to have an informed view about which technologies can be leveraged to deliver business value, while at the same time understanding how to manage the risks associated with the adoption of these.

This digital leader could be in any of the three Leadership Function roles but must be a champion of change and innovation, who understands the value of data and how to use this to inform strategic decision-making.

Set Clear Direction, Strategic Goals, and Available Budget

As mentioned in *Chapter 11 – How The Galapagos Framework Resolves the Common Issues Organizational Factors,* The Leadership Function must define and clearly communicate the strategic direction, the rationale behind this, and the goals that need to be achieved to ensure that everyone is pulling in the same direction. Instilling a sense of purpose across all teams and individuals on The Island will yield many benefits and starting this process at an early stage in The Galapagos Roadmap is a sensible idea. Once the goals are set, the metrics to ensure that the delivery of these is moving in the right direction need to be identified. The systems required for automatically monitoring and reporting on these metrics may take some time to locate and onboard into the organization so it may make sense to start this process now rather than in the *Fill gaps in technology & tooling step of the Delivery phase.*

Every large program of work needs to operate under some financial constraints and digital transformations are no different. The work that The Leadership Function will have done to control the breadth and depth of the scope (see *Chapter 12 – How The Galapagos Framework Resolves the Common Issues Delivery Aspects*) will allow reasonable cost and time estimates to be produced, by the Program Management and Business Analysis teams, and an initial high-level budget to be agreed.

Define the Culture, Capabilities, Skills, Resources, etc., to Drive the Right Outcomes

When making fundamental changes to the way the business operates, coupled with cultural and structural changes to the organization, it is important to involve a very senior HR representative (possibly the CHRO) from day one.

Deliveries of the HR Function

Culture Guide and the Workforce Strategy

The HR Function will not only assist in defining the cultural norms of The Island (contained in the *Culture Guide* of *The Model*) but will also be responsible for the creation of the *Workforce Strategy* (also contained in *The Model*), which will cover items such as the skills, resources, and capabilities required, in which locations, to deliver this and future transformations.

It is crucial that the *Workforce Strategy* includes, where possible, the named individuals that will be used to make the transformation a successful endeavor. Where names cannot be assigned to roles, or where skills gaps exist, the HR function must assist in assigning names and closing the gaps as a priority. This may require casting the net wide to second or attach experienced staff from other areas of the organization onto The Island. Most staff functions will not be required to allocate 100% of their time to The Island and is it critical to strike the right balance of experience and youthful innovation when assigning staff to The Island.

Using a healthy amount of experienced internal staff will yield many benefits, not least of which will be reducing the risk of any surprises cropping up when integrating the structures of The Island back into the parent organization.

Where resource gaps cannot be filled using internal capabilities, then the organization must look at going to market or engaging with a trusted third party, possibly as part of a resource augmentation exercise. The impact and lead time of landing people using this approach must be fully understood and communicated to The Leadership Function to allow it to assess the effect that this might have on the delivery of the transformation.

Organizational Change and Communication Strategy

The creation of The Island will, in most instances, require some form of organizational change to remove silos, increase transparency and improve accountability. These changes will be contained in the *Organizational Structure* section of *The Model*. The management of these adjustments to the way the business operates will need to be handled sensitively to reduce the inevitable resistance to change.

Part of this process will be to define and implement a targeted communications strategy (contained in the *Communication Strategy* section of *The Model*), which will, amongst other things, ensure consistency of messaging, and that the right people are engaged at the right time to drive the transformation forward. The implementation of the *Communication Strategy* may require the skills of The Delivery Function to set up all required communication channels on The Island (e.g., instant messaging, video conferencing, collaborative workspaces, etc.).

Figure 13.2 shows the structure of The Island, which will be covered in detail in *Chapter 14 – The Island* and is presented here to provide context.

Add The Go-To Market and Delivery Function Roles

The Island is divided into two main sections: The Go-To Market Functions and The Delivery Functions.

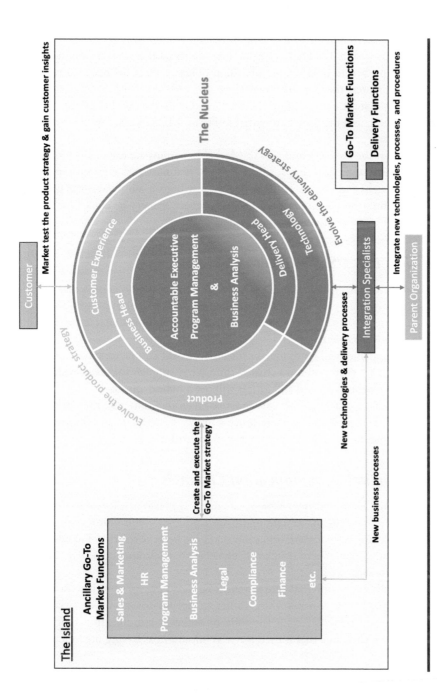

Figure 13.2 The Island structure.

The teams contained in The Go-To Market Functions are primarily concerned with the activities that need to be achieved to successfully launch the product to market, in whatever jurisdictions are applicable.

All groups within The Delivery Functions are focused on everything that needs to be accomplished to build or modify the product to meet the needs of the business, and ultimately the end customer.

The roles that are employed in The Ancillary Go-To Market Functions will vary by organization, and the teams presented in Figure 13.2 serve as a guide and not an exhaustive list.

Given that the Delivery and Go-To Market Functions are responsible for building the product and delivering it to the market, it almost goes without saying that putting the right individuals in the right roles will go a long way in making the transformation a successful endeavor. The *Workforce Strategy* produced by the HR function will be an invaluable asset in respect of this.

Add New Roles/Skills (External)

The *Workforce Strategy* will also be useful in identifying the skills gaps that need to be filled externally to progress the transformation. Each organization will have a different approach to resource augmentation based on existing strategic partnerships and other considerations.

Some companies will go to market for independent contractors, consultants, or permanent staff, others will use a trusted third-party supplier (or several third-party suppliers) to fill the gaps, and still others will use a hybrid approach.

Whichever approach is used, care must be taken to ensure that the right quality of resources are landed and that the process to locate, evaluate, and onboard these individuals does not put delivery timelines in jeopardy.

Deploy Digital Communication Channels

As part of the *Communications Strategy*, mentioned previously, it is important that companies embrace an up-to-date approach to digital communication. This will involve employing the collaboration tools that have become so critical to facilitating effective communication and teamwork, especially in environments where teams are geographically separated.

These tools cover a myriad of different functions ranging from instant messaging to collaborative workspaces, video conferencing, and so on, and every company will have its own preferences for the suite of digital communication tools that it deploys.[2] The technology that is used is not as important as having the functionality

---

[2] No organization should be relying solely on email and telephone for communication in the digital age.

that the organization needs to ensure efficient and effective communication, and collaboration among all individuals and teams involved in the transformation.

Kick-off

Kick-off meetings may seem like a dated concept, but they are an important part of the launch of any program of work as they demonstrate how important this transformation is to achieving a strategic objective. They also provide an opportunity for a senior executive to set the tone and culture that they want to see carried on throughout the transformation.

The kick-off will act as a forum where all members of The Island will have an opportunity to meet with each other, either face-to-face or virtually.

For globally distributed teams, the kick-off event is even more important as not everyone will have met, and the concept of TEAM! (collective success/collective failure, open/honest and friendly communication at all times, etc.) needs to be solidified.

The kick-off must be delivered by a very senior leader (CEO or The Accountable Executive) as this will clearly demonstrate that the initiative has the full backing of the most senior leaders of the company. They will communicate the vision and the strategy and describe how this digital transformation will move the organization forward while at the same time demonstrating that the strategy is aligned with the core values of the organization.

Whoever is leading the kick-off meeting should emphasize the hierarchy of preferred communication styles (e.g., face-to-face, then video call, then telephone/instant message, and then email as the last resort) to ensure that the pace and quality of communication cycles are improved, and it should be made clear that the use of cover ass emails[3] will not be tolerated.

The executive leading the kick-off should also highlight each of the areas involved in the transformation so that everyone understands their role in the execution of the strategy. To emphasize this point, a central reference point could be distributed, with all contact and communication channel details, so that everyone has a common location to allow them to identify the teams and individuals that will help them achieve their goals.

● Delivery

Now that The Island has been sparked into life, it can start the process of delivering on the objectives of the transformation strategy.

---

[3] This type of communication is not just inefficient but can create a defensive culture and promote distrust. Cover-ass emails also stifle open and honest communication and the volume of these (especially, if they contain long CC lists) can lead to information overload.

Fast Evolution of Technology and Processes

The delivery phase of The Galapagos Roadmap is highly iterative in nature and involves ensuring that The Island has everything that it needs to complete its mission (see *Fill gaps in technology & tooling. Develop new processes and procedures* of The Galapagos Roadmap).

In parallel to this, The Island will enter a cycle of deciding what needs to be delivered (*Strategic Action Sessions*), building what has been decided within the next product iteration (*Build*), deploying this to the business users (*Deploy*), assessing what has been built and deployed to check that it is fit for purpose (*Review*), and delivering this product increment into an environment for use by the end customers (*Deliver*).

We will cover these in the following sections.

Fill the Gaps – Technology, Tooling, Processes, and Procedures

In Figure 13.1 we can see that the task of *Fill gaps in technology & tooling. Develop new processes and procedures* comes after the Kick-off event. It is placed here because this could be a very long running process and therefore does not sit comfortably in the *Bringing The Island to Life* phase. However, it is entirely possible that this activity could be started earlier than is shown in the diagram, that is, at some point before the kick-off event.

Every company will have different needs when it comes to filling these gaps. Some organizations will be reasonably mature, with a good portfolio of digital technologies and tooling, others may not be so advanced, and the technology gap may seem more like a chasm.

Regardless of the size of the gap that needs to be filled, it still needs to be filled and the only way to do this is to start work. This effort will be a highly iterative process with the intention of closing the gaps as quickly as possible. Time is never The Island's friend and getting the right tools and technologies in place quickly is essential, as this will improve the productivity of those on The Island significantly.

One of the main reasons for creating The Island structure is to enable the transformation process to be unencumbered by the bureaucracy and red tape of the parent organization. Creating The Island to be as independent and as nimble as possible will ensure maximum efficiency by facilitating quick decision-making and smoothing the path for the implementation of new technologies, tools, and processes.

Technologies

The exact type of technologies that will need to be employed to drive the transformation forward is domain specific. For example, in a manufacturing domain, there might be gaps in robotics/digital twin technologies, whereas in financial services there might be gaps in AI/blockchain/cloud technologies. Given that The Galapagos

Framework is domain agnostic (i.e., it is designed to work across multiple different domains) it is beyond the scope of this book to cover the technologies that might be applicable to specific domains.

However, some example technologies that could be used for web-based applications are provided in *Appendix D – Example technologies and architecture for web-based applications.*

Processes and Procedures

The Island structure also enables the swift adoption of new processes and procedures that will support the delivery of the transformation mission. It is important that The Leadership Function (and others) on The Island take full advantage of *Galapagos Principle 3: Geographic Isolation*, to allow the most appropriate, lightweight, processes and procedures to be adopted to make the operation of The Island as efficient and effective as possible.

Deliver, Deliver, Deliver

Now that the gaps in technology and tooling have been (or are close to being) filled, The Island should be well-formed enough to start the execution of tasks that are directly related to the delivery of the digital transformation. It is important to note that The Island *does not* need to be fully formed for delivery to start, the iterative nature of most of the *Bringing The Island to life* tasks means that these will run on for some time, and delivery work must start as soon as possible.

In true Agile fashion, The Island must aim to deliver small but functioning increments of the final delivery. The focus of the initial iterations should be to deliver quick wins as a priority. If there are any quick wins that would deliver a *WOW* factor, then these should be tackled first.

The successful delivery of quick wins will build stakeholder confidence in the delivery structures that have been put in place and will increase the confidence of the teams on The Island. It will also allow the TEAM! to see what can be achieved by working in a highly collaborative structure, and in these sorts of situations, success breeds success.

Building a *walking skeleton (the basic, bare bones of a delivery)*, a term coined by Gee Paw Hill,[4] will allow The Island to iterate quickly and deliver fast incremental improvements, demonstrating continual delivery at pace. This again will build confidence not just with external stakeholders but within The Island itself and so a virtuous cycle ensues.

---

[4] GeePaw Hill, 'Many More Much Smaller Steps: First Sketch', geepawhill.org (2021), https://www.geepawhill.org/2021/09/29/many-more-much-smaller-steps-first-sketch/ [accessed June 19, 2023].

60-Minute Strategic Action Session (SAS)

As discussed in *Chapter 6 – Emerging Better Practices*, the purpose of the 60-Minute Strategic Action Session is to prioritize what The Island will act on now (Figure 13.3).

Build

Immediately after the Strategic Action Session, The Island will start to execute on the ACT items that have been decided on in the SAS (the ACT items are the deliveries that are the most valuable, easiest to execute, and will provide important early results and increase momentum).

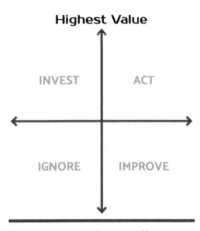

Figure 13.3 Value vs. Effort.[5]

The ACT, INVEST, and IMPROVE outputs of the SAS will act as inputs to the Program Management and Business Analysis functions to allow them to pull together a high-level, prioritized milestone plan to track delivery execution.

Prototype

Every organization will differ in its approach to product build. Having said this, The Galapagos Framework recommends that the first steps in the *Build* phase should involve the production of low-cost prototypes.

These prototypes will be used to validate and refine requirements with business users, in short iterative loops, and this process is repeated until an agreement is reached that the prototype represents what is required. The prototype itself (along with supporting User Stories for additional work that will be required to make the prototype fully functional) then becomes the requirements artifact, in place of any lengthy Business Requirements Definition (BRD) or other requirements documents.

The results of this process are a significant improvement in the quality of requirements being produced and a decreased likelihood of significant changes to

5 Duesbury, S. (2019) 'Figure showing The Quadrants', online figure. Available at: https://www.linkedin.com/pulse/how-top-companies-turn-ideas-action-fast-steve-duesbury/?trackingId=%2FH0MAIeZQduDkB5Jp3URbA%3D%3D [Accessed: June 19, 2023].

requirements once agreement has been reached that the prototype meets the needs of the business.[6]

As soon as these prototypes have been validated, and the associated User Stories for any additional work have been created, they will be used as the basis for building the product. The prototypes may also be used to market test the strategy, and to show customers (and prospective customers) the direction of travel of the organization.

Early iterations of these prototypes can also be fed back into the Strategic Action Sessions to act as the basis for further discussion.

Product Build

Given that high-quality requirements have now been produced (in the form of prototypes and associated User Stories), The Island can progress onto product build, with a high degree of confidence that what is being built is what the business and the end customers want.

The above approach delivers lower-risk, lower-cost, and higher-quality products. It ensures a quality delivery whilst at the same time reducing the risk of rework and associated costs.

It is significantly cheaper to change a prototype than to change any product during the build process (even if the product is in early development or test and has not been released to the market). Some estimates suggest that a change made during the testing phase can be up to 100 times more expensive than if the same change was made in the prototyping phase.

Example

Let's look at a situation where a financial institution wants to deliver a product via new digital channels (e.g., website, mobile application, etc.).

In this instance, pixel-perfect, clickable, User Experience (UX) prototypes of the screens, and workflows between the screens can be produced in a matter of days and replayed back to the business users to confirm that what has been produced is the same as what has been asked for.

If changes are required, these take a short amount of time to apply and are again reviewed by the business.

---

[6] Harkin, B. (5 July, 2023) 'Digital Transformations: The Impact of Leadership, Conflict, and the Mask of Corporate Ambiguity', Fintech Futures, 1 July. Available at: https://www.fintechfutures.com/2023/07/digital-transformations-the-impact-of-leadership-conflict-and-the-mask-of-corporate-ambiguity/ (accessed: 8 September 2023).

In parallel to the production of the UX Prototype a Business Analyst will be tasked with ensuring that the data that is displayed on the screens, and the processing that will be required to support the functionality of the screens can be delivered.

In this cycle, we see the Customer Experience, Product, Technology and Business Analysis functions working in concert, iterating quickly to produce a UX prototype (and supporting User Stories) that becomes a requirements artifact/document for the product.

The prototype, and associated User Stories, can then be committed to programming code, (which is a much more expensive process than building a UX prototype) with a high degree of certainty that what is being developed is exactly what has been asked for.

Deploy

If the product that is being built is a software product, then the delivery phase will require the product to be deployed to an environment that the business can access for review. If this is a physical product, for example, then this phase will cover the manufacturing of the item.

Review

In a software context, the review process is *not* a formal User Acceptance Testing (UAT) phase. If the correct automated testing processes are in place and there is a high degree of automated test coverage (e.g., > 80%) then the need for formal UAT should be dramatically reduced (hopefully to zero) and this process should just be sanity checking that the product features work as expected.

In manufacturing, this phase may involve whatever Quality Assurance (QA) processes are required to ensure that the product is fit for purpose.

The *Review* process should not be limited to the product itself but should also assess how The Island has operated to deliver this product increment.

Analogous to a retrospective in an Agile Scrum[7] approach, this review process should assess what went well, what can be improved, and what improvements to the process will be delivered in the next iteration.

Reviewing the efficacy of The Island as part of each iteration will allow The Island Itself to improve the quality and effectiveness of all the resident functions.[8] Analyzing the performance of The Island allows it to embark on a journey of continuous empirical process improvement. With each iteration, The Island becomes

---

[7] Scrum.org, (no date), https://www.scrum.org/ [accessed June 19, 2023].

[8] This is a review of the processes, operating procedures, communication tools, etc. and not a performance review of the people.

more efficient and effective. This process also allows The Island to quickly adapt to any changes in the surrounding environment.

Deliver

The delivery phase is essentially supplying the product/product feature or service to the end customer. This could mean deploying the code to a production environment (software) or manufacturing and delivering the physical product.

Repeat

Now that this product increment is complete, we start the process again with another Strategic Action Session.

Integrate

When any of the organizational, technical, or process-related elements of The Island are deemed to be in a stable state then these should be integrated back into the parent company.

It is recommended that the process of integrating successful Island elements into the parent company is conducted early in the *Delivery* cycle and frequently thereafter. If this does not happen, then a backlog of integration tasks will build up over time and The Island runs the risk of becoming significantly divergent from the parent organization. The longer The Island waits to incorporate these elements back into the parent company the more the risk increases of the integration process becoming more complex, costly, and susceptible to failure.

It is likely that some of the elements of The Island will be ready for integration before others and thus the integration process will be iterative rather than a *big-bang* approach (where all the tools, technologies, processes. and procedures are integrated into the parent company at the same time). A big-bang approach should be avoided if at all possible.

As other elements in use on The Island become ready then these too will be integrated, possibly in parallel to other *Delivery* activities that are moving the transformation forward.

This cycle will continue until all technologies, tools, processes, and procedures that are in use on The Island have been fully integrated back into the main organization.

Given that there exists a global state of change, an argument could be made for creating The Island and then running through a perpetual cycle of *Integrate* and *Continue to transform* to cater for the volatile worldwide environment, and continuous state of flux in which organizations find themselves today.

However, this decision will differ from organization to organization, location to location, and market to market.

Integration Specialists

Under normal circumstances, there will be many integrations throughout the life of the transformation initiative, and The Integration Specialists will be front and center of all integration-related activities.

As part of The Integration Specialists remit, they will have provided oversight of all the technologies, tools, and processes that The Island has adopted and will have worked with the relevant entities of the parent company to ensure that there is a clear path/plan for integrating each of these back into the parent organization.

Chapter 14

The Island[1]

What Is The Island?

As mentioned previously, The Island is the organizational structure that is tasked with delivering on the transformation strategy and is wholly responsible for the execution and delivery of the entire digital transformation (for the *Transformation Context*[2] within which The Island exists). It is logically separate from the parent company, which allows it to be unencumbered by the bureaucracy and red tape of the main organization.

The entire delivery capability is contained within The Island.

Coalition of the Willing

The Island is a cross-functional group of individuals, both existing and hired into the organization, who have the remit to deliver on a well-defined transformation objective/set of objectives in the most efficient and effective way possible.

At its core, The Island is a coalition of the willing that acts as a central hub to drive the digital transformation effort forward.[3] It will deliver the leadership,

---

[1] "...small islands were particularly conducive to the engendering and transmutation of species." De Paolo, C. (2010). 'Darwin and the Galápagos Islands: An Annotated Guide to the Primary Texts', Victorian Web. Available at: https://www.victorianweb.org/science/darwin/depaolo2.html (accessed: 5th September 2023).

The Island will quickly evolve its approaches to find the optimal way to deliver this transformation.

[2] See *Chapter 4 – The Function of The Galapagos Framework – Scaling Up – The Transformation Context*

[3] As stated in Galapagos Principle 3: "*The Island does not have to be physically separated from the parent organization ... However, if The Island exists in the same location as the parent organization it must be a logically separated team (i.e., it should be identified, and operate, as an independent entity).*"

DOI: 10.1201/9781003404217-20

Figure 14.1 A tropical island.

culture, organization, skills, technologies, tools, processes, procedures, and metrics that are required to achieve all of the strategic transformation goals. It is also tasked with ensuring that all artifacts used on The Island can be integrated back into the main organization.

The Island will set the standard for digital transformations that will be used across the organization.

A Means of Improving Delivery and Delivery Satisfaction

The Island will not just improve overall delivery; it will, crucially, improve delivery satisfaction across both internal functions (those within The Island and the parent organization) and external parties (customers, third parties, and other key stakeholders outside of The Island and the parent organization).

It is anticipated that most/all of the elements employed on The Island will be re-used to deliver subsequent transformation objectives, thus, the approaches and techniques used here can form a cookie-cutter approach for digital transformations across other areas of the business.

A Self-contained/Autonomous Entity

The Island is made up of multiple different teams, all of which are aware of each other (and the work that other functions are performing) and operate in concert to deliver the transformation. Some teams and individuals will interface with the parent organization, but this is not a requirement for all functions.

Each of the functions and teams within The Island contain all the resources (people, tools, technologies, processes, etc.) that they require to deliver on their objective(s).

Thus, The Island, as its name suggests, is a predominantly self-contained body with links back to the parent organization.

What Is the Structure of The Island?

The diagram in Figure 14.2 shows the key elements that make up The Island.

The Nucleus

At the center of The Island is The Nucleus. The Nucleus is the core of The Island and is central to the successful delivery of the transformation initiative. It is The Nucleus that satisfies *Galapagos Principle 2: Customer Proximity* which (via The Customer Experience Function) aims to *reduce the distance between the end customer and the engine room of delivery.*

Principle 2: Minimizing the number of links between the end customer and the product development and delivery functions will reduce costs and increase profit. Increasing the number of links will have the opposite effect.

The Nucleus ensures that the tools, technologies, and processes that are used on The Island can be re-integrated back into the parent organization (via close collaboration with The Integration Specialists).

The power of The Nucleus derives from its simplicity, which allows it to scale easily and provides the flexibility to allow The Island to pivot quickly based on changing needs.

The functions contained within The Nucleus are described below.

The Leadership Function

The Leadership Function bears ultimate responsibility for the entire transformation strategy and also the delivery of the transformation. The leadership team must

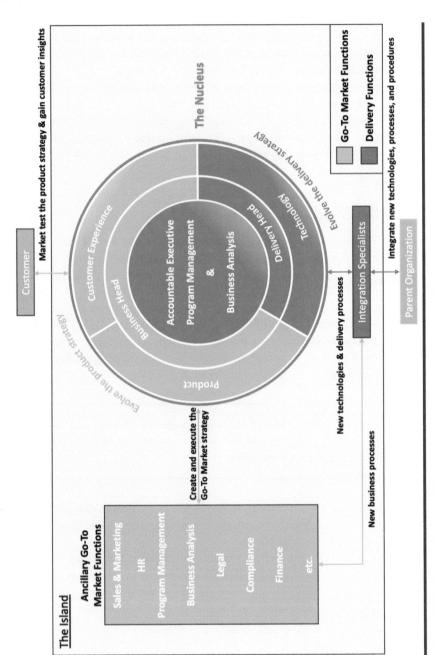

Figure 14.2   The Island structure.

ensure that the strategy is clear and unambiguous, that a consistent leadership style is adopted across The Island, and that the right culture is in place to deliver the desired outcomes.

The Leadership Function will be aware of other likely targets of transformation within the organization and will ensure that the outputs of The Island do not paint the organization into a technological/organizational/operational *cul-de-sac*.

Simplifying the leadership structure to just three roles (the Accountable Executive (AE), the Business Head, and The Delivery Head) ensures that the decision-making process is efficient and communication is streamlined and consistent across all teams on The Island.

The Accountable Executive (AE)

Ultimately answerable for the success or otherwise of the entire transformation, this role must be held by a senior "C" suite executive who will set clear direction and drive the cultural and organizational changes required to ensure success.

Given this, the AE has the final say in any strategic decisions that must be made and will act as the ultimate arbiter of any contention between The Business Head and The Delivery Head roles.

The Business Head

The Business Head role is responsible for all activities required to launch the product/product feature/service into the market (i.e., The Go-To Market Functions). All teams that are concerned with the engagement of the end customer, product strategy, Sales and Marketing, Legal, Compliance, Finance, etc., and ensuring that the product that is delivered is fit for purpose, are within the purview of The Business Head.

This role is another senior executive position, which will be responsible for coordinating many different functions, and therefore must be held by someone who has a positive profile within the business, is well respected, and is highly collaborative in their approach.

The Delivery Head

Responsibility for the product build, security considerations, all tools, technologies, and delivery processes used on The Island (and ensuring that these can be easily integrated back into the parent organization) reside with The Delivery Head role.

Whereas The Business Head role is primarily outward facing (towards the end customer), The Delivery Head role must face in both directions (delivering the product for the end customer but also ensuring that the integration of elements used on The Island back into the main company is smooth).

Due to the criticality of the outputs from this function, this is the last role that must be occupied by a senior executive and preferably an executive that possesses a sound understanding of the technological considerations.

Program Management (Nucleus)

For any program to operate effectively there needs to be some form of co-ordination, and within The Nucleus, the Program Management Function fulfills this role.

The Program Management Function, within the context of The Nucleus, is solely concerned with coordinating and reporting on the deliveries out of The Nucleus itself (including any activities relating to integration back into the parent organization).

For larger transformation programs, this role is distinct from the Program Management Function that drives the deliveries out of The Ancillary Go-To Market Functions, as the skills required for each of these areas are markedly different.

If there is a need for a Program Director to ensure consistency and coordination across both areas of program management (in The Nucleus and Ancillary Go-To Market Functions), then this role will reside within The Nucleus.

Business Analysis (Nucleus)

The entire analytical capability of The Island is controlled by the Business Analysis Function of The Nucleus. All Business Analysts (BAs) across The Nucleus and Ancillary Go-To Market Functions will be coordinated from here (possibly via a set of lead BAs if the size of the program warrants it).

Having both the Program Management and Business Analysis capabilities of The Island controlled from The Nucleus ensures consistency and quality of output from these functions.

The Business Analysis Function within The Nucleus is not only concerned with the overall coordination of business analysis activities (across The Nucleus and The Ancillary Go-To Market Functions) but also with the analysis activities that relate to The Nucleus itself and those relating to product build and integration.

The Island, The Customer, and The Parent Organization

There are three key Go-To Market and Delivery Functions, within The Nucleus, that manage the relationship between The Nucleus itself, the end customer, The Ancillary Go-To Market Functions, and the parent organization, namely, The Customer Experience Function, The Product Function, and The Technology Function (via The Integration Specialists).

Customer Experience Function

Unsurprisingly, the relationship with the customer is managed through, and owned by, The Customer Experience Function which is responsible for all customer engagement.

It is important to note that other functions will also be in direct contact with the customer (e.g., Sales and Marketing). However, they must liaise closely with The Customer Experience Function to ensure that there is consistency in communication and that the relationship with the customer is managed carefully (e.g., confirming that there are not multiple different teams speaking to the same customers at the same time on different topics).

Customer Experience is the new currency; it guides and informs the product strategy and roadmap by feeding customer insights of early prototype demonstrations back into The Product Function. Furthermore, it ensures that there is a consistent, efficient, and effective customer experience across all products and services.

The Customer Experience Function is critical to the delivery of *Galapagos Principle 2: Customer Proximity* (see *Chapter 3 – Introduction to The Galapagos Framework – The Galapagos Principles* and *Chapter 26 – The Customer Proximity Principle* for more detail).

Product Function

All aspects of product strategy, roadmap, design, feature definition, market research, pricing, product launch, promotion, after-sales support, service, etc., fall within the remit of The Product Function.

This function liaises closely with the all The Go-To Market and delivery teams within The Island (both The Nucleus and Ancillary Go-To Market Functions).

Product and Customer Experience

The interaction between The Product and Customer Experience Function will, for example, include the early market testing of the product strategy and gaining actionable customer insights to inform the product strategy and design. Further, this interaction will also inform how the organization services the end customers' needs and requests.

Product and Technology

The collaboration between The Product Function and The Technology Function will drive product development and move the products' evolutionary cycle from concept to the creation of something tangible that can be consumed by the end customer.

As such, this relationship will include, among other things, the development of the product roadmap, the delivery of product requirements, and ensuring that the deliverables meet the needs of the business, the end customer, and are delivered on time and within budget.

Product and Ancillary Go-To Market Functions

There are often a myriad of other departments and teams that are required to get a product out to market. These functions are ancillary to, but no less important than, The Nucleus functions.

In fact, some of these functions could prevent a product ever being released to the market (e.g., Legal and Compliance could demonstrate that the product does not comply with the laws and regulations of the market that it is intended for) or could prevent the product being built in the first place (e.g., Finance highlight that the ROI is not significant enough to warrant the investment).

The Product Function is central to ensuring that situations, such as those outlined above, do not occur and will work with Legal and Compliance (to ensure that the product does not breach the rules and regulations that govern the market), Sales and Marketing (to ensure that the product will generate the required revenue), and Technology to ensure that the cost of build, and ongoing running and maintenance costs, when combined with projected revenue result in a reasonable profit.

The Technology Function

In any digital transformation, the technology operation is critical, and this is no different in The Galapagos Framework, where The Technology Function is responsible for moving the product strategy from a conceptual idea to a consumable item. Technology here is used in its broadest possible sense, it could encapsulate anything from manufacturing technology to biotechnology (in the pharmaceutical industry) to information technology (IT) and everything in between.

Fundamentally, this is the function that builds the product and delivers, not just the product itself, but everything that is required for the product to function (it would be a bad customer experience to deliver a smartphone without a battery, or a software product without the required infrastructure to make it run effectively).

The Technology Function is also tasked with identifying and deploying the digital communication channels that are used on The Island and filling any gaps in the suite of technologies and tools that will be used to deliver the transformation strategy.

In the case of software products, this group must also ensure that any new applications that are built, are not tightly coupled to the legacy systems of the parent company. Instead, any new digital products should be integrated with these *classic* systems via clean APIs (Application Programming Interfaces) as and when required.

Similarly, stand-alone solutions (i.e., products that do not either feed data into or take data out of the parent company) should not be built as these will not be easily integrated back into the main organization (see the *Technology and Integration Specialists* section below).

The technology team will encourage the wider use of lightweight and Agile processes that should become the norm on The Island. These processes, coupled with an appropriate, and current, technology stack should be positively regarded as enablers of change and strategic agility.

Technology and Integration Specialists

Another key responsibility of The Technology Function is to ensure that the technologies and delivery processes that have been used to create the product can be easily integrated back into the parent organization. Therefore, both The Technology Function and The Integration Specialists must work closely together to ensure that this is the case.

Ancillary Go-To Market Functions

As mentioned above, The Ancillary Go-To Market Functions (e.g., Sales and Marketing, HR, Legal, Compliance, etc.) are there to support the delivery of the product to market and are in no way subordinate to any other function. These functions will be covered in more detail in *Chapter 18 – The Island – Ancillary Go-To Market Functions*.

Ancillary Go-To Market Functions and Integration Specialists

It is worth noting that any new business processes or operating model changes coming out of The Ancillary Go-To Market Functions must be validated by The Integration Specialists to confirm that these can be reused in the parent organization.

Integration Specialists

Put simply, The Integration Specialist's role is to act as a reality check on the processes, tools, and technologies that are being used on The Island and to ensure that these can be re-integrated back into the parent organization without incurring significant cost/effort.

There is little point in The Island delivering a transformation using technologies, tools, or processes that cannot be easily adopted by the parent organization.

What Is The Island Responsible for?

Fundamentally, The Island is responsible for the entire transformation. Everything from defining the strategy, to ultimately delivering the product(s) that meet the strategic need, and everything in between, is the concern of The Island.

Predominantly, a self-contained environment, The Island is tasked with delivering the transformation for the business area(s) that it serves covering all aspects of the initiative including, but not limited to, leadership, culture, organization, skills, technologies, metrics, processes, and workforce strategy. The Island will also produce a lightweight digital transformation/operating model (*The Model*, see *Chapter 19 – The Model* for more detail on this), that may be used by other transformations in the future.

It is critical to the success of the transformation that The Island is empowered to identify and fill gaps in skills/resourcing/technology/tooling whilst ensuring that any technology/tools that are used to deliver the transformation can be integrated back into the parent organization. The Integration Specialist role will be key in ensuring the success of this integration process.

Additionally, The Island will explore new approaches, techniques, and technologies to solve the common issues[4] associated with digital transformations in a more efficient and effective way.

Membership of The Island

Digital transformations touch on a significant number of areas of an organization, and these need to be represented on The Island. Most of these roles will not spend 100% of their time allocated to The Island, and a good mix of experienced and innovative individuals is essential. Some of the areas of the organization that may be represented on The Island are shown in Tables 14.1 to 14.3.

TABLE 14.1   The Nucleus Functions Roles and Deliverables

The Nucleus Functions	
Role	**Deliverables**
Accountable Executive	Sets clear direction and drives organizational change (simplifying processes/operating models, removing silos, increasing transparency, and improving accountability). Implements a targeted communication strategy and instills a sense of urgency.
The Business Head	Responsible for all the Go-To Market activities required to launch the product to market. Including Product Development, Sales & Marketing, Legal & Compliance, Finance, Customer Experience, etc. The coordination of all these activities lies with The Business Head.

(Continued)

---

[4] Highlighted in *Chapter 2*.

TABLE 14.1 (Continued)

The Nucleus Functions	
Role	**Deliverables**
The Delivery Head	Responsible for all product build activities required to construct, test, and deploy the product. Delivery will comprise program management, business analysis, technology, testing, etc., and the coordination of all these activities lies within The Delivery Functions.
Customer Experience	Responsible for everything related to the customer experience, for example, delivery of value models covering: Where is/can value be created? What are the drags on value creation? What are the key customer journeys and what are the pain points in these? Rapid product prototyping, iterating prototypes in the market before any build effort (even MVP[a]), and working with customers on the prototype to inform the product strategy are all the responsibilities of The Customer Experience Function.
Product	Responsible for the product strategy and roadmap, product launch, revenue, profitability analysis, etc.
Technology	Improve/increase process automation and use of digital/collaboration tools. AI and modern architectural concepts (e.g., cloud first, containerization, microservices, etc.). Delivery of digital products.
Program Management	Roadmap planning, change management/managing change, define and track key metrics to feed into the strategy process (KPIs, scorecards, etc.), and financial control.
Business Analysis	Analysis of requirements (Themes, Initiatives, Epics, and User Stories), process maps, business rules, etc.

[a] Minimum Viable Product

TABLE 14.2 The Ancillary Go-To Market Functions Roles and Deliverables

The Ancillary Go-To Market Functions	
Role	**Deliverables**
HR (CHRO)	Workforce Strategy, define and promote the desired cultural changes, enhance capabilities, skills, and resources, and define the structures to drive rapid decision-making/the right behaviors/mindset and outcomes.

(Continued)

TABLE 14.2   (Continued)

The Ancillary Go-To Market Functions	
Role	**Deliverables**
Sales/Marketing	Promotional/marketing campaigns, lead generation, sales, and market research reports, etc.
Legal/Compliance	Changes to existing client legal agreements to deliver products via new channels/technologies (e.g., cloud). Are there any legal implications in different geographic regions?
Finance	Cost/profit and loss allocation/disbursements, etc.

TABLE 14.3   The Ancillary Delivery Function Roles and Deliverables

The Ancillary Delivery Function	
Role	**Deliverables**
Integration Specialists	These individuals exist within The Delivery Function and are tasked with ensuring the smooth integration of processes, technologies, and new operating models back into the parent organization.

Chapter 15

The Island: The Leadership Function

Unsurprisingly, The Leadership Function sits at the core of The Nucleus. However, more surprisingly, this function is comprised of only three roles: The Accountable Executive (AE), The Business Head, and The Delivery Head (Figure 15.1).

Having such a small leadership team facilitates rapid decision-making and issue resolution. It also serves to ensure that the strategy and direction are clear and unambiguous, a consistent leadership style is adopted across The Island, the right culture and communication methods are in place to drive the desired outcomes, reporting lines are simplified, and consistent messaging is delivered.

This focused and targeted group is responsible for ensuring that the leadership failings that blight so many digital transformations do not happen in this instance (see *Chapter 11 – How The Galapagos Framework Resolves the Common Issues – The Organizational Factors – Failures in Leadership*).

The simplicity of the structure of The Galapagos Framework is what makes it so effective.

The overall accountability for the transformation lies with The Accountable Executive (AE).

All functions responsible for getting the product to market and the integration of any new business processes, relating to The Go-To Market Functions, back into the parent organization fall under the remit of The Business Head.

Similarly, all functions relating to the building and delivery of the product and the integration back into the parent organization of new operating models/processes/procedures and technologies, relating to The Delivery Functions, are the responsibility of The Delivery Head.

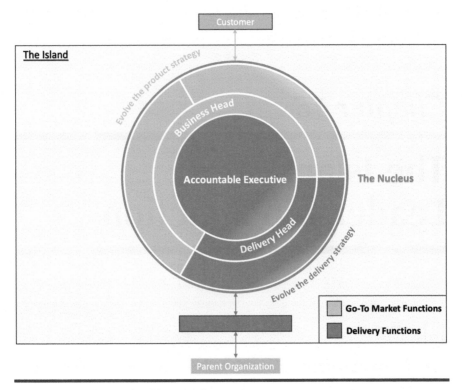

Figure 15.1 The Leadership Function.

The Accountable Executive (AE)

The individual in the role of Accountable Executive is ultimately responsible for the successful delivery of the entire digital transformation and will be the final decision-maker in matters that affect the strategy, direction, and delivery of the transformation program.

To ensure that delivery velocity is not compromised, The AE will also act as an arbiter when an impasse is reached, or there are disagreements, between The Business Head and The Delivery Head. Quick and effective decision-making is key in digital transformation programs, and The AE is essential to that process working well.

Reporting progress to the executive sponsor(s) and other key stakeholders (residing in the parent organization) is a critical function of The AE role. Key Performance Indicators (KPIs), Objectives and Key Results (OKRs), delivery progress, financial measures, and other salient metrics relating to the transformation should be delivered by The AE in an easily digestible format.

Transparency is key to building trust, and it is therefore incumbent on The AE to make sure that the lowlights, as well as the highlights, are reported on.

The Business Head

The Product, Customer Experience, and ancillary Go-To Market Functions all fall under the remit of The Business Head role.

Essentially, any task that relates to getting the product out to market, and generating revenue from the product, falls within the scope of this role. The Business Head role also covers evolving the product strategy and informing this evolution via customer insights gained from market testing the product/product strategy/product features with the end customers.

For larger transformation programs, there is likely to be a Program Management and Business Analysis Function aligned to The Business Head. These are separate to, and distinct from, the Program Management and Business Analysis Functions that manage The Nucleus itself and the deliveries related to the product build.

The development of the product strategy falls within the remit of The Business Head, covering everything from target market, value proposition, product positioning, and roadmap to the pricing and marketing strategy, etc.

Given the scope of The Business Head role, this individual needs to be a strategic leader with exceptional collaboration and people skills and who possesses a solid financial acumen.

The Business Head must be able to partner with a diverse range of groups such as Sales and Marketing, HR, Legal and Compliance, Finance, Product, and Customer Experience in order to bring all parties to the table.

The Delivery Head

Responsibility for all tasks relating to product build, new operating models, processes, procedures (used within The Delivery Function), and technologies used within The Island reside with The Delivery Head role.

Crucially, The Delivery Head is also responsible for the integration of any new processes/technologies back into the parent organization via The Integration Specialists. There is little point in adopting new ways of working or technologies if these cannot be usefully employed by the parent organization.

The evolution of the delivery strategy falls within the remit of The Delivery Head. This covers everything from delivery, development, testing, deployment, security, and support/operational processes to operating model and technology stack changes.

The program management and business analysis skills required for The Delivery Function are markedly different from those required within The Ancillary Go-To Market Functions' sphere of responsibility, and as such it is important that these coordination/analysis functions are conducted by different individuals.

The AE, The Business Head, and The Delivery Head – Working Together

The Leadership Function is set up in this way to solve for the common leadership failings of *Strategy and Direction are not clear and are not anchored in the businesses core values and competencies*[1] and *Complex and sometimes conflicting reporting lines,*[2] and to adhere to *Galapagos Principle 2: Customer Proximity* (i.e., the aim to reduce the distance between the end customer and the engine room of delivery).

In respect of The Leadership Function, the aim of The Galapagos Framework is to reduce the number of different lines of communication to a minimum, not just between the end customer and delivery but also internally so that the strategy, direction, and culture are set and communicated by as few people as possible.

The Framework is not opinionated about the minimum number of people that perform the roles in The Nucleus, which allows the framework to scale from small transformations through to transformations covering large-scale multinational organizations.

At the smallest end of the transformation spectrum, it is entirely possible that all the roles in The Nucleus could be carried out by two individuals, for example, The AE, Business Head, Product, and Customer Experience could be covered by one individual and The Delivery Head and Technology Functions handled by another individual.

At the other end of the spectrum, though, the framework is opinionated. Regardless of the size of the digital transformation, there should only ever be a maximum of six individuals comprising The Nucleus (excluding the Program Management and Business Analysis Functions) – The Accountable Executive, Business Head, Delivery Head, Product, Customer Experience, and Technology.

---

[1] See *Chapter 7 – How The Galapagos Framework Resolves the Common Human Issues: The Human Element, Issue*: Strategy and direction are not clear and are not anchored in the businesses core values and competencies.

[2] See *Chapter 11 – How The Galapagos Framework Resolves the Common Human Issues: The Organizational Factors, Issue: Complex and sometimes conflicting reporting lines.*

Chapter 16

The Island: Go-To-Market and Delivery Functions

Customer Experience

The Customer Experience Function is the primary interface between The Island and the end customer. This function may have its own executive (e.g., a Chief (Customer) Experience Officer) but must, at the very minimum, contain a Customer Experience (CX) or User Experience (UX) team.

The Product Function and Business Head work closely with The Customer Experience Function to iteratively evolve the product strategy and roadmap. It is important to the overall success of the delivery that the Product strategy is tested in the market prior to committing significant investment in early iterations of product build.

Market testing can be achieved by demonstrating a UX,[1] or other, prototype to the customers showing what the early phases of delivery will produce. This process allows The Island teams to check that what is about to be built has value in the market and will also allow The Island to gain early feedback on any functional gaps in the product (which may result in improved revenue generation later).

The Product strategy and roadmap may change as a result of customer insights/ feedback gained from these demonstrations, which in turn can result in cost savings as there will be a high degree of confidence that what is being built is what the

---

[1] For software products, UX prototypes are relatively low cost and should be built in such a way that allows the customer to click around to check the various user journeys that have been produced.

DOI: 10.1201/9781003404217-22

135

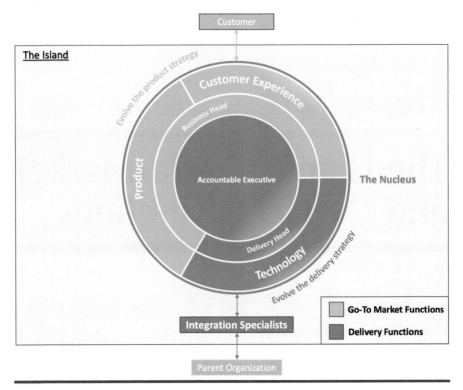

Figure 16.1   The Go-To Market and Delivery Functions.

customers want/need. This will, therefore, avoid situations where money is spent on building functionality that is used very infrequently or not at all.

The process of iterating prototypes in the market should continue for any major releases of the product, both to sanity check the strategy but also to keep the customers engaged. This level of customer involvement in the product development process should result in a higher degree of customer satisfaction and may result in a wider portfolio of revenue opportunities.

The Customer Proximity Principle

One of the key principles of The Galapagos Framework is the principle of *Customer Proximity*, which aims to reduce the distance between the end customer and the engine room of delivery. It is the responsibility of The Customer Experience Function, which exists within The Nucleus of The Island, to deliver on this principle.

The Customer Experience Function ensures that both the customer, and employee satisfaction are brought to the fore. This team tackles some of the issues associated with more traditional customer engagement models, resulting in a reduction in the cost to serve existing customers, and the improvement of customer and staff retention.

Reducing Wasted Effort

Ensuring that the organization delivers products, services, and features that have the most significant and positive impact for customers, is another responsibility of The Customer Experience Function. As touched on previously, prototypes of the product will be used to demonstrate proposed functionality, and other changes, to the end customer.

The process of testing prototypes with the customer allows for early feedback on the product/new product features/services directly from the customer and facilitates the fine-tuning of functionality to align more closely with what the customer wants. This is done without incurring the full development cost of building the functionality first, and then demonstrating this to the customer at the end of the process (only to find out, at this much later and more costly stage, that changes are required).

Having The Customer Experience Function in The Nucleus (and therefore very close to the build functions) dramatically reduces the risk of anything being lost in translation between the end customer and the individuals building the product. This increases the likelihood that what is being built is more closely aligned with the customer needs.

The fast, iterative cycles of building low-cost prototypes, and replaying these back to the customer, allows The Island to develop a hypothesis and test this with existing and potential customers, without incurring the high cost of building the full product/feature.

Reducing Wasted Time

Locating The Customer Experience Function within The Nucleus of The Island places this role in direct contact with the product build functions on a daily basis. In addition, having close, frequent links to the end customer shortens feedback loops. In this way, the organization is automatically more responsive to the customer's needs, and this will significantly reduce time wasted in building something that is potentially not useful to the customer.

Increasing Customer Buy-in

Another effect of shorter feedback loops is that the customer feels more connected to the product and its development. Taken to its logical conclusion this would result in the customer feeling invested in the product and is likely to improve customer loyalty.

If We Are Right, How Will We Know? – Metrics

Metrics are key and need to be in place before The Island starts to function in order to create a baseline of the existing situation. The information collected must be selected to provide realistic measures of performance that directly relate to the ultimate goals of the transformation and the collection process should be as automated as possible (not onerous or difficult to replicate). The metrics used need to be tracked to allow an objective assessment of the performance of the transformation, and to allow any changes to be made based on the data and not anecdotal evidence.

These metrics should feed into the evolution of the strategy, with this feedback loop allowing the strategy to be modified as required to meet the objectives of the transformation.

Product

The Product Function plays a crucial role in the success of any organization and is key to ensuring that the company produces and markets products and services that are of the right quality to effectively meet the needs of the target customer.

The design, development, and delivery to market of products and services, as well as the promotion of these is the responsibility of The Product Function. They will also produce several supporting artifacts that range from the product roadmap, strategy, and feature definition to market research, pricing, and ultimately product launch.

This function must liaise closely with all The Go-To Market and Delivery Functions (e.g., Customer Experience, Delivery, Sales and Marketing, Legal & Compliance,[2] Finance, etc.) to ensure that the product being built is the one that is needed, and that any barriers to a successful product launch are removed.

To effectively carry out its role, The Product Function must work closely with The Customer Experience Function and have a strong understanding of the target customer's needs, and preferences, as well as having a clear understanding of the competitive landscape to identify potential advantages. This involves analyzing customer feedback, market trends, sales performance, and competitor products and services.

Lastly, the post-product launch responsibilities of The Product Function will also cover after-sales support and service of the product.

The Product Head and The Business Head

The Galapagos Framework does not specify whether The Product Head and The Business Head are the same individual, and in smaller transformations it is likely that this will be the case.

---

[2] The Legal and Compliance teams will have to work closely with The Product Function to ensure that standards, laws, and regulations are adhered to (this can become a complex task if a product is to have a global distribution).

Delivering a Clear Product Strategy/Roadmap

With the prototype demonstrations that The Customer Experience Function has conducted, the customer now has a clear line of sight of the direction that the Product Strategy and Product Roadmap are taking, since the evolving prototypes are being replayed to the client.

If customer feedback on the prototypes is incorporated into the Product Strategy, and the product changes as a result, the customer will feel that they have been listened to and can see how they have directly influenced the product direction/ delivery. This process allows the Product Strategy and the Roadmap to be adjusted based directly on feedback from the customer.

Technology

The Technology Function is, of course, critical to the delivery of digital products/ services or products via digital channels. However, within The Galapagos Framework, The Technology Function is also responsible for all new tools that have been adopted for use on The Island (either to facilitate communication/collaboration or to deliver the product(s)/service(s) themselves).

A library could be filled with the books covering the subject area of technology relating to *digital* alone and with the increasing pace of technological change, by the time this book is read, it is likely that any technologies discussed will have been superseded and so it is not the intention of this book to cover specific technologies.[3]

Delivery Processes

It is important to note that The Technology Function is not only responsible for the deployment of the digital products but also for any new internal processes that are used by The Delivery Functions.

Agile Program Management

Agile principles of program management have made the transition from the IT department to almost all other business areas, and this is a very good thing.

Agile delivery is becoming increasingly prevalent across all organizations, and Agile principles should now be regarded as more of a philosophy than a set of development practices or methodologies.

The mindset and behaviors of a truly Agile delivery function sets these teams apart from their colleagues in other types of delivery operation.

---

[3] Some example technologies and architecture for web-based architecture are covered in Appendix D – "Example Technologies and Architecture for Web-Based Applications."

Daily meetings (which used to be confined to crisis management situations) are now commonplace with 15-minute stand-ups undertaken across a wide range of areas.

Whether the organization uses Scrum, Kanban, SAFe (or any other of the Agile methodologies) is not as important as embracing the principles of Agile delivery.[4]

If run properly, teams operate more effectively in an Agile environment over any other form of delivery.

Integration Specialists

It would not be a very fruitful exercise if a digital transformation was successful but there was no way of integrating the operating model/processes/procedures/technologies back into the parent organization. It is the responsibility of The Integration Specialists to ensure that the techniques and technologies that are being employed on The Island can be integrated back into the parent organization.

The Integration Specialists are individuals who still work predominantly in the parent organization and are likely to be allocated to The Island for much less than 100% of their time (i.e., this is not their main role). These individuals exist within The Delivery Function and are critical to ensuring a smooth re-integration of The Island's outputs back into the main organization. They will act as a bridge between the traditional and digital parts of the business and will help foster stronger internal capabilities amongst colleagues in the parent organization and reduce any view that The Island is an *ivory tower*.

Anyone assigned to the Integration Specialist role must have a good network across the parent organization, and may include members of the technology teams, business analysts, and so on. They are likely to come from horizontal,[5] cross-business functions (i.e., functions that support the operations of the company across various verticals or product lines), as roles in these teams will have a larger organizational footprint than any vertical functions, though this very much depends on the individual and their profile within the organization.

The Integration Specialists will be included at the earliest opportunity in The Island's creation and will act in an advisory capacity as new processes/procedures/operating models and technologies are being considered for adoption on The Island. Before any purchasing decisions are made, or new operating models implemented,

---

4 Agile Alliance, "12 Principles Behind the Agile Manifesto," agilealliance.org, (no date), https://www.agilealliance.org/agile101/12-principles-behind-the-agile-manifesto/[accessed June 19, 2023].

5 Horizontal functions are cross domain/department (e.g., IT, HR, Procurement, Legal, Compliance, Finance, Sales & Marketing, Risk, etc.). Vertical functions are business specific areas (e.g., Product).

the key question that this role will ask is, *How can this be incorporated back into the parent organization?*

There may be situations where the answer to this question is, *We don't know*, in which case it will be The Integration Specialists who bring the relevant experts from The Island, the parent organization, and possibly 3rd party vendors, together to work out how the new technology/processes/operating models could be integrated back into the parent organization.

The process, plan, and cost estimates for integrating all techniques and technologies used on The Island back into the parent organization must be documented thoroughly and will form part of The Model outputs.

Technology integrations can be particularly troublesome and thus, it would be a sensible approach to test any integration as early as possible to identify, and resolve, any issues that were not initially anticipated.

Chapter 17

The Island: Coordination Functions

Program Management

Whilst The Island aims to deliver some quick wins, it is important to remember that this is a transformation program, and the Program Management Function should manage stakeholder expectations away from demanding instant results. All parties need to understand that a certain amount of time will be required before The Island fully springs into life.

The Program Management teams in both The Nucleus and in The Ancillary Go-To Market Functions are key to ensuring the coordination and smooth running of the end-to-end delivery. These functions have been deliberately split out as the Program Management skills that drive The Nucleus functions are markedly different from those driving The Ancillary Go-To Market Functions.

The knowledge and competencies required to coordinate the more operational functions (e.g., HR, Legal, Compliance, etc.) are not the same as those required for the change functions (e.g., senior executives, Technology, Product and Customer Experience). It's not just the knowledge of how each of these different functions operates that is important, it's the cadences of each of these areas. For example, Legal and Compliance will, for very good reasons, have a markedly slower cadence than some of the other areas, and from a delivery timeline perspective it is important to understand how the different teams operate.

For a transformation of anything but the smallest size, combining The Nucleus and Ancillary Go-To Market coordination activities into one Program Management role (with potentially only one individual performing the role) is a mistake. Any cost savings made by adopting this structure, other than in very small transformations, are far outweighed by the delivery risks that will be introduced as a result.

                    DOI: 10.1201/9781003404217-23

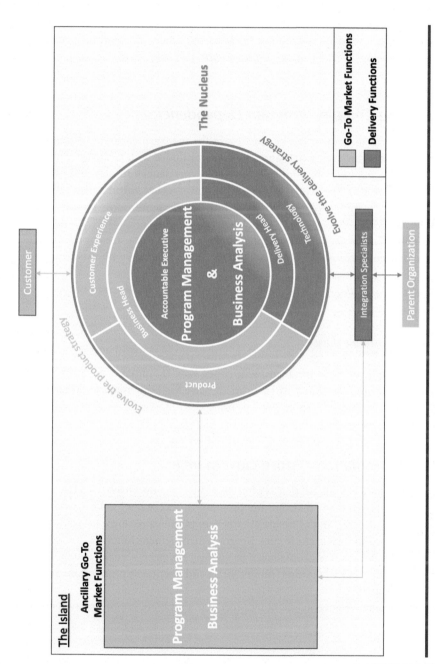

Figure 17.1   The Coordination Functions (Program Management and Business Analysis).

The Galapagos Framework is not opinionated about the use of a Program Director to oversee the two Program Management Functions, but it is important that the Program Management Functions are separated and run by different individuals.

If there is a need for a Program Director role, then, as mentioned in *Chapter 4 – The Function of The Galapagos Framework*, this role should reside within The Nucleus.

Managing Complex Program Dependencies

Dependency management is a key process in the management of most transformation programs. However, The Island structure, combined with *Galapagos Principle 4: Sequential Transformation*, minimizes the interdependencies in play and, therefore, reduces the risk of issues in one stream impacting other streams of work, or the wider transformation program. The Island, therefore, significantly reduces delivery risk (Figure 17.2).

Figure 17.2 shows how interdependencies between work streams of a program can, and often do, cause problems and delays (in conjunction with the Business-As-Usual, BAU, activities).

As stated in *Galapagos Principle 4: Sequential Transformation*, the complexity and risk of running multiple, concurrent, and interrelated streams of work far outweigh any benefit that is derived – *The most efficient path is not a straight line (nor is it multiple parallel streams of work)*.

For a medium or large-scale transformation, parallelism will not deliver the end goal faster and, in most instances, will either slow the process down or result in features, or a product, that falls far short of what has been asked for (i.e., delivery scope is often reduced in an attempt to bring the program in on time and close to budget).[1]

Good Governance ≠ More Governance

Good governance is a phrase that is often used by Program Directors/Managers and there is no disagreement that, for any program to succeed, a level of governance is required and the tracking of financials, delivery progress, resource utilization, risks/issues, etc., are all important for any program management function.

However, what some people mean by *good governance* is actually *more governance* (more meetings, more planning, more artifact and document production, and more program bloat).

Throwing more governance/more process at a problem is almost never the right solution.

---

[1] See *Chapter 4 – The Function of The Galapagos Framework – Scaling Up* for more information on how The Galapagos Framework works in large-scale transformation programs.

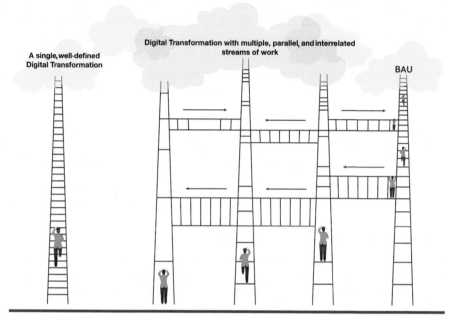

Figure 17.2 Multiple, Interdependent Work Streams.

Light-Touch Governance

The Island is a self-sufficient, independent structure and should define its own approach to governance without compromising either the delivery of the transformation itself or the parent organization's reputation. The Island structure lends itself to a *light-touch* governance model where financial, delivery, risk/issue tracking, and reporting are performed in a predominantly automated fashion.

A light-touch approach to governance ensures that The Island is as nimble as possible, in its decision-making processes, and can react quickly to unexpected situations. It also ensures that reporting is near real-time, as the data that is being reported on should be collected in an automated fashion.

Compromises may have to be made regarding the format of reporting to ensure that the project/program managers focus their efforts on delivery and not on producing a large number of different formats of reports to satisfy slightly different audiences.

All elements of The Island need to focus on delivery, and spending time and effort producing reports in different formats is not the best use of a Program Manager's time (see *Chapter 3 – Introduction to The Galapagos Framework* – The Galapagos Principles – *Principle 9: Establish and automate metrics and reporting early*).

For example, to make financial governance as light touch as possible, approval for all budget spend stops with The Accountable Executive. Similarly, The Accountable Executive will hold ultimate accountability for other governance considerations such as hire/fire decisions or major changes to project timeframes. This role should be able to approve all spending and other major decisions, within the allocated budget, without going back to the parent organization for additional approvals.

Obviously, in the case of budget overruns, or exceptional spending, then additional approval from the parent organization may be required.

Business Analysis (BA)

The Business Analysis Function that resides within The Nucleus is used to provide all of the analytical capabilities required by The Leadership, Product, Customer Experience, and Technology Functions. They may also become involved with The Integration Specialists providing analytical support, where required, for integrating new processes/procedures/operating models and technologies back into the parent organization.

If BA capability is required by The Ancillary Go-To Market Functions, then this should be supplied and managed out of the BA Function in The Nucleus. It is anticipated that the vast majority of business analysis will occur within The Nucleus as this is where the new products and services are designed, built, and delivered to the end customer, and where feedback and insights from the end customer are gathered and evaluated.

Business analysts are critical to any transformation initiative and are responsible for requirements gathering/evaluation/analysis and specification. BAs may also be involved in data analysis, solution design, quality assurance (QA) testing, workshop facilitation, and project management (see below section *Business Analysis/Project Management*) among many other things.

Many elements are produced from The Business Analysis Function, and these may include items such as requirement artifacts (e.g., Use Cases, User Stories), Gap Analysis, Workflow Analysis, Data Analysis, Cost–Benefit reports, etc.

The business analysts should be involved in all stages of the program, from initial research to product delivery, and ongoing evaluation and maintenance of the product. It is also not uncommon for BAs to organize change management, helping to ensure that changes are implemented smoothly and effectively.

Business Analysis/Project Management

Some organizations combine the Business Analyst (BA) and Project Management (PM) roles into one, creating a BA/PM role. The combining of these two roles appears to stem from a cost-saving rather than a performance-improvement perspective. However, the jury is out as to whether the BA/PM role yields any benefits from either a cost or a performance standpoint.

Chapter 18

The Island Ancillary Go-To Market Functions

As each digital transformation is unique across business domains (e.g., a digital transformation in the context of Investment Banking will be very different from a digital transformation in Health Care, which in turn will be very different from a digital transformation in Construction), The Ancillary Go-To Market Functions will also differ depending on the business domain that the transformation is taking place in (Figure 18.1).

Below are examples of some teams that may form part of The Ancillary Go-To Market Functions.

Sales and Marketing

The Sales and Marketing Function is an integral part of any business and has the principal remit of generating revenue by stimulating/driving customer demand and generating awareness of the product/new product features in the market.

Sales and Marketing will ensure that the messaging and content used to promote the product align with the organization's values and core objectives, and will cover activities such as market research, brand building and positioning, promotion (via advertising, public relations, corporate communications, etc.), sales strategy, customer relationship management (CRM), customer service, etc.

The Sales and Marketing Function and The Customer Experience Function must work closely together to ensure that existing, and prospective, customers have a consistent and positive experience.

DOI: 10.1201/9781003404217-24

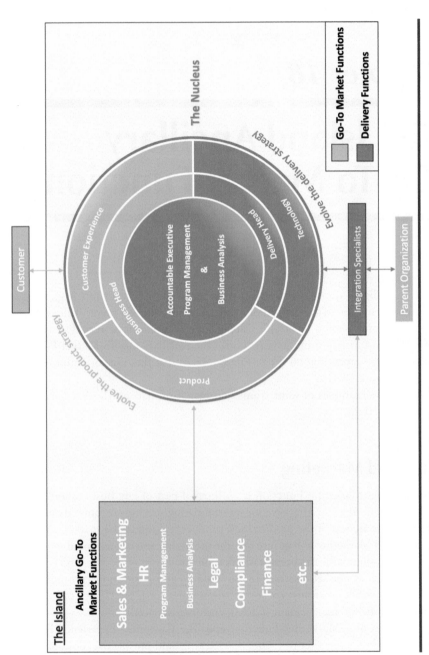

Figure 18.1 The Ancillary Go-To Market Functions.

Generating Actionable Customer Insights

Both The Sales and Marketing and The Customer Experience Functions will consume customer and prospect insights (via the early use of UX and other prototypes of new products/product features, sales pipeline conversations, etc.) and feed these into The Product Function for incorporation into the product/product strategy/product roadmap. It is important that the insights provided are actionable (i.e., insights provided must be clear and specific enough to inform direct decision-making).

Pricing Strategy

The Sales and Marketing Function and The Product Function must also work closely together to form the pricing strategy that is to be adopted for the new product/product features/services to ultimately deliver revenue and generate profit.

Human Resources

The Galapagos Framework represents a more human-centric and inclusive approach to transformational change, and therefore the Human Resources (HR) Function is key to putting the human at the center of the strategy.

It would be a mistake to assume that the HR Function is any less important than the functions that exist in the Nucleus of The Island just because it exists within The Ancillary Go-To Market Functions. In fact, the HR Function will be at the center of the organizational and cultural changes that will be required to ensure the success of any transformation.

Workforce Strategy

A short-, medium-, and long-term Workforce Strategy is one of the key artifacts contained in The Model (explored in more detail in *Chapter 19 – The Model*) and it will be the responsibility of the HR Function to produce this. The workforce needs of the transformation in the immediate term may be very different from those required in the medium to long term.

For example, it may be that the organization has a shortage of a particular skill set that is required either to start the transformation or for the successful execution of the transformation. However, in the medium to long term, these skills would almost certainly form part of the permanent, full-time employee headcount.

Thus, to ensure that the current transformation gets out of the blocks quickly, and to build momentum, it might be that the organization goes to market for temporary/contract staff to satisfy the immediate need, with a view to either converting these to or replacing these with permanent staff in the medium- to long-term. This may be done to create a sense of company loyalty, promote consistency in delivery, and/or achieve a high degree of staff retention.

Similarly, there might be a need to develop existing staff to support the Workforce Strategy going forward and the HR Function will be at the heart of this process, identifying training plans that should be undertaken to grow the internal capabilities of the organization and ensure the efficient and effective utilization of the organization's human capital.

Incentivizing Staff

Aligning incentives and compensation strategies to the vision underpinning the transformation and tying compensation to collaboration (via, objectives setting or other means) are essential to ensuring that all functions/teams and individuals are pulling in the same direction, and these responsibilities are within the remit of the HR Function.

Organizational Change

Organizational changes to remove silos are crucial in improving collaboration but cultural transformation will take time and require the close cooperation of the executives in The Nucleus of The Island and HR Function.

Transformational change is people change – the diversity, skills, and collaboration of the humans involved in the change are central to its success. It is therefore essential that the HR Function is integrated into the change team at the earliest opportunity.

The HR Function is critical to the success of any digital transformation. They are central to ensuring that the organization's employees are engaged, motivated, and productive and will assist in creating the structures that foster an environment of collaboration, creativity, and innovation.

Program Management (Ancillary Go-To Market Functions)

As mentioned previously, the Program Management skills that drive The Nucleus functions are markedly different from the Program Management skills required to drive The Ancillary Go-To Market Functions.

For anything but the smallest of transformation programs, attempting to achieve cost savings by combining the Program Management roles in The Nucleus and The Ancillary Go-To Market Functions is a fool's errand. If cost pressures exist (and they always do), then The Leadership Function should look elsewhere to achieve efficiencies.

Why Are the Two Program Management Roles So Different?

Before we focus on why the roles are so different, let us first examine where the roles have commonality.

Aside from the artifacts produced, the principal area of overlap, between the Program Management Function in The Nucleus and the Program Management Function in The Ancillary Go-To Market Functions, is that it is the responsibility of Program Management to bring all the different areas together in a fashion that allows each to understand the ways of working and the pressures that the others are working under.

Now let us look at the differences.

The Program Management role in The Ancillary Go-To Market Functions must understand some of the accounting complexities of the Finance team, and the limitations of the internal Legal team, and recognize if/when external counsel may have to be sought (and the associated cost and time impacts of this on the budget line).

They will also need to appreciate how the Sales pipeline works, likely conversion rates, associated revenue projection calculations, and the interdependencies of the various functions (e.g., Marketing and Legal/Compliance).

For larger organizations, all the above becomes more complex as the Program Management Function must consider the impact of regional differences across each of the different areas.

These skills are sufficiently different from the more delivery-focused skills of the Program Management Function in The Nucleus that they should (in most/all instances) be kept separate.

Light-Touch Governance

As discussed earlier, The Galapagos Framework advocates a light-touch governance model. Often, the idea of light-touch governance sits more comfortably with some areas of the organization (e.g., Sales and Marketing) than others (e.g., Legal and Compliance).

Frequently, these teams are dependent on each other (e.g., marketing materials may need to be reviewed by Compliance and/or Legal) and so it is imperative that each knows how best to interact with the other to achieve the desired results. The Program Management team within The Ancillary Go-To Market Functions may, therefore, be required to enter more of a facilitation role to grease the wheels between departments whose working practices are, naturally, very different.

Legal and Compliance

The Legal and Compliance Functions will almost certainly need to be involved when bringing a new product/service to market or delivering an existing product via new digital channels.

It is therefore very important to involve these functions at an early stage; the last thing anyone wants to find out, late in the process, is that there are legal/compliance blocks to getting the product to market. Impediments of this nature often cannot be circumvented and, due to the complex nature of the laws and regulations that these functions must navigate, can take a long time to resolve.

The functions that the Legal and Compliance teams perform are covered, at a very high level, below.

Legal

The Legal Function is responsible for protecting the organization and its interests, both inside and outside the company, and as such it is responsible for providing advice and assistance to the company on a wide range of legal matters, including contract negotiation and drafting, legal compliance, dispute resolution, and risk management.

Also, ensuring that the company follows all applicable laws and regulations and providing legal protection for the company's assets, contracts, and operations are all within the purview of the Legal Function.

Compliance

The Compliance function is responsible for making sure the company conforms with all applicable rules and regulations, internal policies and procedures as well as setting up and maintaining a comprehensive compliance program which will include policies, procedures, training, and monitoring systems that are designed to ensure compliance with the applicable rules and regulations. The compliance program should also be regularly updated to stay current with changes in regulations.

The organization's operations and activities must be regularly assessed to identify potential areas of noncompliance and it is the responsibility of the Compliance team to develop corrective action plans to address any issues and ensure adherence to the established program.

The Compliance function will also be responsible for responding to regulatory enquiries, preparing reports, and other documents, for submission to regulatory agencies, and for creating a culture of compliance within the organization including promoting ethical behavior, creating a safe and respectful environment, and ensuring that employees understand the importance of compliance.

Finance

In larger digital transformations or in situations where The Island is either a separate legal entity from the parent organization, or there is a need to closely track The Island's P&L separately, the Finance team will play an important role in providing the necessary financial analysis and overseeing the transformation's budgeting, accounting, and financial reporting and planning.

The Finance Function will monitor current, and forecast future, revenues and expenses, perform cash flow analysis, analyze any financial risks/returns, develop strategies, and make recommendations regarding the best course of action to take to ensure that the transformation meets its financial goals.

Overall, the Finance function plays a vital role in ensuring the financial health of the transformation program and will present financial reports to the board of the parent organization and other stakeholders.

Chapter 19

The Model

What Is The Model?

One of the key outputs of The Island is The Model which is a living, lightweight, and comprehensive guide to the digital transformation. It is one of the first artifacts to be created on The Island as the Workforce Strategy and the associated Skills Matrix sections of The Model will be critical inputs into the decision regarding whether to proceed, delay, or halt the transformation based on any skills gaps identified (in either the number, quality, or location of the resources currently in the organization).

When complete, The Model will essentially be the new operating model that The Island uses to deliver the transformation and will include, amongst other things, the strategic objectives, leadership approach/style, metrics, processes, procedures, technologies, organizational structure, and culture that have been adopted.

The Model will be used (and altered) by subsequent transformations to ensure a successful transformation for the next business area that embarks on their digital journey. It is important that The Model must not try to solve potential issues in other domains outside of the current transformation, as each Model will have unique and specific elements relating to the business domain within which it was created.

There will, however, be some common transformation elements across business domains (e.g., culture/leadership/collaboration tools/metrics, etc.), and as such The Model will make subsequent transformations more efficient as these items will not have to be created from scratch as each new transformation is undertaken.

DOI: 10.1201/9781003404217-25

What Should The Model Contain?

The Model is tailored to the specific needs of the current transformation that is taking place and will include the appropriate tools, processes, and structures needed to achieve the desired objectives.

The Model will be used as an artifact of collaboration between transformation initiatives allowing for future changes and improvements as it evolves.

Leadership Guide

The leadership guide will provide information on how this specific digital transformation initiative is being/has been directed. Effective leadership is essential for driving any transformation initiative and ensuring that it aligns with the organization's strategic objectives. The Leadership Guide offers practical tips, best practices, and advice on organizational structure, culture, and leadership styles to help subsequent leaders successfully navigate future digital transformation initiatives.

More detail on the Leadership Guide is provided in *Appendix A – A guide to the Leadership Guide.*

Workforce Strategy

The Workforce Strategy is a plan to ensure that the company has the right type, number, and quality of skills in the right locations at the right time to deliver the transformation. A strong Workforce Strategy should be in place to develop the talent pipeline that will drive the success of this and future transformations, through a combination of recruitment and development initiatives.

Any Workforce Strategy that is produced must be aligned with the goals and objectives of the transformation whilst at the same time ensuring that the organization develops, attracts, and retains the best talent for current and future deliveries.

The future-proofing of a Workforce Strategy is extremely difficult in a rapidly changing digital landscape, but having a robust talent pipeline in place will allow the organization to be more nimble, and adaptable to advances in technology and remain competitive in an ever-changing environment.

There are myriad operational efficiencies that can be derived from having a well-trained and motivated workforce, ranging from reduced costs (better quality staff tend to produce output faster with reduced levels of rework), to effectively leveraging new technologies that will improve productivity.

Some of the elements that could be contained in a Workforce Strategy document may include programs to identify and attract top talent, establishing career paths, promotions and rewards to retain and develop current staff, programs for implementing continuous learning and development, how to utilize technology to increase employee engagement and productivity, using data and analytics to measure the impact of workforce initiatives, developing flexible working arrangements to increase job satisfaction and reduce turnover, and how to create an inclusive and diverse workplace environment, etc.

Skills Matrix

An important artifact in any Workforce Strategy is the skills matrix, which will be used to assess the organization's current and required capabilities. It will contain the skill sets, and level of proficiency, that the organization needs to achieve a successful transformation.

The skills matrix will highlight where the organization has the right number and level of skills required, but more importantly, it will show where the organization is lacking in a particular skill or lacking a number of individuals with that skill. This will allow the organization to make an informed decision as to how to fill these gaps (e.g., upskilling, cross-training, hiring, etc.).

Table 19.1 shows a very simple example of a current skills profile, covering some of the existing capabilities within The Island (additional data items such as city/

TABLE 19.1   Example of a Skills Matrix Covering Some Existing Capabilities on The Island

Current Skills Profile					
Location	**Function**	**Area**	**Skill**	**Resource**	**Level**
Nucleus	Go-To Market	Customer Experience	CX Manager	Bella R	Expert
Nucleus	Go-To Market	Customer Experience	Customer Service	Mason W	Junior
Nucleus	Go-To Market	Customer Experience	UX Designer	Roisin H	Intermediate
Nucleus	Go-To Market	Product	Product Manager	Logan R	Expert
Nucleus	Go-To Market	Product	Product Designer	Amelie P	Junior
Nucleus	Go-To Market	Product	Product Researcher	Toby T	Intermediate
Nucleus	Delivery	Program Management	Program Director	Elijah J	Expert
Nucleus	Delivery	Program Management	Program Manager	Scarlett W	Expert

(Continued)

TABLE 19.1 (Continued)

Current Skills Profile					
Location	**Function**	**Area**	**Skill**	**Resource**	**Level**
Nucleus	Delivery	Project Management	Project Manager	Ryan T	Intermediate
Nucleus	Delivery	Business Analysis	Lead BA	Mia C	Expert
Nucleus	Delivery	Business Analysis	BA	Ethan H	Intermediate
Nucleus	Delivery	Technology	Cloud	Milly B	Intermediate
Nucleus	Delivery	Technology	Dev Ops	Jaxon J	Expert
Nucleus	Delivery	Technology	Big Data	Charlie B	Intermediate
Nucleus	Delivery	Technology	Cyber Security	Aaron H	Intermediate
Nucleus	Delivery	Technology	Back-End Dev.	Freya M	Intermediate
Nucleus	Delivery	Technology	Front-End Dev.	Zoe G	Expert
Nucleus	Delivery	Technology	Scrum Master	Carson F	Intermediate
Nucleus	Delivery	Technology	Database Admin.	Daisy I	Expert
Ancillary	Go-To Market	Program Management	Program Manager	Ella B	Intermediate
Ancillary	Go-To Market	Project Management	Project Manager	Lucas S	Intermediate
Ancillary	Go-To Market	Business Analysis	Lead BA	Ava K	Expert
Ancillary	Go-To Market	Business Analysis	BA	Noah A	Intermediate

geographic location, department, additional skills/competencies, etc., would normally be added to provide a more comprehensive view). If a gap analysis is conducted and another matrix is created detailing the skills that The Island needs to complete the transformation (see Table 19.2 for an example skills gap matrix), then the organization will have a complete skills matrix of the existing capabilities and the number and level of skills that must be filled to successfully complete the transformation.

A summary of this gap analysis might look like the example provided in Table 19.2.

TABLE 19.2 Example Skills Gap Grouped by Proficiency Level, Area, and Skill Type

Skills Gaps					
Location	**Function**	**Area**	**Skill**	**Level**	**Gap**
Nucleus	Go-To Market	Customer Experience	Customer Service	Intermediate	1
Nucleus	Go-To Market	Customer Experience	UX Designer	Expert	1
Nucleus	Go-To Market	Product	Product Designer	Expert	1
Nucleus	Delivery	Program Management	Program Manager	Intermediate	2
Nucleus	Delivery	Program Management	Project Manager	Expert	1
Nucleus	Delivery	Program Management	Project Manager	Intermediate	1
Nucleus	Delivery	Program Management	Lead BA	Expert	1
Nucleus	Delivery	Program Management	BA	Expert	1
Nucleus	Delivery	Program Management	BA	Intermediate	1
Nucleus	Delivery	Program Management	BA	Junior	2
Nucleus	Delivery	Technology	Cloud	Expert	1
Nucleus	Delivery	Technology	Dev Ops	Junior	1
Nucleus	Delivery	Technology	Big Data	Expert	1

(Continued)

TABLE 19.2 (Continued)

Skills Gaps					
Location	**Function**	**Area**	**Skill**	**Level**	**Gap**
Nucleus	Delivery	Technology	Cyber Security	Expert	1
Nucleus	Delivery	Technology	Back-End Developer	Expert	3
Nucleus	Delivery	Technology	Back-End Developer	Intermediate	1
Nucleus	Delivery	Technology	Back-End Developer	Junior	1
Nucleus	Delivery	Technology	Front-End Developer	Expert	4
Nucleus	Delivery	Technology	Front-End Developer	Intermediate	2
Nucleus	Delivery	Technology	Front-End Developer	Junior	1
Nucleus	Delivery	Technology	Scrum Master	Expert	2
Nucleus	Delivery	Technology	Database Admin.	Intermediate	1
Ancillary	Go-To Market	Program Management	Program Manager	Expert	2
Ancillary	Go-To Market	Program Management	Project Manager	Expert	2
Ancillary	Go-To Market	Program Management	Project Manager	Intermediate	1
Ancillary	Go-To Market	Program Management	Lead BA	Expert	1
Ancillary	Go-To Market	Program Management	BA	Expert	2
Ancillary	Go-To Market	Program Management	BA	Intermediate	1

As can be seen from the example provided in Table 19.2, The Island is short of 40 resources, across various areas, and a range of skill types, that are required to deliver the transformation. More interestingly, The Island considers that it needs 24 expert-level resources across several Go-To Market and Delivery areas. Filling a gap of this size in expert-level resources is likely to be time-consuming and costly, but it is better to understand the skills shortage before the organization embarks on a transformation initiative than to find out after the transformation has started and the entire delivery is put at risk.

Organizational Structure

As discussed in *Chapter 4, The Function of The Galapagos Framework – The Island Structure* and again in *Chapter 11, How The Galapagos Framework Resolves the Common Issues* the organizational structure of The Island is very simple, with all functions below The Leadership Function operating in an entirely flat structure.

The flat structure below The Business and Delivery Heads facilitates open and honest communication and collaboration and furthers team cohesion.

Having said this, the flat reporting structure of The Island will still operate using several different, cross-functional teams each tasked with delivering on different aspects of the current transformation, and the makeup of these should be documented in the Organizational Structure artifact.

Culture Guide

The Culture Guide is a short document that provides the organizational culture that has been adopted on The Island and shows how this aligns with the core values of the organization and aids in delivering the Transformation Strategy. The cultural attributes and behaviors that are being fostered (e.g., increased collaboration, open, honest, and friendly communication, psychological safety, etc.) should also be examined. Likewise, it is important to draw attention to the fact that every employee should contribute to nurturing and improving the culture of The Island.

The style of teamwork, along with the idea that The Island is operating as a unified TEAM!, should be highlighted, as should the approach to diversity and inclusion, the importance of interpersonal relationships, and how a positive approach to work–life balance is being managed.

The approach to leadership that is being adopted on The Island will be covered in the *Leadership Guide* section of The Model, but how the leadership style promotes the culture that is expected on The Island should be documented here.

Other elements that could be included within the *Culture Guide* section of the model are approaches to recognition and reward (and how this aligns with the culture on The Island), learning and development (opportunities for personal and professional growth), and the working environment.

Transformation Strategy

Most digital transformation strategies are put in place to improve operational efficiencies, reduce costs, meet the ever-increasing frequency of changing customer needs, or create new revenue streams. The Transformation Strategy document will detail which objectives are being targeted and will contain numerous different elements many of which will be unique to the organization, industry, and market context.

However, some general areas that the Transformation Strategy might cover are; vision and objectives (the objectives might be in the form of KPIs or OKRs), digital business model, customer experience and engagement, data and analytics, technology and infrastructure, governance, operations, innovation, digital skills and so on.

The Transformation Strategy should be inspirational as well as providing a north star for the entire program. It will serve not only to motivate the teams on The Island, and beyond, but will also be used as the basis for all decision-making related to the transformation.

As such, the Transformation Strategy is a critical document and needs to be clear, concise, and compelling in providing the rationale underlying the transformation, painting a picture of how this initiative will satisfy the long-term objectives of the organization (normally in the form of a single sentence mission statement), and setting the direction for the entire program.

Given the significance of the Transformation Strategy, it must be communicated widely to ensure that everyone knows why the transformation is of strategic importance, how this will be delivered, and the benefits that the transformation will bring to the entire organization.

Along with setting the strategic vision, objectives, and strategies to deliver on these objectives, the Transformation Strategy should also highlight how the successful implementation of the strategy will result in strategic differentiation between the organization and its competitors.

Clarity and Alignment to Values

Whatever the underlying reasons for the initiative, the Transformation Strategy must be clear and unambiguous. As mentioned in previous chapters, care must be taken to ensure that the strategy is rooted in the core business values and competencies of the organization. Doing this will allow all members of staff to understand why the transformation is taking place and will bring employees along on the digital journey.

It is not enough, though, to have a clear Transformation Strategy that is aligned with the core values and competencies of the company if this is not effectively communicated to all staff.

Communication, Communication, and Communication

The communication of the Transformation Strategy must come from the top (the CEO or as close to the CEO as possible). Only in this way will all layers of management understand that the strategy has the full backing of the CEO. This will go a long way to reducing the resistance to change which can so often result in strategies not being implemented effectively or, in some cases, failing.

OK, so there is a clear Transformation Strategy that is aligned with the core values and competencies of the organization, and it has been communicated to all staff by the CEO. This is good, but it's still not enough.

In the early stages, the communication of the key elements of the strategy must be frequently and consistently repeated not just by the CEO but also by other senior leaders. In doing this, The Leadership Function can avoid the *corporate amnesia* that often plagues many businesses. As the implementation of the strategy progresses, the frequency of communication can be reduced but must still be delivered, as an *aide memoire*, and to ensure that those implementing the strategy are still clear on the direction of travel and the rationale behind this.

Metrics

Finally, the metrics that will be used to demonstrate progress on the strategic objectives of the Transformation Strategy should be set out. Whether these take the form of KPIs, OKRs, or some other measures, is not as important as ensuring that progress on, and success in meeting, the strategic objectives is quantitatively and qualitatively measured.

Transformation Roadmap

There are instances where the Transformation Roadmap will be included as part of the Transformation Strategy, but it is separated out here for clarity and ease of reference.

The Transformation Roadmap will use the Transformation Strategy to provide the key principles that will inform and guide the roadmap. Each roadmap will be unique to The Island that is creating it but will normally be in the form of a Gantt chart, or timeline, with initiatives and actions distributed over time in the form of key milestone deliveries.

A high-level example of a section of a Transformation Roadmap is shown in Figure 19.1.

Transformation Roadmap vs. The Galapagos Roadmap

It is important to state at this juncture that the Transformation Roadmap is not the same as The Galapagos Roadmap.

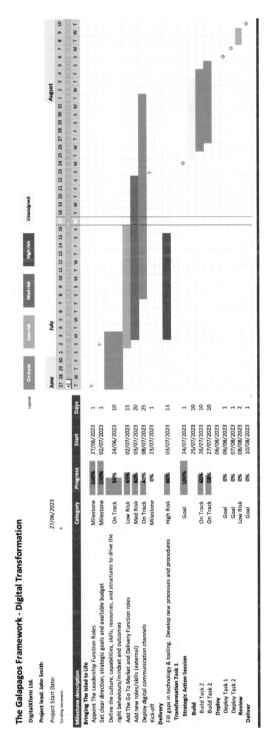

Figure 19.1 Example section of a Transformation Roadmap.

The Galapagos Roadmap is a guide to setting up The Island structures (i.e., *Bringing The Island to Life*[1]) and demonstrating the iterative nature of the *Delivery* cycle and is applicable to *all* transformations.

The Transformation Roadmap is specific to one particular Island and will show the milestones that need to be achieved to successfully deliver on the strategic objectives of this distinct transformation. The Transformation Roadmap will, therefore, provide milestone dates for each of the activities of the *Bringing The Island to life* section of The Galapagos Roadmap. It will also provide the high-level tasks, and associated milestones, that are required to successfully deliver the transformation (i.e., those tasks contained within the *Delivery* section of The Galapagos Roadmap).

Given the above, the Transformation Roadmap shows a finer level of detail than The Galapagos Roadmap and will also provide indicative dates (which The Galapagos Roadmap does not).

Digital Transformation Readiness Review

As discussed in *Chapter 25, Digital Transformation Readiness Review and Digital Maturity Assessment*, The Galapagos Framework considers a Digital Transformation Readiness Review to be a lightweight evaluation of the organization's preparedness to embark on a digital transformation journey.

The readiness review will include a high-level assessment of some of the measures used in the Digital Maturity Assessment (DMA, described below). However, at a minimum, the review should cover areas such as Vision and Strategy, Leadership and Culture, Skills and Capabilities, Technology and Infrastructure, Data (the availability, quality, and management of data), Processes and Operations, Agility, Risk, Compliance, and Cybersecurity (an evaluation of the robustness of cybersecurity measures).

Digital Maturity Assessment (DMA)

Organizations that are sure that they are in a good position to start a digital transformation may choose not to conduct a readiness review but will certainly want to baseline their current digital position, in terms of maturity, and this is what a Digital Maturity Assessment (DMA) will provide.

A DMA is a more thorough assessment of the organization's digital capability (both qualitative and quantitative), than the Digital Transformation Readiness Review provides, and is discussed in *Chapter 25, Digital Transformation Readiness Review and Digital Maturity Assessment*.

The DMA will cover a significant number of measures relating to the organization's existing digital capabilities, and the target digital state that the company wants to achieve across these measures.

---

[1] See *Chapter 13, How does The Galapagos Framework Work in Practice?*

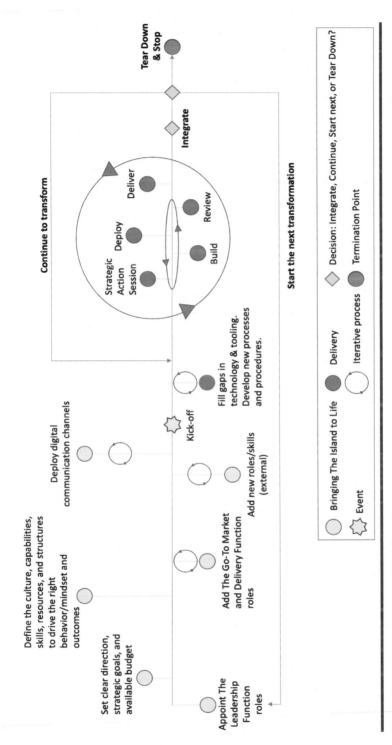

Figure 19.2   The Galapagos Roadmap.

Some dimensions that may be included in the DMA are Vision and Strategy, Leadership and Culture, Skills and Capabilities, Technology and Infrastructure, Data (the availability, quality, and management of data) and Analytics (the tools and skills available for data analytics and insights generation), Customer Experience (CX), Processes and Operations, Agility, Innovation Ecosystem (the company's approach to fostering innovation), Risk and Compliance, Cybersecurity (an evaluation of the robustness of cybersecurity measures), Financial Preparedness (Budget allocation, ROI expectations), etc.

The Digital Maturity Assessment will measure each of the dimensions and assign a grade (e.g, from 1 to 5, where 1 = low level of maturity and 5 = fully digital), and potentially benchmarked against competitors, or other industry targets. The assessment of each dimension will be further decomposed, to provide a finer-grained view of the appraisal, and give further insight as to the detailed elements that make up the aggregated grade.

Given the above, the DMA provides a much deeper analysis of the organization's digital capability than the readiness review; however, both will feed into the Transformation Strategy highlighting areas requiring attention.

Communication Strategy

The purpose of the communications strategy is to promote transparency and improve engagement, both of which are essential to building trust.

There are various templates available for Communication Strategies, the size and nature of the organization/transformation will determine which is most appropriate, however, sections within the communications strategy document may include the following:

Objectives

What the strategy aims to achieve (e.g., improve targeted communication relating to the transformation, reduce the number of emails that the members of The Island receive, streamlining the flow of information across The Island, ensure two-way communication becomes the new norm across all levels of staff, to communicate the ultimate goals of the transformation and keep everyone focused on the main goals, etc.).

These objectives could be tracked by using some Objectives and Key Results (OKRs).

Key Messages

The main themes of the communications strategy (e.g., highlight the benefits of the transformation and how this aligns with the values of the business, enhance the overall efficiency of The Island by improving communication between teams and individuals on The Island, reducing the volume of communication that is not directly related to the transformation, etc.).

Communication Channels

Describe the best communication channels to use in particular circumstances. This could also contain a hierarchy of effective communication (e.g., face-to-face, video conference, telephone, instant messaging, and only after all of these options have been considered email).

Frequency of Communication

How often will The Leadership Function communicate to The Island members and when will these communications be scheduled? Regular updates are important to keep staff engaged and informed.

Roles and Responsibilities

Who will be responsible for crafting and delivering these communications? Ensure that all of the key responsibilities are listed, and allocated, and ownership of each task/outcome is clear.

Feedback Mechanisms

Identify the means by which the staff on The Island can feedback on communication or contribute their own ideas.

Measurement and Evaluation

The metrics that have been established to assess the impact of the communications strategy.

Continuous Improvement

Based on the metrics and feedback, how changes and improvements to the communication strategy will be applied.

Metrics

Data-driven decision-making is crucial when directing successful transformational change. In the past, change strategies and programs have been led based on conjecture, hunch, experience, and gut feel, and this, in part, has led to a very patchy success rate.

The metrics used in any digital transformation will assist the organization in baselining the *as-is* situation and will help answer the question *How will we know if we've been successful?* Further, these metrics will help the organization quantify the degree of success of the transformation initiative.

Getting the right metrics in place early and automating the generation of these as much as possible, will have a substantial impact on improving the overall efficiency of the transformation initiative by enhancing decision-making, reducing risk, and ultimately driving better outcomes (see *Galapagos Principle 9: Establish and automate metrics and reporting early*). It also provides for a better use of Program/ Project Manager's time and allows them to focus on ensuring the transformation is tracking to plan/budget, and managing risks and issues, rather than generating metrics by hand and then reformatting these in various ways for inclusion in any number of reports for any number of different audiences.

A set of example metrics is included in *Appendix C Example Metrics.*

Technologies Matrix (tool and function)

The collaboration tools, as well as the technologies used to deliver the transformation itself, should be included in the Technologies Matrix. The purpose of this artifact is to identify all the tools and technologies used in the transformation, describe the function of these tools, and highlight their impact on delivery (either positive, negative, or neutral). It is beyond the scope of this book to provide a list of digital technologies that could be used, as by the time the book comes to print this list is likely to be out of date. However, an example matrix is provided in *Appendix B - Example Technology Matrix.*

Processes and Procedures

All new processes and procedures (both business and delivery) that are being used on The Island must be documented and included as part of The Model to ensure consistency, efficiency, and understanding across transformations.

The intention is to make the process/procedure clear and easily understood by anyone who needs to use it, and should not, where possible, include jargon or technical terms. Where these are used then definitions must also be provided.

All documents relating to new processes or procedures should include their purpose, scope (in which area(s) does this process/procedure apply), which team is responsible for the execution of the process, and the steps that should be taken in the normal flow of the process as well as the steps that need to be followed when exceptional circumstances arise.

There should also be a clear change history attached to each document.

Integration Process, Plan, and Costs

The Model should contain a comprehensive plan and associated costs for the integration of all new processes, procedures, and technologies used on The Island back into the parent organization.

It is imperative that any significant issues encountered, with any aspect of the integration processes, are included in the *Lessons Learned* section of The Model to allow other transformations to learn from these. The background/rationale for the approach that was taken to resolve these issues should also be provided.

All integration plans, projected and actual timelines, and projected and actual costs must be included within this section to make future transformations aware of any slippage in timelines, or increases in the cost of the integration process, and the reasons for these.

Lessons Learned

The aim of the Lessons Learned document is to act as a knowledge-sharing artifact for future transformations (that take place either within this Island or on other Islands). As such it will assist in the continuous improvement of the entire trans-formation program (which may involve more than one *Transformation Context* and therefore, more than one Island) by allowing The Leadership Function(s) to reflect

TABLE 19.3 Example of Lessons Learned

Phase	Situation	Lessons Learned	Impact	Recommendation
Bringing The Island to life	The budget took too long to finalize.	Start this process earlier.	Negative	This process should be started at the earliest opportunity to avoid impact on landing external resources.
Delivery	Issues with the implementation of new teamworking and collaboration tools.	The new technology did not meet the security requirements of the parent organization.	Negative	Involve Integration Specialists in all product selection.
Delivery	Testing the product strategy in the market via prototypes was well received by both existing and prospective customers.	Regular engagement of customers using prototypes led to better customer satisfaction and increased sales.	Positive	Maintain the process of validating prototypes with customers and prospects.

and learn from their experiences while promoting accountability and transparency by showing that The Island is willing to improve its practices.

The Lessons Learned document is separate from any RAID[2] logs that are being maintained by the Program Management Functions and is used to highlight significant issues that have arisen, the impact of these, and how they were resolved or mitigated.

Each Island will manage its own version of this document, therefore, the content of the Lessons Learned artifact will vary from Island to Island. A very high-level example of what could be included in a Lessons Learned document is provided in Table 19.3 for reference. Please note that a real Lessons Learned table will have many more data points covering items such as *Action Taken, Assignee, Projected Due Date, Actual Due Date,* etc.

---

[2] Risks, Assumptions, Issues and Dependencies (RAID).

FURTHER CONSIDERATIONS

Chapter 20

The Working Environment

It is beyond the scope of this book to delve too deeply into the working environment in which The Island exists, but the relevance and impact of the workplace are briefly touched upon in this chapter.

A Collaborative Space

The global COVID-19 pandemic has changed the ways in which people work, with some individuals and teams working from home full time, others working in some form of hybrid model between home and office, and still others back in the office full-time. It could, therefore, be argued that the working environment is less relevant now than it has ever been, and a lot of people will agree with this view.

That said, as the impact of the pandemic recedes, there is already a push from some companies (e.g., Twitter,[1] now called X, JP Morgan,[2] etc.) to get more people back into the office, in a full-time capacity, sooner rather than later.

Undertaking a digital transformation using The Galapagos Framework, provides an opportunity for organizations to improve their workspace design to enable a more collaborative and communicative approach to delivery.

---

[1] Kurt Wagner and Bloomberg, 'Musk Orders All Twitter Staff Back to Office in First Company-Wide Email', Fortune, 10 November 2022, https://fortune.com/2022/11/10/musk-orders-all-twitter-staff-back-office-first-company-wide-email-exceptions-need-personal-approval/, (accessed 6 September 2023).

[2] Lananh Nguyen and Niket Nishant, 'JPMorgan managing directors asked to work in office five days a week: memo', Reuters, 12 April 2023. Available at: https://www.reuters.com/business/finance/jpmorgan-managing-directors-asked-work-office-five-days-week-memo-2023-04-12/, (accessed 2 October 2023).

DOI: 10.1201/9781003404217-27

It is true that staff can work anywhere; however, some spaces are more pleasurable to work in than others, and in those situations where staff are physically present most/all of the time in the same office, the quality of these spaces becomes increasingly important. The thrum of collaborative working is difficult to achieve in a traditional office environment, where team members are either arranged in banks of workstations (or worse enclosed from each other in little cubicles), with a lack of break out/collaboration spaces and no whiteboards/white walls to jot down ideas or high-level thoughts/designs.

The esthetics and design of a working environment are important as people need a workspace that is uplifting (after all people can spend a significant amount of their time here). There is a substantial body of research on the impact of the built environment on the occupants' well-being, productivity, and health (in relation to the number of workdays lost to illness), and the WELL building standard[3] is now widely used to improve workspaces.

The spaces provided do not even have to be in the same building as the parent organization (and some would suggest that it is better if they are not in the same building as the parent company), and they need not cost the earth to set up. There are a plethora of companies supplying these kinds of collaborative working spaces for relatively little cost.

The office space that staff work in is important, and the positive impact of a collaborative working environment can be significant and is explored further in the *Working Environment* case study in *Chapter 32*.

In short, if organizations are encouraging their staff back into an office environment, then the setting needs to support collaboration, communication, innovation, and creativity. If, however, there is no push to get staff back into the same office, then the organization needs to ensure that the collaboration tools provided are outstanding (more on this in *Chapter 21, – A Few Essentials – Essential Tools – Collaboration Tools*).

---

3 'WELL Building Standard', *International WELL Building Institute*, [online]. Available at: https://standard.wellcertified.com/well (accessed 2 October 2023).

Chapter 21

A Few Essentials

Essential Tools

Collaboration Tools

Collaboration tools have become a necessity in today's digital age, and their adoption has been hastened by the impact of the global COVID-19 pandemic and the need for more people to work from home. It's no exaggeration to state that many organizations would have struggled to retain (let alone grow) their business during the pandemic without the effective use of tools that allowed staff to work and collaborate while not being physically located in the same office.

Though there are some strong arguments to be made that face-to-face communication and collaboration are more effective than collaborating in the virtual world, there are some instances (outside of the pandemic) where this is simply not possible. For example, there are a significant number of companies where it is commonplace to have globally distributed teams.

This remote-working business model, which was once only operated by large multinational organizations, has now been enthusiastically adopted by smaller start-ups and FinTechs in the search for efficiencies whilst simultaneously accelerating business growth. Collaboration tools (e.g., Slack, Microsoft Office 365, Jira, Confluence, Google Workspace, SharePoint, etc.) are the technological enablers of this change in the way in which business is being conducted, and new businesses moving to a globally distributed working model could not have been successful without the effective use of these tools.

The world has moved on from solely face-to-face working, in the same office, to a hybrid or fully remote model becoming the new norm. New businesses have seen significant growth and reduced costs by moving sections of their operations to lower-cost locations, using collaboration tools for instant messaging, voice and video calling, shared whiteboards, centralized information management platforms (for document sharing and storage), distributed project management and productivity tools (for task tracking and workflow management), notifications/reminders and calendar integrations; the list goes on.

These new business models and ways of working could not have been achieved without the ever-reducing cost and increasing depth of functionality provided by the collaboration tools available today.

Successful digital transformations require significant amounts of effective collaboration, and companies striving for success in this area must have the tools in place to support mutual engagement, open communication, and the pooling of skills and resources to deliver on the organization's transformational objectives.

Essential Processes

Agile

It should come as no surprise that The Galapagos Framework advocates an Agile approach to delivery. It is important to note that The Framework supports this approach across all the Delivery and Go-To Market Functions of The Island (*Agile* is no longer just an approach that the IT function follows).

The Framework is not opinionated about which flavor of agile is used (Scrum, Kanban, SAFe, Scrumban, etc.) as long as an agile mindset is adopted.

The advantages of an agile approach are many and varied, but in a fast-paced transformation initiative, these benefits really come into their own.

The flexibility and adaptability that an agile attitude brings allows The Island to swiftly respond to challenges and adjust its priorities and resources to address new developments or unforeseen circumstances.

The virtuous cycle of delivering value by continuous, close collaboration and communication, coupled with actively seeking feedback on delivery and performance, leads to a higher degree of satisfaction, not just for the end customers but also for internal stakeholders and the delivery teams themselves.

Better decision-making and problem-solving are a direct result of improved collaboration, shared responsibility, and the fact that the individuals who are solving the problems are the same individuals who are closest to them. This shared responsibility fosters a sense of unity and trust resulting in better teamwork and better-quality outcomes.

Aiming for perfection at the outset of any transformation is an unachievable goal. Evolving solutions by adopting an iterative and incremental (*Digital Acceleration*) approach allows the transformation to realize value earlier and adjust the approach based on real-time/near-time metrics. This process also results in improved risk management as we validate assumptions earlier in the cycle which allows the transformation to minimize the impact of unexpected issues.

Continuous Improvement

The constant effort to optimize processes and ways of working by identifying, and implementing, incremental improvements over time is key to any modern delivery function. A continuous improvement approach fosters a culture of learning and growth within the organization and encourages teams to constantly refine their methods to improve outcomes.

As with the use of agile, The Galapagos Framework is not opinionated about which, if any, continuous improvement methodology is used (e.g., Kaizen, Lean, Six Sigma, Total Quality Management (TQM), etc.) as long as the principles are followed, and iterative and incremental improvements are achieved.

Focusing on the end goals of the transformation and understanding the strategy will allow the individuals on The Island to more easily identify areas for improvement that will have the most significant impact. Tackling small manageable changes that can be quickly implemented will reduce risk, build momentum, and encourage a culture of learning and adaptation.

As mentioned previously, metrics are key. Continuous improvement relies on objective data and measures to identify areas that should be enhanced, and to assess progress. By adopting a metrics -driven approach, the transformation can ensure that changes are targeted at the areas that will deliver the greatest impact.

It is imperative that the transformation regularly evaluates and reflects on the impact of improvements to allow it to refine and adjust its approach as required.

The Importance of the Correct Tools and Processes

Successful transformations rely on excellent teamwork, a flexible approach to delivery, and a desire to constantly seek out areas for enhancement. The adoption and effective use of collaboration tools, an Agile approach, and a continuous improvement mindset are key to delivering a positive transformational change.

Chapter 22

Current Approaches and Why They Don't Work

The Transformation Is Being Driven by the IT Function

It is often the case that the CEO or other senior leaders within the organization throw any digital transformation strategy over to the IT function, *It's digital, isn't it? Well, it must belong to IT!*

However, transformational change is human change, yes it can and will involve the integration of new technologies, but driving the entire strategy out of the IT function is a mistake that can result in a technology-centric approach that fails to address the broader organizational needs.

Even if the IT function does not drive a technology-centric approach to the transformation, there is still a significant risk that the broader organization will perceive the transformation as a technology-driven initiative, which may result in other departments feeling excluded, which in turn can lead to a lack of collaboration and an increased resistance to the program.

Third-Party Engagement

When embarking on digital transformations, most organizations will engage external third parties to a greater or lesser degree.

DOI: 10.1201/9781003404217-29

Too Much Third-Party Engagement Combined with Too Little CEO Engagement

There are, of course, many situations where an external partner acting as a trusted advisor can, and often does, play a critical role in transformation initiatives. However, given that any digital transformation is likely to be one of the most important strategic priorities (if not *the* most important), it seems incongruous that any third party should be driving the change without the deep and direct involvement of the CEO; however, this is often the case.

Whether this lack of CEO engagement is down to a perceived personal/reputational risk (if things don't go well), a lack of expertise, or any other factor, is unimportant. What is important is that the CEO must be deeply involved and not only *drive*, but *be seen to drive*, the transformation strategy forward.

Strengths of Positive Third-Party Engagement

In situations where the CEO is non-technical a trusted third party can provide support and give the CEO the confidence to make the right decisions, but it is still critically important to the success of the transformation that the CEO is seen to be leading the program.

Where a company's internal teams might lack expertise in certain areas, again, third parties can augment the internal capabilities and bring in any expertise that might be required and, since they are external to the organization, will bring a degree of objectivity by being detached from internal politics or preconceived ideas.

Potential Risks of Third-Party Engagement

Whether or not engaging a third-party will improve the speed of delivery, or cost-effectiveness of the transformation, is much less clear and some external parties can adopt a *land and expand* approach to engagements, where they will seek out additional areas within the organization to develop their influence and grow their footprint (adding more staff and therefore cost to the company as a whole).

Wholesale Organizational Change

There may also be situations where third parties encourage wholesale, organizational change (or as one consultancy has put it *a holistic transformation*[1]) as part of the digital transformation program. A large-scale change is a far more lucrative contract than an isolated digital transformation. If the organization progresses down this

---

[1] KPMG. (2021) 'Time to take a new vantage point on transformation,' KPMG, available at https://home.kpmg/uk/en/blogs/home/posts/2021/10/time-to-take-a-new-vantage-point-on-transformation.html (accessed: 18 July 2023).

route, then care must be taken to ensure that the scope is well understood, and that the company does not bite off more than it can chew by adopting a *universal* approach to the transformation.

Don't Do Everything, Everywhere, All at Once

The Galapagos Framework is not opinionated about the level of involvement of external third parties, but it is opinionated about transforming small discrete areas of your business in an iterative fashion (see *Galapagos Principle 4: Sequential Transformation*). Organizations do not want to be in a position where they engage a large consultancy and then find themselves committed to a multimillion-dollar roadmap and associated contract(s) that they can't get out of.

An iterative and incremental, *Digital Acceleration*, approach to transformational change allows organizations to be more fleet of foot and adopt a flexible attitude to the inevitable challenges that they will encounter.

The Lack of a Human-Centric Approach

The perception that digital transformations are principally about, or fail because of, technology is inaccurate. These are human changes, often conducted within the context of organizational structures that do not lend themselves to digital change.[2]

The human, whether that be the staff within the organization, the end customer, suppliers, or other third-parties, needs to be at the center of the change strategy.

Just Another Cost-Cutting Exercise

Often, digital transformation programs are a thinly disguised cost cutting exercise. This is not to say that digital transformations cannot, or will not, result in cost efficiencies or productivity gains and, if done well, the outcome will certainly be a more efficient and effective organization, but transformational change is not just a simple numbers game.

As Lou Gerstner (ex-IBM CEO) states, *Transformation is fundamentally changing the way the organization thinks, responds, and leads.*

A Human-Centric Approach to Transformational Change

The organization is not some amorphous entity. The organization is made up of humans that think, humans that respond to change (positively or negatively), and humans that lead.

---

[2] Harkin, B. (28 February 2023) 'Digital Transformations: The Case for Change and Why They Fail', Fintech Futures, 1 February. Available at: https://www.fintechfutures.com/2023/02/digital-transformations-the-case-for-change-and-why-they-fail/ (accessed: 8 September 2023).

It is the humans that lead (The Leadership Function), that determine if the response to the transformation is positive or negative. If the transformation is perceived as just another cost-cutting exercise, then there will be a difficult task ahead to encourage those who are delivering the change to respond in a wholly positive way.

Deriving profitability from your core business is one thing, but deriving profitability from transformational change requires a human-centric focus. *There are a lot of transformations that claim to be people-centric but lack human-centric goals/outcomes resulting in huge expenditure with low or negative return on investment (ROI).*[3]

Why the Current Approaches Don't Work

In summary, the current approaches to digital transformations don't work because they are not driven from the top of the organization, they have the wrong level of external/third-party involvement, they attempt wholesale organizational change, including the operating models of the company's core business (often acting on the advice of external third parties), and they do not put the human at the center of the change strategy.

The Galapagos Framework addresses these issues by mandating very senior executive sponsorship from the outset (see *Galapagos Principle 6: Senior executive sponsorship is a must*), an iterative and incremental approach to the transformation (see *Chapter 5 – Moving from Digital Transformation to Digital Acceleration*), changing a discreet area of the business before progressing on to other parts of the operation (see *Galapagos Principle 5: Transformation Context*, starting small now to win big later), and putting the human at the center of the change story (see *Chapter 3 – Introduction to The Galapagos Framework – A human-centric & inclusive approach to deliver successful transformations*).

---

[3] Richard Jeffries – Founder CX ALL.

Chapter 23

The Role of Social Media in Digital Transformations

Social media plays a significant role in modern life, and some would make the bold claim that it has changed the world. Whether or not it has in fact *changed the world* is open for debate but what is unarguable is that it has changed the way people consume news and information, communicate, find work, and interact with one another.

Use of Social Media between the Customer and the Organization

In *Chapter 1*, *digital* was defined as the *convergence of people and technology* and social media is a prime example of this convergence. As such, it has become an important tool in managing the relationship between the end customer and the organization.

Trust

There is a perception amongst consumers that social media is a more reliable source than other information channels and, for certain sections of the demographic, they will turn to social media first to get information about products and services.

Organizations, therefore, put a lot of time and effort into the quality of the information that they put on social media channels, understanding that better quality information will increase the perception of trust amongst consumers.

DOI: 10.1201/9781003404217-30

Data-driven Marketing

Given the ever-accelerating and increasing rate of customer demands, regarding the products and services they receive, social media is a crucial tool that allows organizations to generate vast amounts of data to gain insights into customer preferences, behaviors, and trends. Automated customer analytics provide near real-time feedback on customer activities, and this allows marketing departments to better understand the customer and refine their strategies based on real-world, real-time information.

This data, and supporting analytics, allow content and promotional campaigns to be tailored to meet the individual customers' needs and desires, providing a more compelling and personal level of service.

Customer Service

The way in which organizations engage with customers, and prospective customers, has changed radically with the use of social media, and these channels allow businesses to provide highly responsive customer service.

The impacts on the service that organizations provide to their customers, on an almost daily basis, is evident for all to see on platforms such as X (previously Twitter) where accounts with large numbers of followers use the platform to complain about perceived failings in the service provided by companies. The social media/customer service team on the other end of the complaint responds immediately with something along the lines of, *DM me and we will look into this issue for you…*

This level of customer service is more than most mere mortals can hope to receive, but it is an example of the impact that social media has, and how reactive organizations are having to become on these platforms to reduce the risk of bad publicity.

This highly responsive approach serves to demonstrate how seriously organizations are taking social media in terms of how they aim to improve their customer service (or at least improve the perception of their customer service). Traditional communications channels are unsuited to this type of dynamic and highly interactive engagement, and these new channels are now an essential instrument for organizations to listen, respond and adapt to customer feedback.

Customer Reach

At the time of writing, there are 4.76 billion people, or 59.4 percent of the world's population,[1] using social media. It is, therefore, unsurprising that brands, keen to

---

[1] Statista. (2023) 'Digital population worldwide', Statista, available at https://www.statista.com/statistics/617136/digital-population-worldwide/ (accessed: 18 July 2023).

reach as wide an audience as possible, are sharing content across multiple social media platforms. The intention, in this instance, is to increase brand awareness and use promotional campaigns to guide traffic to specific websites with the aim of driving higher conversion rates, from prospective customers to actual revenue-generating customers.

A highly desirable outcome is a marketing post/campaign that goes viral, reaching a large number of people in a short amount of time. A viral post is not just cost-effective (the return on investment can be high compared to traditional advertising methods) but can also increase trust because it's being shared by real people and not pushed via paid-for advertising.

Any increase in participation between an organization and the end customer will help to stimulate interest and maintain relationships between the customer and the organization. This increase in customer stickiness will improve the Lifetime Value (LTV) of the customer to the organization and allow companies to assess how much they should invest in acquiring and retaining customers.

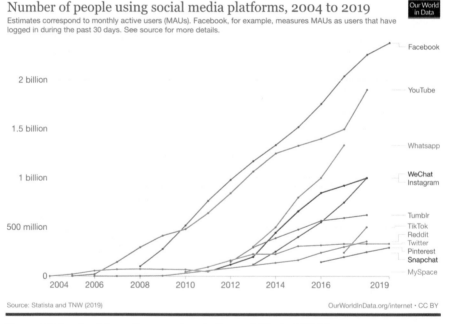

Figure 23.1   Social media users by platform, 2004 to 2019.[2]

² Roser, M., Ritchie, H., and Ortiz-Ospina, E. (2023) 'Rise of Social Media', Our World in Data, available at https://ourworldindata.org/rise-of-social-media (accessed: 18 July 2023).

Social Media Influencers

It should come as no surprise that those aged between 18 and 49 are the most active users of social media (see *Figure 23.2*). This is a huge age range and covers the years when most people will have their highest disposable income, making these channels even more appealing to marketing departments. The younger end of this age range has given rise to the phenomenon of social media influencers who have the power to shape consumer behavior.

The influencer marketing industry has grown significantly in recent years and has become an essential part of many marketing strategies. Positioning brands to collaborate with these individuals aims to enhance product credibility, standing, reach, and impact amongst a younger customer demographic.

Thought Leadership and Community Building

Many companies are using social media channels to support growth over the long term by employing community-building and thought leadership approaches. Brands posting thought leadership pieces can be perceived as more credible and trustworthy, whilst investing time and effort in community building can improve brand promotion and loyalty.

Without social media channels, these activities would have been consigned to magazine articles, for thought leadership pieces, and conferences, for community building. Neither of these offers the same potential for immediate marketing momentum, at the same scale, as social media platforms.

Use of Social Media between the Organization and Potential Employees

Social media has transformed the hiring process, with platforms such as LinkedIn allowing companies to find, and connect with, potential candidates directly rather than advertising or going via 3rd parties. Similarly, these platforms allow candidates to contact their network to explore if a prospective employer's culture aligns with their values.

This is a win for both sides of the hiring equation resulting in candidates being more informed about potential employers, and employers being more effective in targeting potential candidates, both of which should result in a better match between employee and employer.

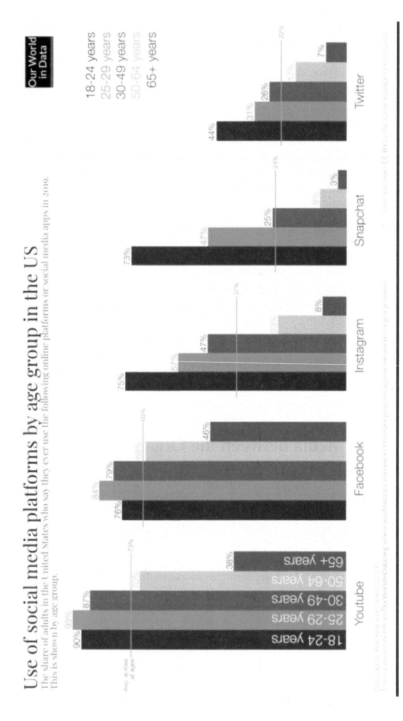

Figure 23.2 Use of social media platforms by age group in the US.[3]

[3] Roser, M., Ritchie, H., and Ortiz-Ospina, E. (2023) 'Rise of Social Media', Our World in Data, available at https://ourworldindata.org/rise-of-social-media (accessed: 18 July 2023).

Use of Social Media within the Organization

Enterprise Social Networks

Though social media platforms are generally public-facing, organizations are increasingly adopting internal social media channels, also known as enterprise social networks (e.g., Microsoft's Yammer, Workplace by Facebook, etc.), specifically to improve communication and collaboration across their business areas.

These platforms often include features like instant messaging, group discussions, file sharing, and so on, aimed at fostering innovation, and information exchange, to help the business develop new ideas, products, and services to meet the evolving needs of their customers.

The speed of communication facilitated by these enterprise social media channels enables internal teams (that may be globally distributed) to respond to time-critical situations in real time (e.g., system outages or other corporate crises). This is especially important in situations where organizations have large sections of their support functions working in low-cost locations, but their main internal business users are based in high-cost locations (think business users in Wall St. with support functions in India).

Speed of response in these situations can be business critical, for example, investment banks unable to trade due to a systems outage may be losing millions of dollars per minute.

Social Media: A Driving Force in Digital Transformations

Social media platforms are a driving force in digital transformations and their use, in both B2C (Business-to-Consumer) and increasingly B2B (Business-to-Business) contexts, is affecting various aspects of business operations, customer experience, and market conditions.[4] The use of social media channels in digital transformations allows organizations to be more responsive and adaptable to the needs of the customer and, to stay relevant and competitive, businesses need to embrace these platforms and regard them as an integral part of their digital strategy.

---

[4] Harkin, B. (30 August, 2023) 'Social Media: A Driving Force in Digital Transformations', Fintech Futures, 1 August. Available at: https://www.fintechfutures.com/2023/08/social-media-a-driving-force-in-digital-transformations/ (Accessed: 8 September 2023).

Chapter 24

The Leadership
Game Plan

The purpose of The Leadership Game Plan is to act as a quick and easy reference to allow leaders to avoid some of the most common pitfalls of digital transformation initiatives.

The game plan provides *Top 10 Tips* and a *Checklist for success*, which covers 20 questions that need to be answered to ensure that some of the common issues that affect digital transformations are avoided.

How to Avoid Digital Transformation Disasters

TABLE 24.1   Top 10 Tips to Avoid Digital Transformation Disasters

Top 10 Tips to Avoid Digital Transformation Disasters	
1. Create The Island and use The Galapagos Framework.	7. Anchor the change story to the core business of the organization.
2. Foster a culture of collaboration.	8. Close the skill gaps in capabilities and resources.
3. Assign digital leaders to the top team.	9. Ensure the right metrics are in place and automate these. Measure, measure, and measure again.
4. Limit the scope of the transformation.	
5. Clearly define the scope of the transformation.	10. Fail fast and learn from mistakes.
6. Communicate the rationale for the change to all.	

DOI: 10.1201/9781003404217-31

A Checklist for Success

20 Questions to Drive Successful Transformation

What follows is a simple checklist to allow organizations to ensure that they are set up to avoid some of the most common issues that plague digital transformations, and to give companies the best chance of achieving success in these endeavors.

TABLE 24.2   Checklist for Success

The Human Element		
Culture	Does the organization encourage cross-functional collaboration?	☐
	Is the organization accepting of the risk of failing fast?	☐
	Are all parties on board?	☐
Communication	Has the change story been communicated to all by a very senior executive?	☐
	Has the Communication Strategy been defined?	☐
	Is the organization using digital channels for communication and collaboration?	☐
	Does the organization actively encourage two-way communication?	☐
Skills	Is the Workforce Strategy clear?	☐
	Has a sober analysis of existing resources and capabilities, across locations, been conducted?	☐
	Are gaps in skills and resources being closed?	☐
	Are incentives across all teams aligned to the strategic goals?	☐
	Are digital leaders assigned to the top team?	☐
The Organizational Factors		
Leadership	Is there clear and visible sponsorship of the transformation from the CEO or another very senior executive?	☐
	Is the strategy clear to all and anchored in the core business of the organization?	☐

(Continued)

TABLE 24.2 (Continued)

	Has the frequency of the Strategy Review Cycles been agreed?	☐
	Are metrics in place (and automated) to baseline the current situation and to measure the performance of the transformation?	☐
	Has the allocation of an experienced Delivery Lead to focus solely on the transformation been considered?	☐
The Delivery Aspects		
Scope	Is the scope sufficiently limited?	☐
	Has the scope been clearly defined with minimal room for ambiguity?	☐
	Is the scope understood by all?	☐

Broader Collaboration

The first principle of The Galapagos Framework is that *Culture is king*, and at the heart of this principle is a culture of *collaboration*.

The rapid pace of change makes it extremely difficult for any one company to cover *all* new technologies that may deliver a competitive advantage. As such, organizations should not just encourage collaboration internally but should seek out opportunities for external collaboration.

There may be potential to form innovation partnerships with independent entities (e.g., Universities, Business Schools, or other Higher Education establishments) to further technology adoption, product development, and innovation. These partnerships can offer a relatively low-cost acceleration path for organizations embarking on a digital transformation.

The ideal innovation partner should be complimentary to your business but with little chance of becoming a competitor and as such, Universities and other Higher Education establishments may offer a good fit.

Chapter 25

Readiness Review and Digital Maturity Assessment

Before embarking on what might be an expensive digital transformation journey, the organization must understand if it is ready to progress an initiative of this size and, as such, a digital transformation readiness review/digital maturity assessment should be undertaken.

These tools will allow the organization to evaluate its preparedness for a digital transformation exercise (in the case of the readiness review) and assess the current state of the business's digital capabilities (in the case of the maturity assessment) and will therefore be included in *The Model* (see *Chapter 19 – The Model*). The digital maturity assessment will also allow the organization to measure how far up the digital maturity curve it is and therefore how much work there is still to do to reach the desired digital goals.

Both the readiness review and the maturity assessment are important for informing the organization's digital journey, but they serve different purposes and focus on different aspects.

For those companies that are clear that they are in a good position to start a digital transformation process, they may choose not to conduct a readiness review but will certainly want to baseline where they are currently, in terms of digital maturity and where they hope to be during and after the transformation process, and this is what a digital maturity assessment will provide.

As mentioned in *Chapter 19 – The Model – Transformation Strategy*, some of the areas covered by the Transformation Strategy may include items such as vision and

DOI: 10.1201/9781003404217-32

objectives (the objectives might be in the form of KPIs or OKRs), digital business model, customer experience and engagement, data and analytics, technology and infrastructure, governance, operations, innovation, digital skills, and so on. Most, if not all, of these elements will be measured as part of any digital maturity assessment, but only a subset of these may be assessed in any readiness review.

Digital Transformation Readiness Review

From the perspective of The Galapagos Framework, a digital transformation readiness review is an executive tool that provides quick insight into the organization's current readiness to embark on a digital transformation initiative. It is typically a lightweight appraisal of the company's current competencies covering areas such as digital strategy and leadership, talent and skills availability, digital channels and platforms, technology, culture and innovation, communication, funding, governance, and so on.[1]

The readiness review is not a replacement for a digital maturity assessment (see the Digital Maturity Assessment section below); it is merely a high-level tool to facilitate discussions around what areas need attention before the organization embarks on a digital transformation program.

The purpose of this review is to give the organization rapid feedback on areas where they will need to improve to increase the likelihood of success in a digital transformation initiative. If the company is found wanting in several areas, then it makes little sense to embark on a transformation until such time as the issues in these areas have been addressed. This readiness review would be a key artifact in any Go/No–Go decisions as to if/when to embark on a transformation process.

At its most basic level, this review could simply take the form of a short questionnaire that is sent out to some key individuals across the organization with results fed back on a near real-time basis.

The output of the review is likely to be a prioritized set of actions, and associated roadmap, that will allow the organization to get itself to a position where embarking on a digital transformation change initiative is feasible.

Digital Maturity Assessment (DMA)

A digital maturity assessment is a more rigorous evaluation of an organization's digital capabilities and will involve interviews, questionnaires, and other analysis techniques to measure the current digital strengths and weaknesses of the organization across several different dimensions such as leadership, strategy, digital business

---

[1] See *Chapter 19 – The Model* for additional areas that may be included.

model, organizational structure, customer experience, data and analytics, technology and infrastructure, organization and culture, funding and governance, operations, innovation, skills, and so on.[2]

Gaps in capability will be identified and ranked and a roadmap of initiatives will be produced showing how and when these gaps could be closed.

The digital maturity assessment helps organizations understand their current digital position and will facilitate the creation of strategies to help the organization achieve its transformation goals.

The output of this assessment is an overall maturity score showing the current digital state of the company and its desired target digital state. This overall maturity score is further decomposed by each dimension measured and the DMA[3] will identify areas for improvement and development within each dimension.

---

[2] See *Chapter 19 – The Model* for additional areas that may be included.

[3] There are a number of consultancies that provide assessment frameworks (e.g., 3pointsDiGI-TAL's DMA framework delivers a comprehensive assessment of an organizations digital capability and readiness for change). www.3pointsdigital.com

Chapter 26

The Customer Proximity Principle

One of the key tenets of The Galapagos Framework is reducing the distance between the end customer and those who are delivering the product/service for the customer. This is the foundation of The Galapagos Framework's Customer Proximity principle (*Galapagos Principle 2*) which states:

Minimizing the number of links between the end customer and the product development and delivery functions will reduce costs and increase profit. Increasing the number of links will have the opposite effect.

Why Do We Need to Bring the Customer Closer to Delivery?

The fact that the number of hops between the end client and the product and delivery functions is so easily measurable makes this a very powerful metric to track and should be included in any KPI's that are used to assess the transformation initiative.

Moving the customer closer to the teams and individuals that are servicing their needs is a positive step for several, qualitative and quantitative, reasons. These will be touched on below and are also discussed in *Chapter 16 – The Island – Go-To Market and Delivery Functions – Customer Experience*.

DOI: 10.1201/9781003404217-33

Cost Reduction

Delivery efficiencies will result from minimizing the distance between the customer and the change functions of the organization.

Reducing Wasted Effort and Time

At large scale, data analyses on consumer behaviors, trends, and needs allow organizations to monitor what their customers want without having to speak to individuals directly. These analyses can then be used to inform the direction and feature set of the product.

At smaller scale, organizations can gain actionable insights on product direction and strategy by demonstrating early prototypes of new products/new product features directly to the customer. These insights can be used to finesse the product/product strategy to ensure that it is more closely aligned with the customer's needs. All of this without incurring the cost of building the product/product features first and then finding out later that these don't deliver what the customer wants.

Shortening the feedback loops between the customer and the areas delivering changes for the customer, reduces the risk of miscommunication and loss of information fidelity, which in turn reduces the risk of misaligned requirements, and the deliveries resulting from these not meeting the customers' expectations.

Every link in the chain between the customer and the functions that are servicing and delivering to the customer carries a point of inefficiency and the risk of a *broken telephone*[1] situation developing.

Removing Hurdles

By removing the barriers to communication between the customer and the organization, the flow of information is made more efficient. However, the quality of the information flow is extremely important, and care must be taken to ensure that the organization does not get swamped by a significant volume of spurious requests and contacts from customers that do not add value.

Increasing Revenue Opportunities

Improving the quality of the product strategy and the interactions between the customer and the company should result in an increase in the portfolio of opportunities for revenue generation.

---

[1] In the broken telephone game, participants sit or stand in a line or a circle with one person whispering a message to the person next to them. That person then whispers the message to the next person, and so on. The game demonstrates how easily information can become distorted as it is communicated from person to person.

Customer Satisfaction, Buy-in, and Retention

Involving the customer in the early phases of development, and direction will foster a sense of ownership for the final product. The customers are not just invested in the product, but the process of product development. People can see how their input has shaped the product and this will result in greater customer loyalty.

There will also be a higher degree of satisfaction among the customer base for the product/product features that have been requested because the needs of the consumer will have been met successfully (due in no small part to the fact that the risk of misunderstanding has been minimized by improving the flow of communication).

Qualitative Measures

As well as the quantitative measures outlined above, there are other, qualitative measures, that should be taken into account.

Employee Satisfaction

The successful application of The Customer Proximity Principle will be better for the employees as there will be no chasm of morale when staff have worked hard to deliver a product (or set of product features) only to learn that, through no fault of their own, their efforts have come to nothing as what they have delivered is not what the customer wants.

Staff morale improves when they deliver something that they can be proud of, that meets the customers' needs, and has a direct and positive impact on the company's profit and reputation.

Reducing Costs, Increasing Revenue, and Improving Customer and Employee Satisfaction

The Galapagos Framework recommends an iterative and incremental (*Digital Acceleration*) approach to increasing the proximity of the customer to The Product and Delivery Functions. This will allow course corrections to take place quickly, with minimal impact, while allowing for empirical process improvement throughout the journey of bringing the customer closer to delivery.

In bringing the customer closer to the functions that deliver products and services, organizations can increase profits by reducing costs, increasing revenue, and improving the satisfaction of both internal staff and external customers.

The Role of The Customer Experience Function

The Customer Experience Function, which exists within The Nucleus of The Island, is the key to bringing the end customer closer to both The Product and Delivery

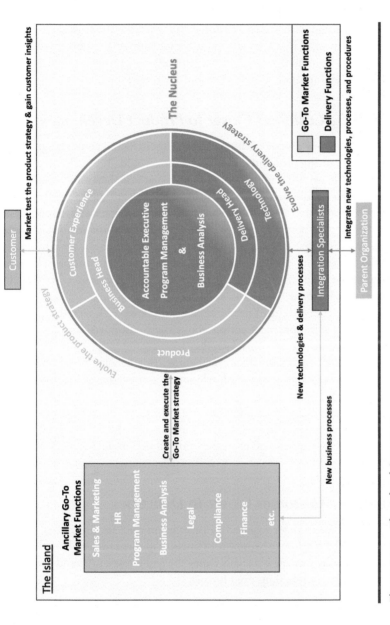

Figure 26.1 The Island Structure.

Functions. The Customer Experience Function will allow the end customer to directly inform the development of the product strategy via The Product Function and the transformation of that strategy into a tangible, saleable product, via The Delivery Function.

The relationship with the end customer is owned by The Customer Experience Function and, as such, this team is responsible for gathering customer requirements, road testing the product strategy with customers and prospects, and feeding any insights gathered into both The Product and Delivery Functions.

Bringing the Customer Closer to Product Development

If the customer knew exactly what product they needed and could design and build this without incurring prohibitive costs, then they would. The customer would also, undoubtedly, change their mind about exactly what it is they want as they progress further through the discovery, design, and build phases.

Organizations exist in a world where a more personal approach to product development is not only possible, at large scale, but in some instances is also expected (the ever-increasing pace of demand and customer expectation again). This forces companies to be more customer-centric and bring the end customer closer to the evolution of the product and, in many instances, involve the end customer directly in product development.

This customer involvement need not be direct, however. Given the huge volume of data that organizations now collect about their customers, and prospects, and the analyses that are run over this data, they have greater insight into the customers' behaviors, needs, and desires than ever before. This detailed insight allows many companies to tweak their product development strategy based on real-world data and not subjective opinion.

The Customer Experience Function will help drive a more personal approach to product development. They will gather and analyze the data to produce actionable customer insights that will ultimately inform the product strategy and delivery priorities.

Bringing the Customer Closer to Delivery

If there are minor changes required to existing product features, these can be fed directly from The Customer Experience Function to The Delivery Function without the need to involve anyone else. This closes the gap between the end customer and the product delivery functions even further.

CONCLUSIONS V

Chapter 27

Closing Thoughts

The Problem Is Big, Very Big

The current approaches to digital transformation are not working, and if the current failure rate of circa 70% continues, then by 2026 there could be a global enterprise spend of **$2.3 trillion** that does not deliver success.

Let's just put $2.3 trillion into some context:

> It is nearly double the UK's total public spending in 2023.[1]
>
> It could fund NASA for 95 years.[2]
>
> It could fund the entire four-year college education for over 16 million US students.[3]
>
> It would be enough to end world hunger[4] and still have $1.94 trillion left over!

---

[1] The ONS estimates that the UK spent just over £1.1 trillion which is roughly equivalent to $1.4 trillion.

Office for National Statistics (ONS), 'Public Sector Finances, April 2023', Office for National Statistics, 2023, https://www.ons.gov.uk/economy/governmentpublicsectorandtaxes/publicsectorfinance/bulletins/publicsectorfinances/april2023, [accessed August 15, 2023].

[2] Based on NASA's Full Year Budget request for 2024

National Aeronautics and Space Administration (NASA), 'Fiscal Year 2024 NASA Budget Summary', 2023, https://www.nasa.gov/sites/default/files/atoms/files/fiscal_year_2024_nasa_budget_summary.pdf [accessed August 15, 2023].

[3] Based on an average cost of $35,000 per year for private college tuition in the US.

[4] Based on $40 billion each year from 2021 to end world hunger by 2030.

World Food Program USA (WFP USA), 'How Much Would It Cost to End World Hunger?', *World Food Program USA*, [August 10, 2022], https://www.wfpusa.org/articles/how-much-would-it-cost-to-end-world-hunger/, [accessed August 15, 2023].

DOI: 10.1201/9781003404217-35

Clearly, a problem of this magnitude requires a fundamental rethink of the way in which organizations approach digital transformations, and The Galapagos Framework delivers this shift in methodology by providing some counterintuitive insights and an important change to the locus around which digital transformations are conducted.

A New and Human-Centric Approach to Deliver Successful Transformations

The Galapagos Framework addresses the fundamental causes of failure in digital transformation programs by adopting a new, more human-centric, approach to transformational change, and solving the common problems that plague these initiatives (across the Human, Organizational, and Delivery dimensions).

By putting the human (be that internal staff, end customers, suppliers, or other third parties) at the center of the change story, organizations will see a seismic and positive shift in the culture, communication, skills, and engagement levels used to deliver transformation strategies. This *human* change will allow companies to use culture as a springboard to deliver competitive advantage.

The Galapagos Framework provides the principles, structures, and artifacts to allow organizations to adopt this more people-focused means of delivering success in digital transformations, without the need to stake everything on a single linear transformation event or transforming the entire organization's operating model. This approach significantly reduces costs, operational, financial, and delivery risks, and increases productivity, delivery performance, and profits.

Key Takeaways

Wholesale Organizational Change Does Not Work

Organizations often find themselves in a position where they think (or have been advised) that the only way to achieve performance improvements that are sustainable over the long term is to adopt a wholesale approach to transformational change.

This is incorrect.

Employing a method that involves many parallel (and interdependent) streams of activity will not get organizations to their end goal faster but will increase the risk of failure.

The Island, Sequential Transformation, and Digital Acceleration Deliver Success

Companies should create a greenfield structure (The Island) within their organization and approach the transformation using fast, iterative cycles of delivery (*Digital Acceleration*) concentrating on one (or at most two) business area(s) at a time in a mostly sequential fashion. Though counterintuitive, this technique will reduce risk and accelerate a successful transformation process.

The use of The Galapagos Framework will improve the organization's ability to perform effectively over a prolonged period, as teams and individuals will be working at a sustainable rate over time.

The Galapagos Principles

The Galapagos Principles underpin the entire Galapagos Framework and inform all the solutions, structures, and artifacts that The Framework provides. These principles should form the basis of every transformation that is undertaken and will act as a guide throughout the organization's digital journey.

The Positive Impacts of Using The Galapagos Framework

Organizational Health

Using The Galapagos Framework does not just result in a positive impact on the delivery of the transformation, it drives behavioral change that benefits the teams involved in the delivery of the strategy by improving motivation, morale, and general well-being.

Reduced Cost

Galapagos Principle 2: Customer Proximity reduces the risk of miscommunication and misaligned requirements, and therefore, reduces the wasted effort spent on building something that does not meet the customer's needs. The Island structure, and the associated cultural changes, promotes a high degree of collaboration and the streamlining of inter-team communication, resulting in more efficient and effective performance.

Reduced Risk

The iterative nature of *Digital Acceleration* allows hypotheses to be tested and developed quickly in a real-world environment, to either succeed or fail fast, and allows transformation concepts to be validated far more rapidly than would be the case with a wholly linear approach. Similarly, employing the *Digital Acceleration* method results in increased flexibility and adaptability to changing circumstances, which is critical in the fast-paced world of digital change.

The use of The Island structure and The Galapagos Roadmap will naturally increase stakeholder engagement, allowing for faster decision-making and course corrections as circumstances change.

Increased Productivity

Operating in The Island environment, which is largely unencumbered from the bureaucracy and red tape of the parent organization, results in significant delivery efficiencies. The Island structure allows teams to create or adopt processes/procedures/technologies that are more appropriate for the delivery of digital change at pace and establishes a more collaborative and communicative working environment.

Increased Profit

The Galapagos Framework does not just deliver reduced cost, reduced risk, and increased productivity but also creates an environment where innovation, experimentation, and creativity thrive, resulting in an enhanced portfolio of opportunities for revenue generation.

The combination of reduced cost, reduced risk, increased productivity, and greater opportunities for revenue creation will deliver increased profits.[5]

Looking Forward

Digital transformation will continue to have a profound and global impact across business, technology, and society in general.

There will continue to be disruption across industries, and the flexibility to change business models will be critical. This corporate agility will allow organizations to remain competitive in a fast-paced market, where the increasing pace of technological change and innovation is not going to slow down anytime soon.

The creation and adoption of new technologies will not only reshape the business landscape but will also result in the increased integration of digital technologies into all aspects of our lives, changing the way we consume information, communicate, find work, make purchases, and interact with one another and the businesses we buy from.

Being flexible and remaining/becoming an eternal student (by continuous learning) will be important skills in order not to be left behind in the swiftly evolving digital world.

Take Control of the Digital Transformation Journey

This book provides the tools that organizations and individuals need to exercise effective control over their digital transformation journey (whether these transformations are already in flight or have yet to begin).

---

[5] See *Chapter 33 – Case Study: The Galapagos Framework and Success*

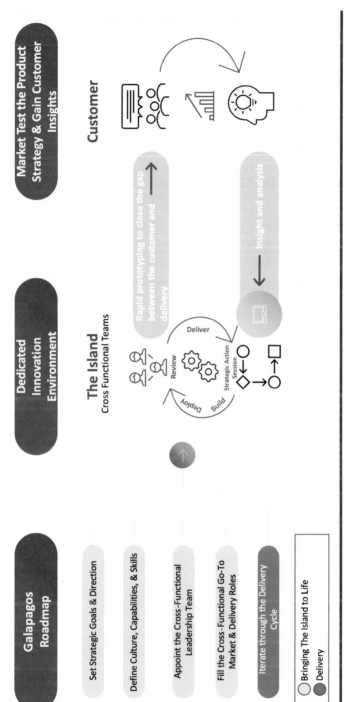

Figure 27.1 The Key to Digital Acceleration Success.

Failing to act will result in businesses being left behind and becoming just another statistic contributing to the 70% failure rate or the $2.3 trillion dollars wasted on digital transformations.

Final Thoughts

Thank you for choosing to invest your time in reading this book and I hope the insights you've gained propel you and your transformation forward.

The digital landscape is ever-evolving, and your contribution is part of the positive change that will allow us to collectively improve the success rate of these initiatives.

As you apply The Galapagos Framework to your transformation endeavors, I encourage you to share your thoughts, successes, and challenges at www.galapagosframework.com or you can email me at brian@digitalxform.co.uk.

CASE STUDIES

Chapter 28

Case Study Rose's Story Part 1: Toxic Culture

AT A GLANCE

- *Rose must deliver on a strategically important digital transformation in an organization where failures in leadership and direction have resulted in a toxic culture and dysfunctional teams.*
- *Rose is familiar with The Galapagos Framework and uses this to construct both short- and long-term action plans.*
- *Rose gains board approval to proceed and puts the organization on a sound footing before starting the transformation program.*
- *Executive support is maintained by providing regular updates to the board using near-real-time, tangible metrics.*

Introduction

Rose is confronted by a significant issue: Frustrated by the lack of progress on a strategically important digital transformation initiative, the chairman of Mythical Deposits Incorporated (MDI), has installed the son of a friend, Paul, to *...sort it out as he knows a bit about IT...*

Paul is clearly out of his depth and grasps at a lifeline in the form of Rose (a skilled digital transformation specialist with extensive knowledge of The Galapagos Framework) to deliver the transformation program.

DOI: 10.1201/9781003404217-37

Rose is a relatively new arrival at MDI but recognizes that the company is suffering from low staff morale, poor delivery, internal politics, and employees in perpetual disagreement. She has traced back many of these issues to failures in leadership, a toxic organizational culture, and many teams operating in a dysfunctional manner.

Toxic culture – The Dinosaur Cafe

Figure 28.1   The dinosaur café.

Overview

Rose has attended several very large meetings where the *do as I say* attitude of some of the leadership team has resulted in individuals and teams being publicly shamed by senior (and very influential) figures.

The relative severity of the perceived indiscretions is seemingly irrelevant with one junior manager being hauled over the coals for the format of a PowerPoint presentation and a senior manager (and his team) equally chastised for the failed release of business-critical software.

These are not isolated instances; most meetings that Rose attends result in someone (or many people) being severely criticized. The individuals delivering the dressing-downs are seemingly oblivious (or do not care) as to the impact that these are having on the delivery teams.

Situational Analysis

Rose conducts a broad appraisal of the current situation across all the teams and functions involved in the digital transformation program and identifies the following issues.

Lack of Trust

It is clear to Rose that there is a breakdown of trust between teams to deliver on dependencies. For example, the software development teams are continually missing deadlines, which means that the marketing function is forced to delay marketing campaigns. This results in the relationship managers having to explain to the end customers that the deliveries that they had been promised will not be on time and then deal with the resulting reputational damage. Similarly, the product development team feels that the sales team isn't doing enough to generate interest (and revenue) for new products and product features being developed.

Culture of Fear

A culture of fear exists, and Rose can see that employees do not feel enough psychological safety to speak up. The situation is leading to every element of even the most minor output being checked, double-checked, and triple-checked to avoid the inevitable consequences should something found to be wrong.

Emails are sent numerous times a day with very large CC lists employed to *cover the ass* of the sender. This defensive use of emails reveals how toxic the culture is.

The company has no tolerance for risk and failing fast is not accepted; everything must be right first time. There is no scope for teams or individuals to solve problems creatively, and MDI is stuck in a rut of *...this is the way we do it here...* resulting in inevitable delivery impacts and the missing of portfolios of opportunity.

Staff are losing confidence and enthusiasm for delivery is waning.

Lack of Collaboration

There is no meaningful team cohesion and Rose sees that there is minimal collaboration between teams. The organizational structure is heavily siloed, and within these silos, there are several Key Person Dependencies (KPDs) that are causing delivery delays. There is an increasing rate of employee absences, due to sickness, and the KPDs are exacerbating this situation as there is insufficient knowledge/skill to cover when a key individual is out of the office.

Politics

Political game-playing is widespread, and individuals and teams are taking up very defensive positions with significant amounts of time and effort being spent in inter-team/inter-function sniping and finger-pointing. Rose knows that when people feel they are under attack, retreating into a silo to seek protection is a natural reaction.

Impact Analysis – Toxic Culture

Rose conducts an impact analysis of the toxic culture and highlights the following.

Reduced Productivity

The toxic culture, and its cascading impacts, is having a direct and significant impact on productivity. The output of the entire delivery function is well below what would be regarded as the norm for a unit of its size.

Morale

Staff morale is very low, and a situation has arisen where highly skilled individuals are spending significant amounts of time and effort on unimportant tasks (e.g., tidying up a PowerPoint deck) rather than on tasks that are directly related to delivery.

These skilled resources are still expected to deliver on commitments with the relatively unimportant tasks proving an unwanted, and time-consuming, distraction which is resulting in staff members working unsustainable hours to get deliveries across the line.

This in turn is leading to …

Sickness

The pressure on staff over a sustained period of time is having the inevitable consequence of an increase in staff sickness. As staff absence, due to illness, increases, a vicious cycle now ensues where the same amount of work must be delivered in the same timeframe but with fewer staff, resulting in yet more pressure.

Which leads to…

Staff Attrition

Unsurprisingly, the point is being reached where many staff are (or are in the process of) leaving the organization to pursue their careers elsewhere.

The cost of the human and intellectual capital that is walking out of the company based solely on a toxic culture is significant.

Waste

Rose's view is that the impact of the toxic culture is significantly increasing the cost of MDI's transformation, in terms of reduced productivity, waste, high staff turnover, and lack of delivery.

Dysfunctional Teams

The internal politics, absence of meaningful collaboration, fear of failure, and lack of trust mean that the teams tasked to deliver on MDI's digital transformation are not performing well, and this is contributing to the company's poor overall performance. The situation is dire, and the impact is significant; delivery risks are increasing, timelines are slipping, and additional costs are being incurred.

The toxic culture has resulted in informal siloes being created, and instances of passive–aggressive behavior between some members of staff, which is further inhibiting free and open collaboration and communication.

Additionally, Rose has discovered that teams are incentivized differently meaning that there is no consistent compensation policy, across the teams delivering the transformation, which is aligned with the goals of the digital transformation.

Action Plan: Toxic Culture and Dysfunctional Teams

The situation is critical but using her extensive knowledge of The Galapagos Framework, Rose creates both short- and long-term action plans to resolve the serious situation that MDI finds itself in.

Short Term

Issue – Create some breathing space

Rose needs to give those delivering the transformation some respite from the current situation.

Resolution – Lower delivery targets

Rose must gain executive support to lower delivery targets in the short term. This will alleviate the pressure on the teams that are already struggling and allow some breathing space for further changes to be applied.

● **Issue - The human issues of a lack of trust, collaboration, and a culture of fear**

The impact of the human issues resulting from the toxic culture is significant and needs to be tackled with some urgency.

● **Resolution – Create The Island and follow *Galapagos Principle* 1: *Culture is king***

Trust and Collaboration

Rose must set up The Island structure. It is essential that The Leadership Function sets the example, emphasizing that The Island creates an environment that promotes a collaborative way of working and that everyone must operate on the basis of mutual trust and respect.

The leadership team must also create and communicate a clear and consistent strategy to ensure that all staff are guided by the same north star.

Psychological Safety

It is incumbent on The Leadership Function to eliminate the fear of failure and forge team cohesion by ensuring that The Island operates in an atmosphere of collective responsibility. That is, The Island works as a unified TEAM! (no individual succeeds/fails only the TEAM! succeeds/fails).

● **Issue – Organizational and skills/incentives issues**

Rose must tackle the organizational and skills issues that are enabling political game playing to thrive and allowing teams to operate in a dysfunctional manner.

● **Resolution – Remove silos and align incentives to the transformation strategy**

The Island

The creation of The Island structure itself will remove the organizational silos. Rose understands that ego and fear drive politics, and tackling the human issues outlined above will eliminate the practices that are allowing politics and defensive/passive–aggressive behavior to flourish.

Approaches to Incentivization

A consistent approach to incentivization will have a direct and positive effect on removing the toxic culture that exists within MDI, and the involvement of the Chief Human Resources Officer (CHRO) is critical to the effective delivery of this.

Incentives and compensation strategies must be aligned with the vision, goals, and objectives of the transformation itself. This is essential to ensure that all functions/teams and individuals are pulling in the same direction.

Long Term

Issue – Maintain the support of the board

Rose must retain continued support from the board for the changes that need to be made.

Resolution – Keep the board informed of progress

Rose has adhered to *Galapagos Principle 9: Establish and automate metrics and reporting early* and will secure the continued support of the board by keeping them updated on progress using the near-real-time, tangible metrics that are being produced from The Island.

Issue – Cultural transformation

There is a clear need for a broader cultural transformation at MDI.

Resolution 1 – Disseminate the culture that has been nurtured on The Island

The Island will create a culture that is conducive to digital change, and this will set the standard for the wider cultural transformation of MDI.

This process will take time but the regular communication of how MDI's core values align with the culture and the vision will ensure that this process does not lose focus.

Resolution 2 – Develop/hire new leaders

MDI may have to look to develop or hire new leaders to inspire and promote the adoption of the new, more collaborative, cultural norms, and tackle the existing leadership issues. These new leaders could be developed from MDI's existing talent pool or hired into the organization from outside.

Conclusion

Rose clearly has a difficult task on her hands, and she knows that successful delivery of the digital transformation requires significant organizational and cultural change within MDI.

Company culture is critical to the success of digital transformation programs. In any company where a non-collaborative culture exists, silos are created, which in turn leads to defensive and political behavior which impacts delivery.

There are many companies where blame and internal politics are prevalent, creativity is stifled, and there are lots of very influential *old-guard* types who are comfortable with the status quo and are reluctant to change (possibly because these individuals have, over the years, become master manipulators and expert politicians).

The successful implementation of Rose's short- and long-term action plans, within the current MDI environment, transforms the culture, improves the way in which the delivery teams operate, and puts the transformation program on a sound footing to deliver success.

All names, companies/organizations, characters, and incidents portrayed in this case study are fictitious. No identification with organizations or actual persons (living or deceased) is intended or should be inferred.

Chapter 29

Case Study Rose's Story Part 2: Leadership Vacuum

AT A GLANCE

- *Rose must deliver on a strategically important digital transformation in an organization where there is an absence of effective leadership, which results in the vision and strategy for the transformation not being communicated effectively.*
- *Coupled with the leadership issues, the organizational structure that currently exists is unsuitable for effective digital change.*
- *Rose is familiar with The Galapagos Framework and uses this to construct both short- and long-term action plans to deal with the situation and deliver transformational success.*

Introduction

In part one of this case study, Rose tackled the issues of a toxic culture and dysfunctional teams operating in a way that was detrimental to the delivery of MDI's (Mythical Deposits Incorporated) digital transformation strategy.

In the second part of this case study, Rose is confronted with ineffective leadership, failures in strategy, and an organizational structure that is unsuited to transformational change.

DOI: 10.1201/9781003404217-38

Absence of Effective Leadership

Rose has noticed that there is a high degree of micromanagement among several senior leaders involved in the delivery of the transformation initiative. These individuals are so wrapped up in the day-to-day details that they are unable to paint a clear and compelling picture of what the future will look like and are therefore struggling to motivate their teams.

This approach is stifling innovation, team development and motivation, and is preventing effective leadership from being exercised.

Action Plan: Absence of Effective Leadership

The current situation is acting as a drag on the delivery performance of the transformation. Once more, Rose uses her extensive knowledge of The Galapagos Framework to create both short- and long-term action plans to tackle the leadership vacuum.

Issue: Leadership vacuum

Individuals in leadership positions are so deep in the weeds of delivery that they cannot provide effective leadership.

Short Term

Resolution – Align leadership incentives to *how* delivery is achieved

The management of incentives for the leaders of the transformation program should be aligned with *how* delivery is achieved as well as *what* is delivered.

Positioning incentives in this way will shine a light on ineffective leadership behavior and allow MDI's board to address the issues and challenge the responsible individuals.

Tackling those that are creating the vacuum will improve delivery velocity and increase staff morale.

Long Term

Resolution – Develop/hire new leaders

Similar to the issue of cultural transformation, presented in part one of this case study, new leaders may have to be developed or hired into MDI to solve the problem of the existing leadership vacuum over the longer term.

Both the issues of cultural transformation and a leadership vacuum have the same long-term solution, that is, develop/hire new leaders.

Vision and Strategy Not Clearly Defined

The lack of effective leadership has resulted in the vision for the digital transformation (and strategies to support this) being unclear and not communicated effectively across MDI. This, in turn, has led to management teams, responsible for the delivery of the transformation, being unsure of:

- How to control conflicting priorities between delivery requests coming from the digital transformation function and requests from other areas.
- The best resourcing strategy to adopt, resulting in a failure to allocate the right number, type, and quality of resources at the right time into key delivery areas to support the transformation.

The disconnect between the vision, the strategy, and the delivery of the strategy makes it almost impossible for MDI to deliver any quick wins with this transformation initiative.

The leadership team of MDI's digital transformation should not be regarded as solely responsible for the failings. The board of MDI must also bear some of the accountability. They have overseen MDI's leadership team and are either unaware of the situation or have not seen it as significant enough to intervene.

Action Plan: Vision and Strategy Not Clearly Defined

The leadership failings that Rose has detected within the transformation initiative are having a serious and detrimental impact on the delivery of the strategy.

Once again Rose turns to The Galapagos Framework and identifies that the failures in leadership within MDI's digital transformation align directly with one of the common issues tackled by The Galapagos Framework (i.e., *strategy and direction are not clear and are not anchored in the businesses core values and competencies*).

Rose understands the criticality of this leadership failure and creates a short-term action plan that should be executed with some urgency, to overcome this problem.

Short Term

> **Issue – Strategy and direction are not clear and are not anchored in the business's core values and competencies.**

All staff must understand the rationale behind the transformation strategy to help mitigate the risk of resistance to change.

| ◉ | **Resolution – Zero ambiguity in the strategy. Communicate it often.** |

The Leadership Function of The Island (created in part one of this case study) must clarify the vision, including the key elements of the culture that need to be adopted. The vision must be aligned and anchored to the core values of MDI. The "C" suite executive(s) must communicate the vision to all areas of MDI to demonstrate that the digital transformation has the full backing of the board.

The strategy must be communicated consistently and frequently (in the short term), by very senior executives, to ensure that the message is complied with.

Organizational Structure

Rose sees that the misfiring performance of the transformation program at MDI is compounded by a complex matrix management structure, which has evolved over time and is contributing to conflict and the political chicaneries that are prevalent within the program. The structure is slowing down delivery and is leading to a lack of accountability and confusion due to conflicting reporting lines.

In the current, relatively small, digital transformation that MDI is embarking upon, Rose has identified no fewer than 12 different teams (ranging from Product Development, through Sales and Marketing, to Technology, Program Delivery, Legal and Compliance, etc.) that all report to different management lines and that are critical to the successful delivery of the digital transformation.

This structure is understandable given that most of these are discrete functions. However, through the use of The Galapagos Framework, Rose knows that this structure is at odds with a delivery philosophy where everyone is driving toward the same end goal, the pace of execution and decision-making must be fast, and there is a need to have most of these functions committed solely to the digital transformation (pretty much to the exclusion of everything else).

A very complex matrix structure can result in behavior that slows down delivery significantly and increases the complexity of program governance.

Rose has identified instances in MDI where the effort of many delivery teams has been discreetly redirected away from the digital transformation to other *more pressing* areas in the hope that this goes unnoticed.

When this redirection of effort becomes apparent, Rose sees situations quickly arising where this becomes an area of conflict between multiple managers. As this struggle continues, the staff on the ground are left unsure of where their priorities truly lie (as ultimately, it's their line manager who is in control of their performance reviews and associated compensation).

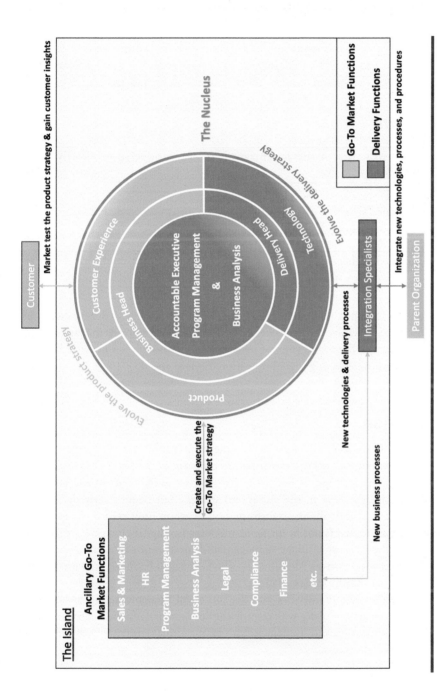

Figure 29.1 The Island structure.

Action Plan: Organizational Structure

The structure of MDI is not supportive of the highly collaborative and communicative working style that is required for effective digital transformations.

Rose looks to *How The Galapagos Framework resolves the common issues. – The Organizational Factors* and creates a short-term action plan to address the problem.

Short Term

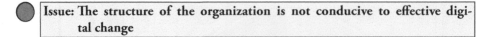

Issue: The structure of the organization is not conducive to effective digital change

A heavily siloed structure exists which is creating an atmosphere of mistrust leading to defensive behavior.

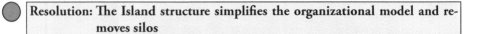

Resolution: The Island structure simplifies the organizational model and removes silos

Rose understands that The Island structure of The Galapagos Framework has been designed to resolve the issues caused by organizational models that are unsuited to digital change. The Island's cross-functional nature promotes a working style that is more suited to delivering digital transformations at speed.

Conclusion

In part one of this case study, Rose tackled the toxic culture and dysfunctional teams that existed within the MDI transformation program.

In the second part of this case study, Rose addresses the issues of a lack of effective leadership, resulting in the vision and strategy not being clearly defined and communicated, and finally the transformation program itself existing in an organizational structure that is not fit for rapid and effective digital change.

Clearly, the issues at MDI are significant and cover some of the *Human Elements* and *Organizational Factors*, identified by The Galapagos Framework, which lead to so many digital transformations failing.

Rose's use of The Framework and the successful implementation of her short- and long-term action plans will resolve the leadership failings, align the teams, transform the culture, and implement an organizational structure that will deliver transformational success.

All names, companies/organizations, characters, and incidents portrayed in this case study are fictitious. No identification with organizations or actual persons (living or deceased) is intended or should be inferred.

Chapter 30

Case Study Joanne's Story Part 1: Leadership Conflict

AT A GLANCE

- *Joanne has been hired into Mythical Deposits Incorporated (MDI) to recover a failing digital transformation program.*
- *The leadership structure at MDI is complex with joint heads of the business and multiple different teams required to support the delivery.*
- *Joanne uncovers an environment where conflict at the top and corporate ambiguity are impeding delivery.*
- *Joanne is familiar with The Galapagos Framework and uses this to construct a short-term action plan to mitigate the delivery risks of this ambiguity.*

Introduction

Joanne has been hired into Mythical Deposits Incorporated (MDI) to recover a failing digital transformation program. MDI has, so far, spent millions of dollars trying to deliver its products via new digital channels.

However, nine months into the program, there has been very little in the way of delivery, and what has been produced falls significantly below the expectations of the joint business heads. Defect rates are high and the functionality that has been presented often meets with the phrase *This is not what we asked for...*

DOI: 10.1201/9781003404217-39

Dave and John are the co-heads of the business; they have risen through the ranks of various organizations, where fast-paced and dynamic environments have valued their confidence and strength as ideal leadership characteristics. Both are highly driven and have very clear, and often very strong, opinions of what deliveries will drive the business forward and therefore take priority.

Joanne has identified some key factors that are leading to the lack of effective delivery of the transformation program.

In part one of this two-part case study, leadership conflict and corporate ambiguity will be explored.

In part two, MDI's heavy-weight governance model and its impacts will be examined.

Overview

Dave and John are both perceived to be very strong leaders with very clear views of what they believe is right for the business. This inevitably leads to differences of opinion and a certain amount of conflict. Tension at the top is to be expected and, in some cases, encouraged to avoid the leadership team from descending into groupthink.

However, the very reasons why Dave and John have reached senior leadership roles are the same reasons why they struggle in a joint-head position. Joanne has discovered that the co-head conflict is inhibiting effective and efficient decision-making which is resulting in time and cost overruns.

The differences of opinion between Dave and John are leading to the co-heads using subtle nuances in wording when each is communicating strategy and requirements to the delivery teams.

What items should be delivered, and the priority of these, changes frequently resulting in some teams working on items that are not the most important. This is causing tension further down the chain between elements of the Delivery Function, who are pursuing differing goals in the face of imprecise direction.

MDI is in danger of finding itself in a vicious cycle of conflict but now at the heart of delivery.

Corporate Ambiguity

Joanne is clear that the conflict between Dave and John is acting as a drag on delivery timelines and leading to increasing costs. There have been several instances where what was delivered was not what the business wanted, and as such, the various delivery teams are now in a position where they are continually seeking clarifications, resulting in further delays and inefficiencies.

This level of corporate ambiguity suits Dave and John as it allows them to adjust their position on strategy, priority, and the detail of delivery items without taking much, if any, responsibility for the impact that this is having on delivery, both in terms of time and cost.

Action Plan: Corporate Ambiguity

Joanne is in a delicate situation and must act sensitively. She knows that having a co-head structure does not lend itself to conducting rapid and effective business change; however, changing the leadership team is not an option.

If left unchecked, it is easy to conceive of a situation where the tensions between Dave and John lead to destructive behaviors that drive political game-playing and maneuvering which ultimately results in one of the co-heads moving on, but not before many months/years of reducing the effectiveness of the delivery teams.

Given that the leadership structure will remain in place, Joanne uses her extensive knowledge of The Galapagos Framework to create a short-term action plan to mitigate the negative effects of corporate ambiguity.

Short Term

Issue – Professional/corporate ambiguity

Joanne must minimize the delays and wasted effort resulting from the professional/ corporate ambiguity that is coming from the joint heads of the business.

Resolution – The Leadership Function must eliminate professional/corporate ambiguity.

Understanding how The Galapagos Framework resolves *The Common Issues – The Human Element – Failures in leadership* allows Joanne to tackle the problem.

First, she identifies all areas of ambiguity that are stemming from the co-heads and highlights these as delivery risks/issues against the transformation program. Each risk/issue is impact assessed and prioritized for resolution.

Within The Galapagos Framework, it is incumbent upon the Accountable Executive (AE), Business Head, and Delivery Head (or in this case Delivery Heads[1]) to ensure that clarity is sought in all matters.

---

[1] Strictly speaking, there should only ever be one individual in the Business Head role. However, there may be situations where The Galapagos Framework is adopted for use in an organization where co-heads exist in the Business or Delivery Head role. In these cases, it may be too much of an upheaval to remove one of the co-heads. This case study shows how to overcome the impacts of conflict in these situations.

Provide Flexibility

Joanne must perform a delicate balancing act by providing the joint heads with the flexibility they need to change tack on delivery items that are not required for some time (without compromising the delivery of the transformation program), while ensuring that there is little/no ambiguity regarding the items that are to be worked on in the immediate and near term.

Given this, Joanne alerts the AE (Tony) to the impacts of the most pressing issues arising from the ambiguity of the joint delivery heads (Dave and John) and Tony convenes a 60-Minute Strategic Action Session to close out the areas of uncertainty.

The outputs of the Strategic Action Session (i.e., the items that will be acted on now) are as follows:

Clearly define the order and priority of delivery items where uncertainty exists

All items where clarification is sought are ranked in terms of priority and order of delivery. This allows Joanne to hone in on the items that are presenting the biggest risks to the delivery of the transformation.

Remove ambiguity on immediate and near-term deliveries

All immediate and near-term deliveries are to be acted on (in priority order) as soon as the Strategic Action Session concludes.

A process of UX-led requirements extraction[2] will be carried out on each of these deliveries.

The UX designer is partnered with a Business Analyst to confirm that the data items that Dave and John want to see on the screens currently exist or can be derived from the data that is already available in the MDI data sources. This minimizes the risk of there being issues when the UX prototype is converted to programming code.

Conclusion

Joanne clearly has a difficult task on her hands. Senior leadership challenges are never easy and should not be confronted head-on; keeping the co-heads on side will be critical to successful delivery.

Joanne must tread carefully to circumvent the issues and mitigate, where possible, the negative impact of conflicts between Dave and John.

---

[2] These are short sessions where a UX designer sits with the co-heads to mockup a visual representation of what it is that they require.

The action plan that Joanne is implementing will remove delivery ambiguity and will result in a clear direction of what needs to be delivered, and in what order, while still providing the co-heads with the flexibility to change tack on delivery items that are not required for some time.

The UX-led requirements extraction will result in a decrease in rework as areas of ambiguity are removed.

In Part 2 of this case study, MDI's complex organizational structure, heavyweight governance model, and the impacts of these on digital transformation will be examined along with the approaches that Joanne will take to resolve these issues.

All names, companies/organizations, characters, and incidents portrayed in this case study are fictitious. No identification with organizations or actual persons (living or deceased) is intended or should be inferred.

Chapter 31

Case Study Joanne's Story Part 2: Heavy-Weight Governance

AT A GLANCE

- *Joanne has been hired into Mythical Deposits Incorporated (MDI) to recover a failing digital transformation program.*
- *Joanne uncovers an environment where a heavy-weight approach to governance is impeding delivery.*
- *Joanne is familiar with The Galapagos Framework and uses this to construct a short-term action plan.*
- *Joanne gains board approval to make the changes that are required to ensure that the digital transformation proceeds in a more efficient and effective way.*

Introduction

In part one of this case study, Joanne addressed the impact of leadership conflict, corporate ambiguity, and the negative effects these were having on the delivery of MDI's (Mythical Deposits Incorporated) digital transformation strategy.

DOI: 10.1201/9781003404217-40

In the second part of this case study, Joanne is confronted with the detrimental effects of a heavy-weight approach to governance.

Heavy-Weight Governance

Prior to Joanne's arrival, and in an attempt to wrestle back some control of cost and timeline overruns of the transformation program, the MDI board has thrown more governance at the problem.

Joanne arrives in a situation where a hierarchy of six Steering Committees and delivery boards are in existence. The administrative overhead in every area of delivery is significant.

Individuals, whose time would be better spent focusing on the digital transformation, are instead asked to produce PowerPoint slides and delivery updates and then to present these to each of the Steering Committees and delivery boards.

Joanne attends the 9 am daily stand-up. This meeting lasts for over an hour and has in excess of 50 individuals in attendance, the majority of whom neither contribute to nor take anything from the meeting.

Things are so bad that it's taking almost two months just to gain approval from the relevant boards and steering committees to hire a single additional resource to assist in delivery (even though the budget is available). By the time the role is released to the market and filled, the elapsed time from the identification of the need to the landing of the resource will be six months!

By throwing more governance at the cost and timeline overruns, the MDI board has exacerbated the situation. They have introduced more inefficiency, more work, and reduced the pace of delivery.

Morale has also been impacted with highly skilled individuals spending significant amounts of their time producing status updates, and attending board and steering committees, rather than performing the skilled roles for which they were hired.

Action Plan: Heavy-Weight Governance

Using her extensive knowledge of The Galapagos Framework, Joanne understands that this issue aligns directly with one of the common issues identified, and resolved, by The Framework (viz. *Heavy-weight governance is increasing costs and reducing delivery efficiency*).

Using The Framework as a guide, Joanne creates a short-term action plan to address the problem.

Short Term

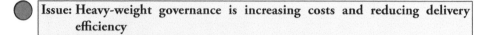

Issue: Heavy-weight governance is increasing costs and reducing delivery efficiency

The impact on cost and delivery timelines of multiple layers of red tape and bureaucracy are significant. In an attempt to take control of the program, MDI's board has actually put the entire transformation in jeopardy.

Resolution 1: Present the facts

Joanne must gather metrics on the cost and delivery impacts of the current heavy-weight governance process and present these back to MDI's board.

Once the full impact is understood, the board may wish to change its governance approach.

Resolution 2: A balanced/lighter touch governance model

Once the MDI board agrees to modify its approach to governance, Joanne must implement a light-touch governance model.

Joanne reviews all meetings and attendees and strictly limits the number of meetings, the time allocated to these, and the number of attendees.

Joanne reduces the number of boards and steering committees from six to two – an operational delivery board and a strategic Steering Committee (which will handle all budgetary approvals above the approval limit set for the Accountable Executive).

Further, Joanne ensures that a risk-based approach to budgetary approvals is adhered to, with large budget requests receiving more scrutiny than smaller requests.

Given the fast pace of digital transformations, Joanne advocates for a principles-based approach to decision-making to allow managers and leaders to make decisions based on broad principles rather than strict rules. This approach will provide flexibility and increase the pace of decision-making.

Resolution 3: Lead, don't dictate

Finally, Joanne ensures that those leaders involved with the transformation do not adopt a micromanagement approach to problem resolution. She promotes a more guidance-based attitude which will allow leaders to demonstrate their trust in the teams tasked with solving the problems.

Conclusion

Joanne understands that throwing more governance at a problem is almost never the right way to proceed. The knock-on effect of this approach can and will worsen the situation. The key challenge Joanne faces here is to reduce the administrative burden whilst still ensuring effective control of delivery cost, time, and quality.

The streamlined process that Joanne puts in place will ensure that governance control, delivery velocity, and quality are all maintained.

All names, companies/organizations, characters, and incidents portrayed in this case study are fictitious. No identification with organizations or actual persons (living or deceased) is intended or should be inferred.

Chapter 32

Case Study Tony's Story: Working Environment

AT A GLANCE

- *Tony is running a delivery team in a hybrid model – using both internal staff and staff supplied by an external consultancy – to deliver a digital transformation program for Mythical Deposits Incorporated (MDI).*
- *Due to the increasing workload, Tony must rapidly expand the size of the team and it is clear that the team will quickly outgrow its current office space.*
- *Tony understands the importance of having the delivery teams in a space that promotes collaboration.*
- *Tony gains approval to move the team to a more collaborative working space and sees a dramatic increase in the delivery output.*

Introduction

Tony is tasked with delivering a large digital transformation program for Mythical Deposits Incorporated (MDI).

The size of the program and the urgency to deliver means that there is a need to quickly increase the staffing levels of the team.

This rapid expansion means that the team will outgrow its current office space and there is no additional space, in the existing building, that can be made available.

The Current Working Environment

Currently, the team works in a standard corporate environment where staff are arranged in banks of desks with a small number of meeting rooms (which appear to be perpetually booked out) available on the office floor. There is very little natural light (with most of the window seats taken up by the managers of the various functions), and there are no breakout areas or spaces where staff can easily hold impromptu meetings to share ideas or talk through complex problems.

The floor is mostly silent and consists of people sitting at their computers working through their tasks with the only conversations taking place at the coffee machine or the water cooler.

It is, in short, a bland and sterile environment.

With the need to rapidly increase the team size, Tony sees the opportunity to move the team from the current environment to a more *collaborative* workspace.

Collaborative Workspace

Research into suitable areas in the current building has drawn a blank and forced Tony to examine the possibility of moving the entire team offsite. Fortunately, there are several companies offering relatively inexpensive (and frankly better) workspaces a short walk from the main office. This is significant as it allows Tony's team to be able to attend meetings in the main office, as and when required, and means the senior leadership team (and members of other teams) can pop in for informal meetings or just check on progress with minimal inconvenience.

The workspaces that Tony evaluates are a world away from the existing corporate environment that the team is currently working in.

These office spaces are specifically designed for creativity, productivity, and collaborative working with plenty of natural light and the ability to arrange the seating away from rows to pods of desks. There are ample breakout spaces and meeting rooms that allow staff to move away from their desk to discuss topics with other team members, without disturbing the rest of the team.

Tony puts forward a proposal and gains approval to move his entire team to the new workspace. Coupled with this, Tony makes the decision to allow the team to dress in casual clothes rather than the mandated formal business attire of the main office.

Impact

After the initial euphoria – of moving away from a staid working environment into a space where there are plenty of collaboration areas, ceiling-to-floor windows, lots of meeting rooms (and the additional benefit of free beer after 4 pm) – has settled down, Tony notices a clear change in how the team is operating.

Figure 32.1 Differences in working environment.

Walking into the new work area, there is a noticeable buzz that had not been present previously, and a more relaxed atmosphere. There are regular huddles of people around computer screens and whiteboards discussing how to resolve issues or move forward with the transformation. Individuals from other teams are keen to attend meetings in the new location and actively seek out reasons to visit.

Tony has been producing productivity statistics for quite some time and when comparing the statistics from before and after the move, he sees a clear increase in the throughput of delivery items after the move. After a couple of months working in this new location, Tony sees that there is a 27% increase in delivery throughput. This improvement in productivity more than pays for the cost of the space that is being used.

When Tony reports the productivity statistics to senior leaders, this starts to cause a bit of a stir within MDI and, with tangible benefits being realized, other teams soon start to follow Tony's lead.

Conclusion

If you are spending a significant amount of your time in a place of work, it is important that the environment inspires you. We are humans and being arranged into rows of desks like automatons to produce *things* robs us of some of our humanity.

In contrast, an esthetically pleasing workspace has numerous *human* benefits; stimulating creativity, improved mental well-being, increased motivation, better communication, collaboration, and so on. More than this, however, the environment in which you work reflects the company culture. A company that does not value the more human aspects of the working environment is unlikely to understand the value of creativity, collaboration, communication, and innovation.

Put simply, people work better in an environment that is suited to their style of work.

All names, companies/organizations, characters, and incidents portrayed in this case study are fictitious. No identification with organizations or actual persons (living or deceased) is intended or should be inferred.

Chapter 33

Case Study Phil's Story: The Galapagos Framework and Success

AT A GLANCE

- Phil has been hired into Mythical Deposits Incorporated (MDI) to deliver a new product via digital channels.
- Phil has extensive knowledge of The Galapagos Framework and uses the principles of The Framework to set the culture and build the organizational structures to ensure success.
- Phil proceeds to use The Galapagos Framework and delivers a WOW factor product in record time.
- Use of The Galapagos Framework becomes the de facto standard for digital transformation programs across the MDI organization.

Introduction

Phil has been presented with an exciting opportunity. He has been hired into Mythical Deposits Incorporated (MDI) to deliver a new product via digital channels. MDI has been burnt by previous failed attempts in other areas to deliver products in this way and as such, the Board of MDI has given Phil a significant level of autonomy to ...*just get this done...*

DOI: 10.1201/9781003404217-42

Phil is a transformation specialist who is extremely familiar with The Galapagos Framework, and he sees this as a perfect opportunity to use The Framework to deliver this program of work.

Greenfield

Phil arrives at MDI and is surprised to find that there is almost no delivery team, no technical infrastructure, no software, and no delivery process.

The resources that have been assigned to this multimillion-dollar initiative consist of the head of the business that requires the new product – Dave, and three current employees who have been with MDI for some time: a technical manager – Steve, a programmer – Ian, and a business analyst – Roger.

The scope of this delivery is clear to Phil and there is an enormous amount to do:

- ■ Implement the structures of The Galapagos Framework.
- ■ Hire the new (globally distributed) delivery team.
- ■ Define and build the product.
- ■ Build the IT infrastructure that will run the new product and make it globally accessible.

First Things First – The Galapagos Roadmap

Phil immediately gets to work by creating The Island structure and follows The Galapagos Roadmap to set up The Island structure.

Bringing The Island to Life

Appoint The Leadership Function Roles

Phil begins the process by allocating The Leadership Function roles.

The Accountable Executive (AE)

Phil gains approval to install the global head of business, Graham, in The Accountable Executive (AE) role.

Combined Business Head and Product Roles

The business head, Dave, is also responsible for defining the product strategy. Given this, Phil decides to combine the Business Head and Product roles and have Dave act in both capacities.

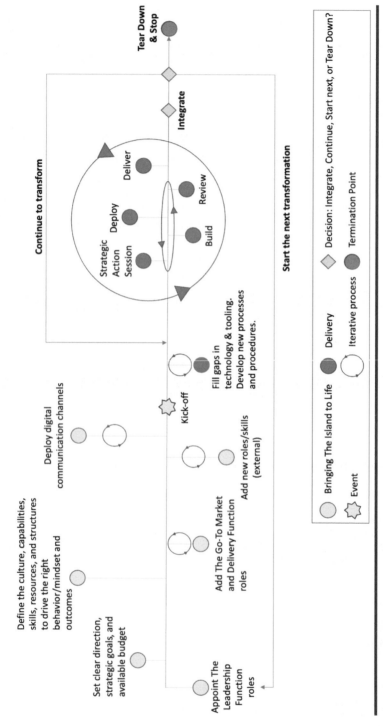

Figure 33.1   The Galapagos Roadmap.

Delivery Head and Technology

Phil himself takes the Delivery Head role and installs the existing technical manager, Steve, as the lead of The Technology Function.

Customer Experience

In the absence of any suitable candidates within MDI, Phil goes to market to fill The Customer Experience Function.[1]

Strategic Action Session: Strategy, Direction, Budget, Capabilities, Skills, and Resources

Following The Galapagos Strategy Review Cycle, Phil kicks off the first 60-Minute Strategic Action Session.

The aim of this session is to ensure that the strategy is clear (and rooted in the core values of MDI), the objectives are set, and the budget has been agreed, is ring-fenced, and is available to spend.

Further, a Workforce Strategy and an action to deliver a plan to close any skills gaps must also be tackled in this session.

Finally, The Ancillary Go-To Market Functions that will be required to get the product to market and The Delivery Functions (including The Integration Specialists) that will be required to build the product must be identified.

The Galapagos Strategy Review Cycle

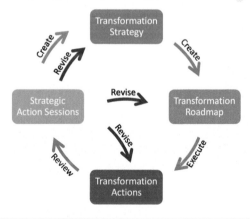

Figure 33.2   The Galapagos Strategy Review Cycle.

---

[1]   Ultimately, Phil hires a customer experience lead who has extensive experience with UX design.

The ACT[2] items coming out of this session are to:

- Create The Model[3] and populate this artifact with the first iterations of both the Transformation Strategy and the Transformation Roadmap.
- Create The Workforce Strategy to allow the skills gaps to be assessed and produce a plan for filling these gaps without compromising the delivery of the transformation program.
- Identify and engage The Ancillary Go-To Market and Delivery Functions.

Processes Used and Artifacts Produced

> **Process**: Appoint The Leadership Function Roles
>
> *The Island has now been created, albeit with only one function at this point.*
>
> **Process**: Strategic Action Session
>
> *The first (of many) Strategic Action Sessions has taken place.*
>
> **Artifact**: The Model
>
> *The Model has been created and has been populated with the first iteration of the following artifacts*:
>
> **Artifact**: The Transformation Strategy
>
> **Artifact**: The Transformation Roadmap
>
> **Artifact**: The Workforce Strategy
>
> **Process**: Ancillary Go-To Market and Delivery Functions
>
> *The teams (and individuals) that will make up The Go-To Market (e.g., Sales and Marketing, Legal, Compliance etc.) and Delivery (e.g., Application Development, Security, Infrastructure, Cloud etc.) Functions have been identified and added to The Island. The Island is now becoming more fully formed.*

At this point the skeleton of The Island has been created, most of The Leadership Function roles have been filled (and Phil has gone to market to begin to fill The Customer Experience Function).

---

[2] See *Chapter 6, Emerging Better Practices – The 60-Minute Strategic Action Session.*
[3] See *Chapter 19 – The Model.*

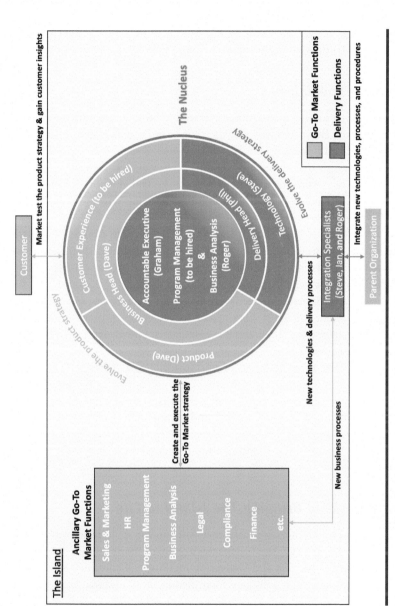

Figure 33.3   The Island structure with individuals assigned to roles.

The Ancillary Go-To Market and Delivery Functions (including The Integration Specialists) have been identified and engaged.

Further, the first iterations of the Transformation Strategy, the Transformation Roadmap, and the Workforce Strategy (identifying the skills gaps that need to be filled) have been created and added to The Model and a plan is being created to fill the skills gaps identified in the Workforce Strategy.

Integration Specialists

As mentioned previously, upon Phil's arrival into MDI there are only three individuals, outside of the Business Head (Dave), that have been allocated to the program (viz. Steve, Ian, and Roger).

Phil understands that these three existing staff members are critical to the successful delivery of the program, as they will help the new members of The Island to build their internal network and connect with the teams and individuals who are required to assist them with the transformation.

The importance of having these individuals in the team cannot be overstated. MDI is a huge organization with key functions (and individuals) spread across the globe. Navigating this enormously complex structure without any internal help will slow the delivery down significantly.

Steve, Ian, and Roger have been with MDI for many years and are extremely knowledgeable about the inner workings of MDI's complex processes and who to contact *to get things done*. They also have extensive knowledge of MDI's internal systems and data sources.

Phil places these three members of staff into the role of Integration Specialists as they will help to foster stronger internal capabilities among the other members of The Island (covering building internal networks of people and navigating complex internal processes and procedures) and, given their excellent understanding of MDI's internal systems, are ideally placed to assess how the systems, processes, and procedures used on The Island can be integrated back into MDI (the parent organization).

Ongoing Tasks in Bringing The Island to Life

There are several highly iterative tasks that will run for some time in the Bringing The Island to Life phase of The Galapagos Roadmap. For example, the staffing of The Ancillary Go-To Market and Delivery Functions will continue, as will the hiring of individuals to fill the skills gaps identified in the Workforce Strategy.

Digital Communication Channels

Fortunately, MDI has an extensive array of digital communications channels and tools that have been in place for some time, and which are required to support the globally distributed nature of the business. There is, therefore, no need for Phil to deploy new digital communication technologies as what is in place currently is fit for purpose.

Kick-off

When most/all of the skills gaps have been filled and The Ancillary Go-To Market and Delivery Functions are fully staffed, Phil asks Graham (The Accountable Executive) to lead a kick-off meeting.

The CEO of MDI, keen to ensure that any resistance to change is mitigated, will open the kick-off by describing how important the transformation is to MDI achieving its strategic business objectives and highlighting that this initiative has his full backing.

The meeting provides Graham with an opportunity to set the tone and culture that he wants to see disseminated throughout the transformation and allows him to communicate the vision and strategy and describe how this transformation initiative will move the organization forward while remaining aligned with MDI's core values.

The preferred communication styles will be highlighted to ensure that the pace and quality of communication are consistently high.

A central repository has been created with all the contact and communication channel details, for the transformation. Graham will use this to highlight each of the areas involved in the transformation so that everyone understands their role in the execution of the strategy. This will also act as a common reference point to allow staff members to contact the teams and individuals that will help them achieve their goals.

Culture

One of the many benefits of building out a new team to deliver a greenfield program is that Phil, Dave, and Graham (The Leadership Function of The Island) can set the internal culture that is to be nurtured.

The culture that The Leadership Function is instilling is one of high collaboration, open, honest, and friendly communication at all times, and the fostering of very close relationships across all the teams and functions of The Island.

The leadership team will ensure that everyone is inspired to communicate openly and to own their mistakes as and when they occur. They lead by example, speaking openly to the team about situations where they could have done things better themselves. This creates a culture of psychological safety and leads to a situation where people don't try and cover up mistakes but are instead open and honest about missteps that occur.

The positive impact on delivery of providing a psychologically safe space is difficult to overstate. When mistakes are made, or unexpected events occur (as they inevitably do), The Leadership Function is aware of these as and when they happen. This allows them to be highly reactive to issues and adjust plans and deliveries to absorb delays with minimal impact on the overall transformation.

A side effect of removing the fear of failure is that the delivery teams provide more accurate estimates of how long tasks will take, as they do not feel the pressure to reduce delivery times to an absolute minimum. Over a short number of weeks, delivery estimates become extremely accurate.

No Surprises

This shift in culture, and the increased accuracy of delivery estimation, allows Phil to commit to stakeholders that there will be *No Surprises* as to what will be delivered and when.

Given the history of failure at MDI in delivering this type of initiative, the *No Surprises* declaration proves an extremely powerful statement to make as a significant factor contributing to previous failures was stakeholder dissatisfaction, in seeing that what was delivered was not what they had asked for.

Team Cohesion, Fast Decision-Making, and Issue Resolution

Phil ensures that there are no barriers to communication across The Island, every team member feels that they can ask questions of, or challenge, anyone else (regardless of corporate grade/position).

This leads to a situation where, as issues are encountered, they are resolved quickly. There are no lengthy feedback cycles, as everyone knows who they should contact for specific information, and they do not hesitate to speak directly to other members of The Island, either face to face or by picking up the phone, as and when required.

Phil ensures that the team is laser focused on delivery. Thus, when a feature has been committed to be delivered by a specified date, this is invariably achieved. In turn, this leads to an increase in confidence (and trust) across all stakeholders as The Island is seen as a team that *can and will deliver*.

Reporting Lines

The Island structure creates clear and simple reporting lines, leading to absolute clarity regarding accountability. Product delivery (covering Technology and Program Direction) is the responsibility of Phil, all The Go-To Market Functions (covering Product Development, Sales & Marketing, Operations, etc.) are the responsibility of Dave and ultimate accountability for the entire transformation rests with Graham.

As well as clarifying accountability, this simple structure allows communication to be streamlined as everyone on The Island (and within MDI itself) knows exactly who they should contact if issues arise in any of The Delivery or Go-To Market Functions.

Geographic Isolation

Galapagos Principle 3: Geographic Isolation, satisfied by The Island structure, brings many benefits to the delivery of the transformation.

The Delivery Function is unencumbered by MDI's existing processes and technologies. Thus, Phil ensures that new lightweight, Agile, delivery processes and visualization technologies are adopted with minimal resistance.

The visualization technologies used allow anyone, at any time, to get a real-time view of where items are in the delivery pipeline.

UX (User Experience) designers work hand in hand with Business Analysts and the business representatives to lead a new UX-led requirements extraction process that improves the quality of the requirements produced.

Another benefit is that the technical teams are not hindered by the technical debt of MDI's legacy systems (as they are building an entirely new product) and integration with existing systems is via a clean set of APIs. This improves delivery velocity and allows product functionality to be delivered in a shorter timeframe.

Processes Used and Artifacts Produced

Process: Integration Specialists have been identified and assigned to this role

Steve, Ian, and Roger (given their extensive knowledge of MDI's inner workings) have been allocated to The Integration Specialists role.

Process: Staffing

The staffing of The Ancillary Go-To Market and Delivery Functions and the hiring of individuals to fill the skills gaps identified in the Workforce Strategy is well underway.

Process: Deploy Digital communication channels

MDI has extensive digital communication channels in place already so there is no additional work required in this area.

Process: Kick-off

The kick-off event has taken place and the teams (and individuals) that make up The Island are all aware of each other and the functions that each performs.

Process: Culture, communication, cohesion, and simple reporting lines

> *The Leadership Function has set in place the culture that is to be adopted on The Island, with communication and a high degree of team cohesion being important elements at the heart of the culture. The simplified reporting structure of The Island has been created and communicated to all.*

Artifact: The Model

> *The Model has been updated with the following artifacts*:
>
> **Artifact**: Culture Guide
>
> **Artifact**: Communications Strategy
>
> **Artifact**: Organizational Structure

Delivery

All of the tasks in the Bringing The Island to life phase of The Galapagos Roadmap have been completed (though some of the more long-running tasks of adding roles to The Go-To Market and Delivery Functions and hiring new skills externally may last for some more time) and Phil must now start on the Delivery phase.

Phil is well versed in The Galapagos Framework and has already started the process of *Fill gaps in technology & tooling* well before the *kick-off* event of the Bringing The Island to life phase,[4] as he knows this process is likely to run for some time and is inherently risky.

As a result of Phil's foresight, enough of the gaps in technology have been filled to allow delivery to begin in earnest.

All the elements of the Delivery phase of The Roadmap are highly iterative and the cycle of **Strategic Action Session**, **Build**, **Deploy**, **Review**, and **Deliver** begins.

Early UX Prototypes

The Customer Experience Function drives the production of early UX prototypes of product features, and these are being tested in the market, with current and prospective customers, thereby validating the product strategy.

As and when changes are requested by customers these are applied to the prototypes and replayed back to the customers *before* they are committed to programming code; this reduces costs and reduces the risk of the product strategy being misplaced, or the product delivery not meeting the customers' need.

---

[4] See *Chapter 13 – How does The Galapagos Framework Work in Practice? – Fast evolution of Technology and Processes and Deliver, Deliver, Deliver section.*

These prototypes (and supporting User Stories), once validated, become the requirements artifacts that the application developers use to develop programming code.

Expectation Management

Phil makes clear that *No Surprises* do not mean that occasionally timelines won't move. It does, however, mean that all stakeholders are made aware of these situations, and the reasons behind the moving timelines at the earliest opportunity. As such, when stakeholders see a demonstration of the product/product feature they know exactly what to expect and are never underwhelmed.

Stakeholder Support

Phil garners strong support from Graham (the AE) of The Island, and senior leaders in MDI, by delivering early iterations of the product on time and exceeding the stakeholders' expectations (on more than one occasion the functionality demonstrated to stakeholders results in a *WOW!* being delivered, much to the satisfaction of the entire delivery team).

This support and trust shield The Delivery Function from external *noise* when things get tough and issues are encountered, as stakeholders trust The Delivery Function to resolve the issues allowing it to focus solely on solving problems and getting the product built without distraction.

Digital Acceleration

The iterative delivery cycles continue until the first full production delivery of the product is released to MDI's customers. This delivery is met with very positive reviews from the customer base who regard the product as *best in class*.

Conclusion

The use of The Galapagos Framework by Phil, and the ensuing successful delivery, results in The Galapagos Framework becoming the *de facto* standard for all new product development at MDI.

There are many reasons why MDI found The Galapagos Framework so effective:

Increased Productivity and Delivery Performance

- ■ The use of The Island structure means that staff do not, for the most part, have to deal with any legacy processes, procedures, and systems that are not fit for

the delivery of digital change. Often these systems/processes were developed many years ago by individuals who have long since left the organization.
- All teams on The Island work in a highly collaborative environment where there is no fear of failure.

Risk Reduction

- Operational and delivery risks are reduced as the product strategy has been validated in the market (via UX prototypes of product features).
- Financial risks are also reduced, as the product features are delivered at a lower cost due in large part to there being no re-work needed once the product/product feature had been delivered, as requirements were not misunderstood.

Increased Profits and Standardization Using The Galapagos Framework

- *Profits are increased as the product and product features meet the business needs and exceeded the customers' expectation resulting in increased sales.*
- The use of The Galapagos Framework and the implementation of The Island structure are key factors that led to the successful delivery of the digital transformation and The Galapagos Framework becoming the standard for all digital transformation programs across the MDI organization.

All names, companies/organizations, characters, and incidents portrayed in this case study are fictitious. No identification with organizations or actual persons (living or deceased) is intended or should be inferred.

A Guide to the Leadership Guide

The Leadership Guide offers practical tips, best practices, and advice on organizational structure, culture, and leadership styles to help leaders successfully navigate digital transformation initiatives. What follows is a guide to creating your own organization's Leadership Guide.

Organizational Structure

The Island operates using a very flat organization with The Accountable Executive, Business Head, and Delivery Head roles leading the entire transformation and every other role on The Island comprising a totally flat organizational structure. The rationale behind this flat structure is to ensure maximum collaboration by breaking down silos and barriers to effective communication.

Roles and Responsibilities

To lead a successful transformation, however, The Leadership Function must also ensure that clear roles and responsibilities are established from the outset. This will create accountability and foster cooperation among the cross-functional teams.

Organizational Culture

As stated in *Galapagos Principle 1: Culture is king,* culture is driven by The Leadership Function (Accountable Executive, Business Head, and Delivery Head). The Island must foster a culture of free and open collaboration, communication, and innovation while removing any fear of failure.

The members of The Island must be encouraged to continuously explore new ideas and solutions by creating an environment that rewards creativity and controlled risk-taking. A continuous learning approach must be promoted to provide employees with the opportunities to explore and acquire new skills. Organizations cannot grow their business if they don't grow their people.

It is the purpose of the Organizational Culture section of the Leadership Guide to highlight the norms, behaviors, and core values of the culture that have been fostered and what effects this has had on the transformation.

Leadership Styles

The Galapagos Framework is suited to transformational/servant leader/collaborative and Agile leadership styles and is not suited to any form of command-and-control approach to leadership. Each leadership style will come into play to a greater or lesser degree depending on how far the transformation has progressed through The Galapagos Roadmap.

The early stages will require a transformational leadership style, providing inspiration and motivation while creating the shared vision and highlighting what this transformation will achieve, and why it is of strategic importance to the organization.

Subsequent stages will place more emphasis on collaborative, Agile, and servant leader approaches, empowering employees and building strong relationships based on mutual trust and respect, while embracing flexibility, adaptability, and continuous improvement.

Combining these leadership styles will promote open, honest, and friendly communication and, in concert with shared decision-making and close teamwork, will create a positive working environment that will be conducive to innovation and success. This, in turn, will allow The Island to swiftly respond in a positive fashion to inevitable changes in the transformation landscape. A high degree of emotional intelligence is required in collaborative, Agile, and servant leaders, and this skill will be brought to the fore during further stages of the transformation.

It is the purpose of the Leadership Styles section of the Leadership Guide to highlight what styles were used at each point of the transformation and with what degree of success.

Strategies for Success

As highlighted in *Chapter 2 – Common Issues*, if the strategy and direction are not clear and not anchored in the core business values and competencies, then this will lead to confusion with teams and individuals not pulling together and, in some instances, can increase the resistance to the transformation initiative itself.

It is therefore critical to create a clear and comprehensive strategy that outlines the organization's digital transformation goals. This will inform the timelines and required resources for the various stages of The Galapagos Roadmap and provide clear direction and focus.

The strategy must be communicated by a very senior executive (the CEO or as close to the CEO as possible) and must be communicated frequently in the early stages of the transformation initiative.

Further to the points highlighted in *Chapter 3 – Moving from Digital Transformation to Digital Acceleration*, a customer-centric approach to the transformation should be adopted. If the transformation is not solving the correct problem for the customer, then what is it trying to achieve in the first place? Organizations must ensure that they prioritize customer needs by focusing on improving customer experience. The purpose of The Customer Experience Function is to ensure that the organization is positioned to increase customer satisfaction and loyalty.

Aligned with a customer-centric approach, the organization must also ensure that the members of The Island develop and leverage partnerships by collaborating with technology vendors, industry experts, and other organizations to gain access to the latest innovations and insights.

Galapagos Principle 9: Establish and automate metrics and reporting early exists to ensure that data-driven decision-making is front and center of directing the transformation. Insights derived from these metrics will help assess progress and impact, identify areas for improvement, uncover new opportunities, and drive a more informed decision-making process. These metrics will help to answer the question of *How will we know if we have been successful?*

The topic of metrics is covered in the *Metrics* section of *Chapter 19 – The Model*.

Conclusion

By following the advice given in the Leadership Guide, leaders of future digital transformation initiatives can successfully drive digital change, positioning their organizations for growth and success. Embracing organizational change, fostering a culture of innovation, and adopting the right leadership styles will ensure that the digital transformation efforts are effectively executed and deliver tangible results.

Appendix B

Example Technology Matrix

Technology Matrix

The example Technology Matrix below provides an overview of some of the multitude of technologies and tools used in digital transformation initiatives, along with their primary function.

This is clearly not an exhaustive list as the digital landscape is continually evolving at a rapid pace as new tools and technologies emerge. Given this, it is likely that the technology column in the table will contain the actual product being used (e.g., Cloud Computing may well be changed to Amazon Web Services (AWS), Microsoft Azure, etc.) rather than the general technology area provided in the table below.

Please also note that the Impact and Relevance will be domain specific and, as such, what is provided below is just an example where ⬆ = High, ⬇ = Low, and ▬ = Neutral.

TABLE B.1   An Example Technology Matrix

Technology	Function	Impact	Relevance
Collaboration Tools	Improves communication, productivity, and efficiency of the team. Covers task management, file sharing, scheduling, document collaboration, project management, integration, knowledge management, etc.	⬆	⬆
Big Data Analytics	Analyzes large, complex datasets to uncover patterns, trends, and insights, driving informed decision-making.	⬆	⬆
Cloud Computing	Facilitates on-demand access to computing resources, including storage, processing, and networking.	⬆	⬆
Application Programming Interface (API's)	Abstracts the complexity of underlying systems to improve maintainability, interoperability, and scalability.	⬆	⬆
Automated Testing and Test-Driven Development	Software tools to execute test cases, compare the actual results with expected results, and report any discrepancies.	⬆	⬆
Dev Ops	Tools to improve integration between development and operations teams, enabling faster deployment, better monitoring, and quicker resolution of issues.	⬆	⬆
Containerization	Tools to package a service and its dependencies into a container, which is a lightweight, standalone, and executable software unit.	⬆	⬆
Container Orchestration	The automated management, scaling, and deployment of containers in large-scale, distributed systems.	⬆	⬆

(Continued)

TABLE B.1 (Continued)

Technology	Function	Impact	Relevance
Service Mesh	An infrastructure layer that handles inter-service communication in a microservices architecture.	⬆	⬆
Artificial Intelligence	Models and machines that are capable of tasks resembling human intelligence (e.g., problem solving, decision-making, and learning).	⬆	⬆
Blockchain	Provides a decentralized, secure, and transparent method for recording and sharing digital transactions.	—	⬇
Internet of Things (IoT)	Connects devices and sensors to collect, analyze, and exchange data, enabling improved efficiency and real-time insights.	⬆	⬇
Robotic Process Automation	Automates repetitive, rule-based tasks, reducing manual effort and improving efficiency.	—	⬇
Virtual Reality	Immerses users in fully digital environments, providing new opportunities for training, collaboration, and customer experiences.	⬇	⬇
Augmented Reality	Enhances physical environments with digital information and visualizations, improving user experiences and engagement.	—	⬇
5G Networks	Offers enhanced connectivity, faster data transmission, and reduced latency, enabling advanced digital services and applications.	⬆	—
Cybersecurity	Technologies and practices to protect digital assets, infrastructure, and data from unauthorized access, theft, or damage.	⬆	⬆

Appendix C

Example Metrics

Example Metrics

Monitoring the success of any digital transformation initiative requires the organization to use several different metrics. Examples of some of the more common metrics are provided below.

Key Performance Indicators (KPIs)

KPIs are quantifiable measures that help track progress toward the strategic goals of the transformation. Table C.1 provides an example of how to track a transformation's progress against various targets. The Current Value column should be updated as you make progress on each KPI. The Status column will indicate whether the KPI is on track, at risk, or off track.

TABLE C.1 Example KPIs

Category	Name	Description	Target Value	Current Value	Status
Customer Experience	Net promoter score (NPS)	Measures customer loyalty and likelihood to recommend your products/services	Increase by 20%		

(Continued)

TABLE C.1 (Continued)

Category	Name	Description	Target Value	Current Value	Status
	Customer satisfaction score (CSAT)	Measures the satisfaction of customers with a product or service	Increase by 15%		
	Customer retention rate	Assesses the ability to retain customers over a specified period	Increase by 10%		
Process Efficiency	Percentage of automated processes	Measures the proportion of processes that have been automated	60%		
	Operational cost reduction	Tracks the reduction in operational costs achieved through digital transformation	Decrease by 25%		
	Error rate reduction	Monitors the reduction in error rates across processes	Decrease by 20%		
Workforce Capability	Percentage of employees upskilled	Assesses the proportion of employees who have been upskilled in digital competencies	80%		
	Number of digital certifications	Tracks the number of digital certifications earned by employees	Increase by 30%		
	Employee turnover rate	Measures the number of employees leaving the organization	Decrease by 15%		

(*Continued*)

TABLE C.1 (Continued)

Category	Name	Description	Target Value	Current Value	Status
Technology Adoption	Percentage of cloud-based applications	Measures the proportion of applications hosted in the cloud	70%		
	Number of integrated systems	Tracks the number of systems integrated as part of the digital transformation	Increase by 50%		
Innovation and Revenue Growth	Number of new digital products launched	Monitors the number of new digital products or services launched	3		
	Digital revenue growth	Measures the increase in revenue resulting from digital transformation initiatives	Increase by 30%		
Cybersecurity and Compliance	Reduction in security incidents	Tracks the decrease in the number of security incidents	Decrease by 40%		
	Compliance with cybersecurity standards	Assesses the level of compliance with relevant cybersecurity standards	100%		

Balanced Scorecard (BSC)

As a framework for translating a transformation's vision and strategy into a measurable set of performance indicators, a BSC can be an effective tool. For example, Table C.2 views a set of KPIs across five perspectives: Financial, Customer, Internal Processes, Learning and Growth, and Innovation. The *Target* column shows the target value for the KPI and the *Actual* column shows the actual performance against the target. The *Status* column is used to indicate whether each KPI is on track, needs improvement, or has been achieved.

TABLE C.2   Example Balanced Scorecard

Perspective	KPI	Target	Actual	Status
Financial	Return on investment (ROI)	15%	13%	
	Program budget adherence	100%	95%	
	Cost savings realized from transformation	$1m	$750k	
	Revenue growth from transformation	20%	17.5%	
Customer	Customer satisfaction	90%	80%	
	Digital channel adoption rate	75%	75%	
	Customer acquisition/retention rate	30%	32%	
	Net promoter score (NPS)	40	38	
Internal Processes	Project completion rate	100%	98%	
	Defect rate in digital products	5%	3%	
	Time to market for new features	60 days	40 days	
	Process efficiency gains	40	38	
Learning and growth	Employee skill development	80%	80%	
	Staff digitally trained	90%	90%	
Innovation	Rate of innovation projects	25%	22%	

Objectives and Key Results (OKRs)

OKRs are high-level objectives combined with a set of key results to measure progress toward each objective. Table C.3 shows that each objective focuses on a specific aspect of the transformation, with key results providing measurable outcomes to track progress.

TABLE C.3 Example OKRs

Objective (O)	Key Result 1 (KR1)	Key Result 2 (KR2)	Key Result 3 (KR3)
O1: Improve customer experience	Increase NPS by 20% within the next 12 months	Reduce customer support response time by 30% within the next 12 months	Launch two new customer-centric digital products within the next 12 months
O2: Enhance employee digital capabilities	Upskill 80% of employees in digital competencies within the next 12 months	Increase the number of employees with digital certifications by 30% within the next 12 months	Implement a company-wide digital mentorship program within the next 6 months
O3: Streamline internal processes	Automate 60% of manual processes within the next 12 months	Reduce operational costs by 25% within the next 12 months	Increase employee productivity by 20% within the next 12 months
O4: Accelerate digital innovation	Launch three new innovative digital products/services within the next 12 months	Increase digital-related revenue by 30% within the next 12 months	Establish two strategic partnerships with technology vendors within the next 12 months
O5: Strengthen cybersecurity posture	Reduce the number of security incidents by 40% within the next 12 months	Implement a comprehensive cybersecurity training program for all employees within the next 6 months	Achieve compliance with relevant cybersecurity standards within the next 12 months

Appendix D

Example Technologies and Architecture for Web-Based Applications

Technology and Architecture

The Technology Function is, of course, critical to the delivery of digital products and services (or products via digital channels).

As stated previously, this topic on its own can (and has) fill(ed) many books. Therefore, only a few areas will be covered here, with the addition of some *honorable mentions* of other areas that the reader may like to look into.

It is entirely possible that by the time of publication, some/all of the technologies below will have been superseded, but that's the nature of the digital world!

Cloud/Cloud First

Whether this is a digital twin used in a manufacturing context or a software product, it is difficult to conceive of a digital delivery in the 21st century that will not be (either in its entirety or partially) deployed to the cloud.

The days when companies whose core business is not IT, build and manage their own IT infrastructure and data centers, are numbered. For many companies, the cost of running and managing their own IT set-up is enormous and can be a huge headache. The thought of removing a sizeable portion of this pain is instantly appealing.

Across the globe, companies are undertaking large IT migration projects to move away from deploying software products on their own *physical tin* (computer hardware) and porting these applications and databases into the cloud (thereby using the cloud providers' *physical tin*).

All of the previously perceived barriers to cloud adoption (e.g., *How can I be sure my/my customer's data is secure? Is it ok to store my customers' data outside of the country in which they exist?*) have either completely disappeared or are being removed/circumvented very quickly.

The elastic compute and scalability that is offered by cloud providers is extremely attractive. Organizations are no longer in a situation where (if their capacity planners get it wrong, or they have a sudden spike in usage/data volumes) they might run out of compute power causing severe service degradation or in a worst-case scenario application failure.

The days where capacity planners used to estimate maximum usage/data volumes then double it and double it again (to get the specification of the hardware that might be required in a worst-case scenario) are again coming to an end (along with the associated high costs and often idle compute capacity).

Rather than planning for what size and type of hardware is going to be required (and placing the orders for this many months before it would be required), the role of capacity planning is now more concerned with how much of the elastic compute is likely to be used over the coming months so that this can be costed (and often bought in advance to secure a reduced cost per unit of compute).

APIs (Application Programming Interface)

When integrating with existing legacy systems, it is important that the newer digital applications are decoupled from the older systems in use within the organization. Not only this but any *integration point* (i.e., other system or resource) that is outside of the direct control of your digital delivery team needs to be abstracted. That is, you want to protect your application from knowing anything about the inner workings of any system upon which your application relies.

This decoupling can be achieved by defining APIs. Any new applications being built only ever communicate with legacy/other applications via these APIs. This means that if one of these legacy/external systems makes a change, it does not affect the new application as long as the API definition remains the same and the data returned is as expected.

Automated Testing and Test-Driven Development (TDD)

There are still a significant number of organizations where automated testing (and the adoption of Test-Driven Development) is still not the norm. If companies want to deliver better quality software, faster, then a very high percentage of automated test coverage is a must.

Dev Ops

Much has been made of DevOps over the years, but it is without doubt that the increasing use of Continuous Integration/Continuous Deployment (CI/CD) pipelines has shortened the cycle time between the code being completed and being deployed to an environment (either a test environment or in some cases direct to production) where it can be used.

A developer will complete their code (including developer testing) and commit this into the development repository, the code is built, automated tests run and, assuming all the tests pass, the code is deployed. This process is usually complete within a matter of minutes.

Some technology companies are deploying code into production many thousands of times per day.

UX to UI (User Experience to User Interface, Zero Distance between the Two)

The advent of increasingly sophisticated User Interfaces has led to the creation of the role of User Experience (UX) designer.

In The Galapagos Framework, the UX team exists as part of The Customer Experience Function, and it is this team that sits with The Product Function and customers (either internal to the organization or external to it) to pull together the User Journeys through the system and what the screens (User Interface – UI) will look like.

Clickable prototypes will be produced by the UX team to allow the Product team and the customers to see what a potential delivery might look like. Feedback can be taken in real time and the prototypes adjusted quickly and replayed back to the interested parties.

All this work can be undertaken before a single line of code is written. It is much more cost effective to make changes to a clickable prototype than it is to make changes once the code has been built and delivered.

However, there are a couple of things that need to be taken into account when using UX teams to produce prototypes. Care needs to be taken to ensure that the data items on the screens that the UX team is pulling together already exists, can be created, or can be derived from existing data. Unless you have a UX designer who already has good business domain knowledge, and knowledge of the underlying systems within the organization, then it is advisable to pair a Business Analyst with the UX Designer to ensure that the UX team is not demonstrating something that can't be delivered. Unconstrained UX results in beautiful prototypes that never make it into production.

The organization must have a good team of quality User Interface (UI) developers/programmers. These are the individuals who will take the UX prototypes and make them real. It is important that there is *zero distance* between what the customer has seen in the UX prototypes and what is delivered in the end application. Both the UX and the delivered UI must be pixel perfect.

Architecture (Microservices)

There are many types of software architecture in use, and each has its own pros and cons. The type of architecture employed, to deliver a software product, is largely dependent on the use case and business domain of the application.

Within a modern web-based application, a Microservices architecture may be adopted in situations where scalability is important, and this approach is becoming more widespread by the day.

Microservices come with their own challenges, but they do offer organizations a clean migration path from one technology stack to another. As each microservice is fully self-contained, the technology stack that is in use within each microservice can be different. So you could choose to migrate some current functions of an existing application (written in one programming language using one particular technology stack) to a microservice (written in another language using another technology stack) without too much impact on the existing systems.

Similarly, you might take the view that any new functions of an existing application that are built will adopt a microservices architecture, possibly using a new programming language and technology stack. Existing functions just need to call out to the new services, thus preserving the existing investment in legacy systems and allowing organizations to try out new technologies that may, ultimately, prove to be better than those that are currently in use.

Containerization

Alongside the microservices architecture is the area of containerization. Microservices often use *containers* to deliver small modules that work together to create more scalable applications.

Containerization is the packaging together of software code with all the other elements that this code requires to work (e.g., libraries, frameworks, etc.). This software module is isolated in its own *container*. A common technology that is used for containerization is Docker.

Container Orchestration

In situations where there are lots and lots of containers, these need to be managed (i.e., they need to be deployed and started/stopped in the case of problems, new instances created to cater for increases in volume, load needs to be balanced across these microservices, and the health of the services monitored, etc.). Kubernetes is a common technology that is used for container orchestration.

Service Mesh

A service mesh is a network of microservices that provides a platform for efficient communication between services, while also enabling service-level observability, reliability, and security. The service mesh normally takes the form of a sidecar proxy that is deployed alongside each service instance. This provides each service instance with a dedicated proxy, which is responsible for managing the service-to-service communication, and provides a secure, reliable, and observable communication channel.

The service mesh layer provides several key benefits, including auto-scaling, improved observability/health checking, and reliability. By providing a dedicated proxy to manage communication between services, the service mesh layer provides a platform for detailed monitoring, logging, and tracing of service-to-service traffic. This is especially important in distributed systems, where service-to-service communication is complex and difficult to debug. The service mesh layer also provides scalability, as it enables services to scale independently, without needing to scale the entire system.

For the reasons stated above, service meshes are becoming increasingly popular within the cloud-native community.

Security

Security is a critical concern for all web-based applications and is important for protecting both the application and its users. Security measures should be tailored to the specific application and its users, but some common security measures include the following.

Authentication

Implementing strong authentication mechanisms ensures that only authorized users can access the application. N-Factor Authentication is a type of Multi-Factor Authentication that requires two or more authentication factors to gain access to a system.

These authentication factors can be something you know (e.g., a password), something you have (e.g., a hardware token/card/mobile phone), or something you are (e.g., a biometric). N-Factor Authentication is sometimes referred to as Multi-Factor Authentication (MFA), Two-Factor Authentication (2FA), or Two-Step Verification (2SV). The *N* in N-Factor Authentication usually stands for *multiple* or *multiple levels* and is used to indicate that there is more than one authentication factor required. N-Factor Authentication helps to ensure the security of a system by making it more difficult for an unauthorized user to gain access.

Authorization

Authorization is the process of establishing roles and permissions to ensure users can only access the resources they are authorized to access.

Encryption

Encryption is the process of encrypting data both at rest and in transit to prevent unauthorized access. End-to-end encryption (E2EE) encrypts messages at the sending end, sends them, and then decrypts them at the receiving end. This prevents anyone in between the two endpoints from reading the messages. It is often used to protect sensitive data such as financial information or personal communications. End-to-end encryption ensures that only the sender and the recipient can read the messages, thus providing a high level of privacy and security.

Security/Penetration Testing

Performing regular security tests to identify any vulnerabilities is an essential component of a comprehensive security strategy, enabling organizations to find and fix issues before malicious actors can exploit them. Regularly scheduled penetration tests, combined with other security measures, help ensure ongoing security and compliance.

This type of testing is often conducted by ethical hackers or cybersecurity professionals who use the same tools, techniques, and processes that hackers use, but with the goal of identifying and rectifying vulnerabilities rather than exploiting them. The techniques used can range from automated scans to more intensive manual tests where testers try to exploit identified vulnerabilities to see if they can gain unauthorized access or perform unwanted actions.

Access Control

Access control is a security measure that regulates who or what can view, use, or modify data within an application and is a fundamental concept in security used to minimize the risk to the organization. This approach to security determines the level and type of interaction an individual user (or system process) can have with a resource or data, such as reading, modifying, or executing.

Effective access control in IT applications ensures that only authorized users can perform actions on the system and helps prevent potential system abuse, data breaches, and other security incidents.

Logging

Logging is the process of capturing, storing, and often categorizing information about events, transactions, or operations within a system or application and provides a chronological record of activities and is used for a number of different purposes (e.g., monitoring, troubleshooting, audit, security analysis, etc.).

Firewalls

Installing a firewall protects the application from malicious traffic.

A firewall is a network security device or software designed to monitor, filter, or block data packets as they travel to or from a network or system. Its primary purpose is to establish a barrier between a trusted internal network and untrusted external networks, such as the Internet, thereby providing a first line of defense against malicious traffic.

Honorable Mentions

Platform as a Service (PAAS)

PAAS is a cloud computing model that enables customers to develop, run, and manage applications without the complexity of building and maintaining the infrastructure typically associated with developing and launching an application.[1] With PAAS, customers are provided with a platform on which they can deploy, run, and manage their applications. This platform typically includes a range of services, such as storage, networking, servers, databases, and more.

API Gateways

An API gateway is a service that is the entry point for backend services. It acts as a reverse proxy, routing requests from clients to services.[2] It may also perform various cross-cutting tasks such as authentication, SSL/TLS termination, rate limiting, and caching.

REST Services

REST (Representational State Transfer) services provide communication standards between computer systems on the web, facilitating easier system interaction. RESTful web services use HTTP requests to GET, PUT, POST, and DELETE data and are lightweight and fast compared to other SOAP-based web services.

WebSocket's

WebSockets are a type of computer communications protocol that provides full-duplex communication channels over a single TCP connection. They allow for

---

[1] Cleary, L. 'Choosing a Cloud Model: SaaS versus PaaS', IT Pro Today (August 21, 2017). https://www.itprotoday.com/industry-perspectives/choosing-cloud-model-saas-versus-paas [accessed 6 September 2023].

[2] 'Microservices architecture: API gateway design', Microsoft Learn (n.d.). https://learn.microsoft.com/en-us/azure/architecture/microservices/design/gateway [accessed 6 September 2023].

a bi-directional flow of data between a server and client, which enables real-time data exchange without the need for constant requests and responses. WebSockets are increasingly used for real-time applications such as chatrooms, online games, streaming data, and collaborative editing tools.

Testing

Quality Assurance (QA) Testing

QA testing, in the context of software development, is the systematic activities and processes designed to ensure that products and services meet specified requirements and are reliable. It verifies that the software meets any organizational standards and ensures that it's free of defects.

User Acceptance Testing (UAT)

UAT, or User Acceptance Testing, is the final phase of software testing performed after QA testing. It involves the end-users or clients of the software testing the solution in a real-world scenario to ensure it meets their needs and requirements.

Performance and Load testing

Performance testing is the process of testing the speed, scalability, and stability of a system. It is used to measure the response time, throughput, and resource usage of a system under various conditions and is often used to identify and eliminate bottlenecks to improve the performance of a system.

Load testing, on the other hand, is concerned with simulating a real-world load on a system to test its performance under normal and peak load conditions. It is used to identify the maximum number of concurrent users a system can handle and to determine the response time and resource utilization of a system under various load conditions. Load testing is often used to ensure that a system can handle a given number of users or transactions.

Disaster Recovery (DR) Testing

This is the process of evaluating a system's ability to recover from a failure or disaster. This type of testing is essential to ensure that business operations can be maintained after a disaster or major event has occurred. The goals of DR testing are to ensure that the system can recover quickly, is able to recover to its most recent state, and that any data or information that has been lost is recovered and accessible. DR testing can involve both manual and automated processes and can include a variety of tests such as backup and restore tests, system recovery tests, and application recovery tests.

Big Data

The term *Big data* is used for data sets that are so large or complex that traditional relational databases and associated processing capabilities are unsuitable. *Big data* can also refer to the use of predictive analytics, user behavior analytics, or certain other advanced data analytics methods that extract value from data, and seldom to a particular size of data set.[3] Companies and organizations use big data to gain insight into their operations, services, and customers.

Big data databases are designed to store large amounts of data that are normally difficult to store, process, and analyze using traditional data management systems. These databases are more powerful and scalable than traditional databases, allowing organizations to store and analyze larger amounts of data.

Logging and Monitoring

Logging is the process of collecting and recording data about the activities that occur in an IT system. This data is used to monitor the performance and security of the system, identify any issues, and ensure compliance with regulations.

Monitoring is the process of actively watching the system for any changes or irregularities. It can involve analyzing the log files to identify potential problems and trends, as well as providing alerts when certain conditions are met. Logging and monitoring are essential components of any IT system and can be used to ensure the system is running smoothly and securely.

Caching

Caching is a technique used in IT systems to temporarily store data in a computer's memory or to reduce the amount of time required to access the same data in the future. Caching reduces the amount of processing power and time required to access the same data and can be used to improve the performance of web applications, databases, and network services.

Caching helps reduce the amount of data that needs to be stored in a database or sent over a network, reducing latency, and improving the overall performance of the application.

---

[3] 'Certified Big Data Professional', ICCP (n.d.). https://iccp.org/certified-big-data-professional.html [accessed 6 September 2023].

Appendix E

Glossary

3D Printing: 3D printing is a form of additive manufacturing that enables the production of three-dimensional objects, created by layering materials in succession, often controlled by computer-aided designs held in a digital file. It is a cost-effective way of producing complex shapes and parts that would have been difficult to achieve with traditional manufacturing techniques.

Artificial Intelligence (AI): AI is a branch of computer science that focuses on the development of computer systems that can think, learn, and act autonomously.[1] AI applications are used in a wide range of industries, including finance, healthcare, and defense.

Big Data: The term *Big data* is used for data sets that are so large or complex that traditional relational databases and associated processing capabilities are unsuitable. Big data can also refer to the use of predictive analytics, user behavior analytics, or certain other advanced data analytics methods that extract value from data, and seldom to a particular size of data set.[2]

Blockchain: Blockchain is a distributed, decentralized, digital ledger that is used to record transactions securely, immutably, and efficiently. It is used in a variety of applications, such as cryptocurrencies, finance, and supply chain management.

CI/CD: CI/CD stands for Continuous Integration/Continuous Deployment. It's a set of software engineering practices that emphasize the regular integration

---

[1] Helmenstine, A. 'What is AI or Artificial Intelligence? An AI Answers', Science Notes (July 15, 2022). https://sciencenotes.org/what-is-ai-or-artificial-intelligence-an-ai-answers/ [accessed 6 September 2023].

[2] 'Certified Big Data Professional', ICCP (n.d.). https://iccp.org/certified-big-data-professional.html [accessed 6 September 2023].

of code changes into a shared repository (CI) and the automatic delivery or deployment of integrated code to a non-development environment (CD).

- **Continuous Integration (CI)**: This practice involves automatically testing code changes from multiple contributors to ensure they integrate smoothly and don't introduce defects.
- **Continuous Delivery (CD)**: Ensures that changes, after passing CI tests, are automatically and reliably released into a staging or production environment, making them ready for release at any time.
- **Continuous Deployment (also CD)**: An extension of Continuous Delivery where changes are not just made ready but are actually deployed to production automatically without explicit manual approval.

Cloud Computing: Cloud computing is a model for enabling ubiquitous, convenient, on-demand network access to a shared pool of configurable computing resources (e.g., networks, servers, storage, applications, and services) that can be rapidly provisioned and released with minimal management effort or service provider interaction.[3]

Containerization: The process of packaging, distributing, and managing applications and their dependencies within a container. Containers are lightweight, standalone, and executable software packages that include everything needed to run a piece of software, including the code, runtime, system tools, system libraries, and settings.[4] They are isolated from each other and from the host system, ensuring consistent operation across different computing environments.

DevOps: DevOps is a set of practices and principles that bridge the gap between software development (Dev) and IT operations (Ops). Its primary goal is to shorten the system development life cycle and provide continuous delivery of high-quality software by promoting closer collaboration between developers and operations teams. This often involves automation, continuous integration, and continuous delivery practices to streamline and improve the process of design, development, deployment, and infrastructure management.

Internet of Things (IoT): The Internet of Things (IoT) is a network of physical devices, vehicles, appliances, and other items embedded with

---

[3] Mell P.M., Grance T., A. 'NIST Definition of Cloud Computing', National Institute of Standards and Technology (September 28, 2011). https://www.nist.gov/publications/nist-definition-cloud-computing [accessed 6 September 2023].

[4] Cohen, B. 'How to Access Docker Dashboard on Ubuntu', DeviceTests (July 22, 2023). https://devicetests.com/access-docker-dashboard-ubuntu [accessed 6 September 2023].

software, sensors, and connectivity, enabling these things to connect and exchange data.[5]

Kaizen: Kaizen is an approach to continuous improvement that emphasizes small, incremental changes that result in sustained improvements over time, rather than large-scale overhauls. Everyone in an organization, from top management to general staff members, aims to continuously improve operations and eliminate waste.

Kanban: Kanban is an Agile methodology originating from Japanese manufacturing, which has been adapted for software development and other tasks. A Kanban board displays tasks or user stories on cards, which move through predefined columns or stages (commonly: To Do, In Progress, Done) to visualize work items and the flow of these through the process.

Kanban focuses on limiting work in progress (WIP) at any given stage, allowing teams to identify bottlenecks and ensure efficient workflow. The primary goal is to enhance efficiency and continuously improve the process.

Key Performance Indicator (KPI): A KPI is a quantifiable measure used by organizations to evaluate the success of a specific activity, operation, or process in relation to its goals and objectives and can relate to various operational aspects like sales, customer service, operational efficiency, and more. They are often accompanied by targets, which provide benchmarks for performance evaluation.

Lean: Lean is a continuous improvement methodology that emphasizes the elimination of waste (non-value-added activities) in all forms and the optimization of system-wide processes. Lean thinking is centered on creating more value for customers with fewer resources, improving flow, and leveling production to meet actual customer demand.

Microservice: A microservice is a software architectural style where a complex application is composed of small, independent, and loosely coupled services. Each service, or *microservice*, is responsible for a distinct piece of functionality and communicates with other services through well-defined APIs (Application Programming Interfaces). These services can be developed, deployed, and scaled independently, and are often organized around business capabilities.

Minimum Viable Product (MVP): An MVP is the most basic version of a product that can still be released to achieve a specific goal, whether that's testing a hypothesis, gaining user insights, or entering a market quickly.

The feedback collected from MVP users informs the next iterations of the product, guiding developers in refining and adding features based on actual user needs and preferences.

---

[5] J. B. Ajith, R. Manimegalai and V. Ilayaraja, "An IoT Based Smart Water Quality Monitoring System using Cloud," *2020 International Conference on Emerging Trends in Information Technology and Engineering (ic-ETITE)*, Vellore, India, 2020, pp. 1–7, doi: 10.1109/ic-ETITE47903.2020.450.

By deploying an MVP, organizations can test their hypotheses in real-world scenarios, allowing for quicker pivots and more efficient use of resources in product development.

Objectives and Key Results (OKRs): OKRs are goal-setting frameworks that help organizations define and track objectives and their outcomes and consist of two components, Objectives (a clearly defined, qualitative goal intended to be ambitious and inspiring) and Key Results (quantifiable metrics that indicate progress toward achieving the objective). Typically, multiple key results are associated with each objective to provide a comprehensive view of performance.

Scaled Agile Framework® (SAFe®): SAFe® is a set of organizational and workflow patterns for implementing Agile practices at an enterprise scale.[6] SAFe is designed to scale lean and Agile practices promoting alignment, collaboration, and delivery across multiple Agile teams. SAFe applies principles from Agile development, systems thinking, and product development flow to provide a detailed and customizable approach to scale Agile.

The framework encompasses roles, responsibilities, artifacts, and activities necessary for implementing lean-Agile operations at enterprise scale, addressing challenges that larger organizations face when adopting Agile methodologies.

Scrum: Scrum is an Agile framework focusing on delivering the highest value work in the shortest time. Scrum employs regular fixed-length iterations, called sprints, typically lasting two to four weeks. The framework introduces roles like the Product Owner (responsible for defining product features and priorities), Scrum Master (facilitates the Scrum process and addresses impediments), and the Development Team (performs the actual work of designing, building, and testing the product).

Key artifacts in Scrum include the Product Backlog (a prioritized list of product features) and Sprint Backlog (a list of tasks to be completed in a given sprint). Regular ceremonies such as Daily Stand-ups, Sprint Reviews, and Sprint Retrospectives are also integral components of Scrum.

Scrumban: A hybrid Agile methodology that combines principles from both Scrum and Kanban, aiming to provide the structured planning and roles of Scrum along with the flexibility and continuous flow of Kanban.

Service Mesh: A service mesh is a dedicated infrastructure layer designed to facilitate service-to-service communication in a microservices architecture. It abstracts the complexity of managing service intercommunication, ensuring reliability, security, and observability, and provides capabilities like traffic management, service discovery, load balancing, fault tolerance,

---

6 Piikkila, J. 'What is SAFe? Scaled Agile Framework explained', Atlassian (n.d.). https://www. atlassian.com/agile/agile-at-scale/what-is-safe [accessed 6 September 2023].

telemetry, authentication, and authorization without requiring modifications to the actual microservice applications.

A service mesh is typically implemented as a collection of lightweight network proxies, deployed alongside application code, commonly referred to as *sidecars*.

Six Sigma: Six Sigma is a methodology that aims to reduce defects and improve the quality of a process. It provides tools and techniques to make business processes better by identifying and removing the causes of defects and minimizing variability resulting in the delivery of better products and services.

Total Quality Management (TQM): TQM is a comprehensive and structured approach to continuous improvement and organizational management that seeks to improve the quality of products and services through ongoing refinements in response to continuous feedback.[7] The TQM process encompasses the culture, attitude, and organization of a company, focusing on the entire quality management process, involving all stakeholders from suppliers to customers.

UI (User Interface): A User Interface (UI) is the point of interaction between the user and a digital device or product – including displays, buttons, icons, touchscreens, keyboards, and more. In the context of software applications, UI is often a combination of visual elements such as screens, pages, buttons, and icons, as well as interactions like swipe actions and clicks, through which users interact with a device.

Use Case: A use case is a formal description of a system's behavior as it responds to a request from an external user or another system. Use cases detail the sequence of events and interactions between the user (or actor) and the system, outlining specific goals or tasks the user seeks to achieve. Use cases define functional requirements by describing the expected behavior under various scenarios, including both typical interactions and potential error conditions.

User Journey: A user journey is a visual or narrative representation of a user's interactions with a product or service over time and across multiple touchpoints. The journey maps out the user's experiences from their initial engagement, through various stages of interaction, to a final outcome or goal. User journeys are often employed in user experience (UX) design and service design, and help teams empathize with users, pinpointing areas for improvement in the product or service.

User Story: User stories are concise, informal descriptions of one or more aspects of a software feature. They are written from the perspective of an end user or a specific role and are designed to focus on user value (i.e., what users need from a system rather than technical details).

---

7 'Total Quality Management (TQM)', QS Study (n.d.). https://qsstudy.com/total-quality-management-tqm/ [Accessed 6 September 2023].

A user story often follows a simple format: *As a [type of user], I want [a specific feature or action] so that [a benefit or value is achieved]*, and should be accompanied by acceptance criteria, which provide details on how the story's functionality should behave to be considered complete.

UX (User Experience): User experience (UX) design is the process design teams use to create products that provide meaningful and relevant experiences to users. UX design involves the design of the entire process of acquiring and integrating the product, including aspects of branding, design, usability, and function.[8] Key elements include usability, accessibility, performance, design/aesthetics, utility, ergonomics, overall human interaction, and marketing.

Web 3.0: Web 3.0 is the term used to describe the next generation of web technology. It is focused on making the web more intelligent, secure, and user focused. Web 3.0 will be powered by technologies such as artificial intelligence, blockchain, and the Internet of Things.

---

[8] 'UX Design', Interaction Design Foundation (n.d.). https://www.interaction-design.org/literature/topics/ux-design [accessed 6 September 2023].

Index

Pages in *italics* refer to figures, pages in **bold** refer to tables, and pages followed by "n" refer to notes.

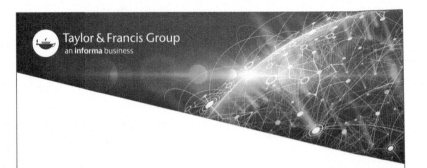